THINKING ABOUT [TLC] LOGO

A GRAPHIC LOOK AT COMPUTING WITH IDEAS

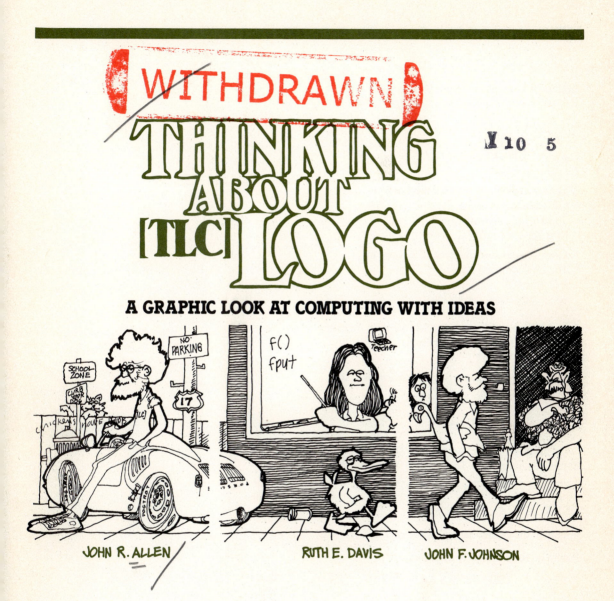

JOHN R. ALLEN   RUTH E. DAVIS   JOHN F. JOHNSON

HOLT, RINEHART AND WINSTON
New York   Chicago   San Francisco   Philadelphia
Montreal   Toronto   London   Sydney   Tokyo
Mexico City   Rio de Janeiro   Madrid

Smalltalk is a trademark of Xerox Corporation
TLC-Logo is a trademark of The Lisp Company, Inc.

Address correspondence about this book to:
   CBS College Publishing
   383 Madison Avenue
   New York, NY 10017

Address correspondence about [TLC] Logo to:
   The Lisp Company
   P.O. Box 487
   Redwood Estates, CA 95044

First distributed to the trade in 1984 by Holt, Rinehart
and Winston, General Book Division.

Library of Congress Cataloging in Publication Data

Allen, John R.
      Thinking about TLC-Logo

      1. Logo (Computer language) I. Davis, Ruth E.
II. Johnson, John F. III. Title.
QA76.73.L63A44 1983   001.64'24   83-10771

ISBN 0-03-064116-0

Printed in the United States of America

Published simultaneously in Canada

3 4 5 6   039   9 8 7 6 5 4 3 2 1

CBS COLLEGE PUBLISHING
Holt, Rinehart and Winston
The Dryden Press
Saunders College Publishing

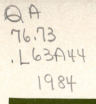

PREFACE

Now what does that mean—a Pre-face? Something coming before the face? A mask, perhaps, or something to hide the real intent? Words often have exactly that purpose. Although that is not the intention of this pre-face, words are part of our plot: words like "computer", and "meaning", and "intelligence", and "communication", and "object." We will play with words, play with ideas, play with turtles, and play with computers. We will show you how to design Logo programs that will perform colorful dances, do mind-boggling animation, and generally turn your dull, tedious life into a sparkling social success.

But this is a serious book, believe it or not. We do have a point in mind. For we are mental dentists, in search of the mind-rotting cavities of computer-phobia, misinformation, and misunderstanding. The appearance and style of this book are the laughing gas that will make the pain of the operation bearable. So brace yourself for some bad puns, old jokes, hard work, and excitement. After the Logotomy you will have a much better appreciation for, and understanding of, the true nature of computation.

THIS IS A SERIOUS BOOK. THE CARTOONS ARE PUT IN FOR THOSE OF YOU WHO DON'T KNOW BIG WORDS.

1

PREFACE

Of course, such a confession on the first page is much like beginning a whodunit by announcing the plot, complete with the villain and the outcome. Indeed, this troubled us a bit. We feared that if we revealed our conspiracy too soon, readers might flee in panic; they might go back to reading the phone book, the sides of buses, or the US budget.

But because this is a serious book, it seemed appropriate to tell you the why-and-wherefore right up front: we want to introduce you to the art of thinking. Thinking—that's what you do when your TV dies.

So who cares about becoming more friendly with an overgrown calculator? Ah! We want to show you that computers are more than adolescent calculators, and more than number-spewing, paper-chewing monstrosities threatening to take over the world.

Though thinking is an ancient art, we want to introduce a modern artistic flair. We want to think about computers. Not the crusty old tools of the 1950s sci-fi movies, but the sneaky little beasties that are coming home with the kids. It used to be dogs, hamsters, or rabbits; now it's computers. This raises several questions:

1. are they good for anything?
2. are they a menace?
3. can they think?

(...and after we answer these questions about the kids, we ask the same questions about the computers.)

Of course, one cannot write a book about thinking using the same approach that would work for a book on brain surgery or sausage stuffing. We have to sneak up on certain subjects rather than confronting them head on. As a result, we have woven our approach to mental dermatology (a cure for flaky thought) throughout the book rather than present it in a one-two-three fashion. However, we can shed some light on three general levels that the book will explore.

The Superficial Level
This is the surface level of the book. An investigation of Literacy, Logic, Logo, and Lunacy.

The Prejudicial Level
Yes, we're prejudiced. Even in the face of massive evidence to the contrary, we believe that humans can—and sometimes

do—think. Clearly, this is the most speculative level of the book.

The Artificial (Intelligence) Level
This is the applications level of the book. Assuming that thought is possible, can we build machines that mimic some of these abilities?

The following sections supply more detailed discussions of these levels.

The Superficial Level
Every book should have at least one purpose, just like every cloud should have a silver lining. Our weather balloons indicate clear skies for those readers interested in learning about Logo, Literacy, and Logic.

PREFACE

LOGO — The Logo programming language is the hatrack on which we hang ourselves. Thus a large part of our book involves gaining experience and confidence with the Logo model of computing. Besides containing the typical programming techniques, Logo contains some ideas that are particularly effective when discussing the mind-fuzz areas like:

What's computation?
What's thinking?
What's a thing?
What's up?

But these questions are exactly "what's" important to becoming literate.

LITERACY — We believe that computer literacy requires a deep understanding of the fundamental principles of computing, thinking, and having a good time. Unfortunately, most approaches to computer literacy involve (1) exercises in how to use computer keyboards, (2) word-processing to write letters to Grandma, and (3) drill-and-kill survival courses to become fluent

in ancient computer languages. Bleaagh! Hardly fun and hardly very useful.

Well, you don't go into terminal sweat when you have to read a new book. If the book has new words, you can look them up in a dictionary; if the book has new ideas, you have to work harder; but if you persist, you can usually understand what's going on. Part of being literate is being able to transfer your knowledge to new situations. Of course, the ability to transfer your knowledge implies that you understand the basic information and how it relates to other things that you know. The more you can relate a new situation to past experience, the faster you can assimilate the new information. This whole process is driven by the models of the world that you have built up in past situations. In particular, the driving concern in artificial intelligence is the development of models of thinking and problem solving. This quest to understand thought is not new; symbolic logic, dating from the early Greek civilizations, deals directly with the formalizations of rules that captured the inner workings of of the human mind. This brings us to our next topic.

LOGIC — The third element of substance that we discuss in this book is logic. The

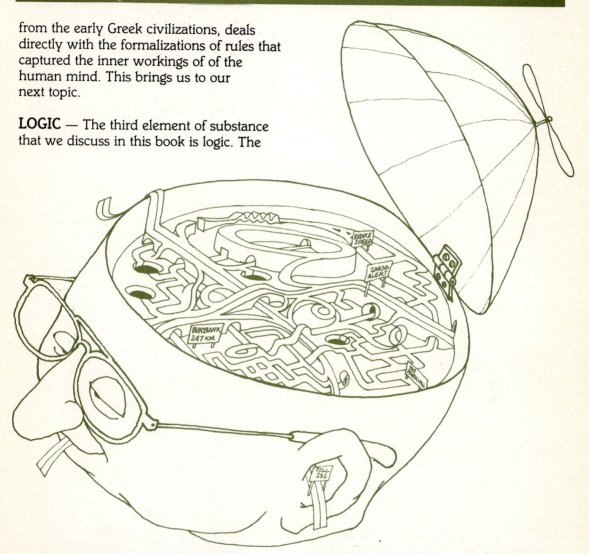

term "logic" has many meanings. Computer "logic" typically refers to the very simple machine-level operations. Never fear; we have no intention of discussing electricity or bits or bytes or floppies or moppsies or cottontails. You see, none of this stuff has anything to do with real

knowledge about computation. These are just the latest technological tricks, soon destined for that great computer hardware museum in the sky. No, our use of "logic" refers to the rules that people seem to use in thinking. For example, if we believe that all turtles have four legs, and later we see a

PREFACE

two-legged animal in a shell, we cannot also believe that this new creature is a turtle. That's logic.

Or assume we have three ducks, of which one is red, one is blue, and one is of unknown color—it's shy and hiding in a box. If we get our ducks—the blue one, the boxed one and the red one—lined up, logic tells us that there is a red duck standing next to a non-red duck. Why? Well, our boxed duck must either be red or non-red. Assume it's red; then it is standing next to a non-red duck (the blue one). Assume our shy quacker is not red; then it is standing next to a red duck. What flawless logic! It is reasoning like this that sets humanity apart. That brings us to the Prejudicial Level.

The Prejudicial Level

People do think. Evidence that will sustain this claim is available in that illusive quality called "common sense". We'll ex-

plore some techniques that people use to solve problems, think about the world, and generally muddle through. We will illustrate some of the general rules of logic that

are common to the way people reason, and we will outline some less well-defined techniques that people use in the creative aspects of problem-solving. The intention is not to imply that "to think is to compute", or that "to compute is to think", but to show similarities and differences between thinking and computing.

For example, a common conception is that computation implies arithmetic; yet most of our thinking doesn't involve numbers. What does thinking involve? Does computation have to involve numbers? If not, why not? Can we use computers to help in the problem solution rather than restrict them to the answer production phase? How do we solve problems? What is problem-solving? How do we recognize that a problem exists? How do we recognize when we have found a

solution? How do we recognize that a problem has no solution? How can we relate any of this mind-fuzz to computing? to Logo? How can individuals hope to gain a sense of perspective on computing if technology is changing so fast? Better yet, why should anyone care? We don't express great concern for "car literacy" or "shovel literacy"; why should we make a big deal out of "computer literacy?" We believe that the home computer offers an astounding new chance for individuals to explore their own humanity. That certainly sounds like a platitude of the first magnitude—a duck-billed platitude if there ever was one.

However, a large part of one's humanity springs from self-esteem and a sense of self-confidence. Too many of us have had that beaten out of us. It happens in schools that have certain expectations of what is correct and what is incorrect, or who is destined to succeed and who is destined to fail. It happens in society where there are those who know "the answer" and those who don't. When self-esteem disappears,

irrationality and escapism take their place. How does one repair the damage or, better yet, stop it from occurring in the first place?

How about finding the most mysterious and awe-inspiring object in our society and stripping away that mystery and awe, showing that, from the correct perspective, most of us can understand it? Well, we tried that but we couldn't figure out the Internal Revenue Service either. That's why we turned to computers. But computers will also satisfy our needs admirably. In the past, computers have:

(1) been the mysterious, powerful ally of the mad scientist,
(2) been understandable only by those people who are "real brains",

(3) threatened to become "intelligent" and take over the world.

Of course, the same people who paint this picture of the Giant E-lec-Tronic Brain That Ate The World will gladly explain that the machine is only able to add and sub-tract numbers, and does so by turning switches off and on. No one with a brain in their own head would believe that a collection of switches could possibly show any kind of intelligent behavior. Yet intelligent machines are coming.

In one of the most striking developments of contemporary computing, the Japanese announced their Fifth Generation Project in late 1981. They declared that their next national goal was the development of practical intelligent machines by the end of this century. This effort is not just a research project. They intend to establish a totally information-based society.

Since the initial announcement, Fifth-Generation projects have been announced in Europe and the United States. How can sophisticated world powers expect to build intelligent machines at all, let alone out of such trivial things as switches. Clearly something is wrong. A contradiction? A dilemma? No; a case of the wrong model for the particular situation.

For example, suppose you were asked if you could cover a chess board with dominoes whose size covered exactly two squares on the board. Thus:

It would be easy to convince yourself that it could be done. Now suppose that we removed two opposite corners of the board:

Is it still possible to cover the butchered board with dominoes? Not clear is it? In fact it is not possible. And how do you convince yourself that it is not possible? An exhaustive search will yield only frustration, while the right model makes the problem trivial.

Just observe that every domino covers a black space and a white space, thus, no matter how many dominoes are on the board, the number of white spaces covered up is exactly the same as the number of black spaces covered. But our nibbling removes two tiles of the same color, leaving an unequal number of black and white spaces to be covered! Thus there will be no way to cover the reduced board.

What's needed to appreciate intelligent machine developments is an appropriate model spelled out in black-and-white.

The Artificial Level

Our problem is that the model of a machine as "a collection of switches that do arithmetic" is not appropriate for modern ideas; it doesn't describe computing at the right level. If we described the brain at the same level of detail—in terms of its axons, and ganglia, and assorted electrical impulses—we'd find it hard to believe that such a mess could think. It's a long way from synapses to Shakespeare's sonnets.

So what's needed is a more descriptive picture of computation in terms of **what** it can do, not **how** it does it. The secret is to get rid of the notion of computers as number-crunchers. Computers don't do arithmetic. Now, we know that opinion is subversive, but it is fact nevertheless.

If you look inside a computer you will not find any numbers other than the serial numbers on the chips. And if you look inside the chips no numbers will be found

there either. Deep down inside these components you will find nothing but tiny dancing electrons. To be sure, there is a regularity in the patterns that these particles weave, but it is up to us to give meaning to these meanderings. Some of these patterns can be interpreted as operations like addition and subtraction. Some of the more interesting patterns represent rules for diagnosing disease, or rules for recognizing mineral deposits, or facts about specific patients in a hospital. Some of the patterns represent rules for transforming one pattern into another.

Somehow it seems that little has been gained. We replaced one simple-minded model (arithmetic) with another one (patterns). Yet this change will turn out to be an important one. We will be able to give descriptions of the logical rules that we humans use in thinking, in terms of pattern manipulations. We will be able to design Logo programs that will carry out these pattern manipulations. We will be able to mirror a lot of what we call intelligence in terms of patterns and their manipulations.

•   •   •

So that's our story. After we build a model of how people solve problems, we will show how to relate that model to the computing ideas surrounding Logo. But do not panic! We have no intention of arguing that you can be replaced by a Logo program. We simply want to show you that there are similarities between the ways we organize and reason with information and the weird and wonderful ways of modern computation. The intent is not to destroy your humanity, or turn you into the next generation of mad scientist, but rather to expose you to several key ideas about intelligence of either the natural or artificial variety.

PUTTING DESCARTES BEFORE DE HORSE.

We believe that it is critical for the typical citizen to have an accurate picture of computers, the potential they offer, and the limitations they possess. If you break out in a rash now when faced with a computer keyboard, expect to be bed-ridden in a few years. Machines that can ask and answer intelligent questions are coming. Yet before such devices can be integrated into any society, they must be understood by the general population. One of the points of this book is to illustrate the basic rules that govern such machines. Furthermore these pattern-driven engines are no more threatening than your car's engine. And though few of us could repair, let alone build, such an engine, there is no large segment of our society that stands in fear of automobiles. Similarly, one should not fear the computing engine. In the quest for this

wondrous goal, we will illustrate two types of models—physical models and mental models—to relate Logo to the human world. First, we will introduce you to creatures called turtles. These objects will be used to think about the physical properties of modern computing. We will deal with them much like traditional computing deals with numbers. We will ask turtles to compute and display various geometric and animated scenes. One particularly useful property of these turtles is that it is easy for a person to translate turtle actions into person actions. Thus, our physical actions translate into models of turtle movement on the video screen.

Our second model—the mental model —involves patterns and recognition of similarities and differences in patterns. Fortunately, the mental model is an extension of the physical model. In particular, we first describe the way a computer carries out the instructions of our turtle, not in the jargon-laden instructions of computerese, but in simple pattern-recognition steps that we could mechanically carry out ourselves. One could argue that this isn't thinking (since even a politician could do it). But it is a first step; we have to make sure we know how to perform an operation before we can analyze how it is done.

Then we ask: "Can we describe the process that we are using to carry out the rules that we are performing?" That is more difficult. Now we're thinking about how we think, and that should start to make your head hurt. The corresponding task for a computer will make many computer languages "hurt" too—but not Logo. Logo has the necessary tools for talking about itself; that is the key to analyzing intelligent behavior.

Next, we consider what to do when the task we are trying to perform won't work.

Now we're getting to something approaching intelligence! When things don't work, you have a problem. Making things work —that is, finding solutions—is problem-solving, and that requires intelligence.

When we get stuck—that is, when a problem arises—we will rummage through our intellectual rubble, thinking about what we've tried in the past, trying to analyze where our superior brain could have tripped up and, hopefully, coming up with alternative plans to accomplish the intended goal. In this process, we use our brains to analyze the workings of that very same brain. We call this process introspection. But how does introspection relate to computing?

In the computing field, problem-solving is called "debugging". The programmer reflects on the remains of a computation, trying to discover the source of the error. Of course, programming and debugging are nothing new; humanity has done such trial-and-error development for centuries. Indeed, the idea of trying to train some other device to do your bidding is old, too; it's just been called "teaching" or "slavery" before. What's novel is that now the slave is made of silicon.

The big QUESTION is:
…if a key part of intelligence is problem-solving (debugging), can we imagine a way that a silicon servant could recognize a problem, find the difficulty and then repair it, perhaps in a manner similar to that a human might use? That is, could we program a computer to analyze its own actions and take corrective measures in case of difficulty? In short, can we design an introspective computer?

The big BUT is:
…if we persist in thinking about computers as over-grown calculators, we'll never get there. If we tried to describe all **our** actions, thoughts, and plans in terms of numbers, we'd look pretty stupid too! We need a reasonable way to talk about the ideas involved in intelligence.

The big IDEA is:
…to look at the notions humans use. How do we organize our minds? We group things together and give them names. For example, a tree is a collection of leaves and branches, bugs and bark. This whole collection becomes an object. Of course, a leaf

is also an object, as is a bug. But when we're talking about trees we usually leave out all this extra detail of twigs and tendrils and concentrate on the major features.

The big WORD is:

...Object. What's an object? An object is a

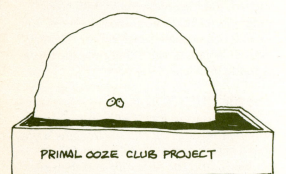

PRIMAL OOZE CLUB PROJECT

thing,...an idea. It's a cloud in the blue sky of the mind. The importance of objects to thought is our ability to use them in controlling complexity, and organizing and classifying information. The importance of objects to computation is the realization that machines can compute with objects just as machines can compute with numbers.

The big DEAL is:

...the mental mud of objects and their representation as patterns. These are the keys to modern computation; and, though the terms are new, these ideas are close to the way we organize our own thinking. The task before us is to make you more at home with the notion of "object".

Our tour through the mental mania surrounding objects is divided into five parts:

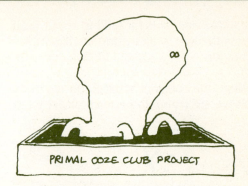

PRIMAL OOZE CLUB PROJECT

Section I: I Object!

This section gives a detailed statement of our objection to the traditional notion of computing as a game of numbers and arithmetic. The section moves on to an informal discussion of objects and object-oriented programming. It discusses problem-solving techniques and how one can achieve goals. It describes how one can think of computation as communication with jovial little beings whose goodwill can be maintained by politely asking them for favors. All this is in preparation for the next sections.

Section II: Eye Object.

This section concentrates on the visual parts of the Logo language. At one level, it builds a physical model, relating the graphical movements of a screen turtle to physical movements of a human. Logo-ites call this "playing turtle". At another level, this section builds a mental model, explaining how to understand the turtle movements in terms of communicating with another being by "sending messages" to it. Finally, at a third level, the section introduces a model that is useful in understanding how a "computer" could execute the messages that are being sent.

Section III: I, Object.

The third section analyzes the mental and physical models of Part II, showing how we can build such models in languages like Logo. The final part of this section outlines the way we could begin to build introspection into a computational system. The wonders are revealed!

Section IV: Aye, Object!

We herein do show that objects are important stuff for mathematics, philosophy, engineering, and other arcana.

Section V: Objection Sustained!

Our parting shot, our shouting part.

Isn't that impressive? The Truth of the Universe, all in one slim volume. And who should be blamed for this?

Acknowledgements

Whether they like it or not, several people are responsible for the existence of this book and its surrounding software.

Michael Davis-Allen, Chris, and Geoff Allen for putting up with this nonsense. The Davis Clan, the Allen Clan. Wendell, Gwenavere, The Depot Hill Athletic & Drinking Society, and Ducks.

Andy Burgess, who supplied many of the ideas contained in TLC-Logo, wrote the Logo system that implements the mind fuzz, and has an incredible caffeine capacity.

Michael E. Burke, who suffered through the birth of the first version of this book and lived to tell about it. His patience and persistence in the face of adversity are greatly appreciated.

Alan Foster, who supplied the Worm-o-rama of Chapter 4, and did a monumental amount of work during this insanity.

The the poor folks who commented on some of this orange crayon journalism: The Knights of the Lambda Calculus—Jim des Rivieres, Greg Nuyens, and Mike Dixon; The Days of Wine and Roses—Ron and Elena Danielson, The Morning [sic] Becomes Eclectic—Lois Flynne; along with a reluctant cast of thousands.

CBS College Publishing's patience as we constructed this mental monolith: Paul Becker, Brete Harrison, and Pat Sarcuni.

The staff at Graphic Arts West, Randy and LaRae; who watched in horror as we pushed bits and fonts into their typesetter.

The staff of Sherry Hagen Graphic Design, Sherry, for producing a book from no copy. Gay, for hiding five pages of copy on one page.

The Teapot Graphics Idea Factory for the new meaning of TGIF.

Ruth E. Davis, who convinced an old Lisp hacker that logic programming wasn't so bad after all. John R. Allen, who convinced her that logic was worth studying in the first place.

CHAPTER 1
THINKING ABOUT [TLC] LOGO

"Thinking about TLC-Logo, indeed. I object!", you exclaim. "Computers have been invading my life long enough. They lose my check every month and find my tax return every year. Now, when I finally bring one home, you want it to invade my head? You want me to **think** about them and their dreadful little languages? Fat chance!"

Well, we hope your reaction to our invitation isn't quite that strong. Yet, objections like these are quite understandable. Each of us can tell tales of computer horror. Bills are sent for products we have not purchased, payments are incorrectly credited, but the IRS computer never sends double the requested refund. And when we ask for an explanation, the response is usually "the computer did it". Such behavior should have made a massive public relations problem for the computer industry. Yet here we are, in the midst of the "personal computer revolution," inviting these strange little devices into the comfort of our own homes. Computer revolution, indeed; it's a minor miracle!

Of course, computers have not been introduced into the home market with the same sales methods as those used in the business, financial, and scientific market. These machines were serious business, with big card readers, big tape drives, big printers, and big price tags. They were hard to use, with complex programming languages, horrible rituals for getting the programs into the machine, and even more tedious techniques required to get any answers back from the monster. But after all, this was work. Work isn't supposed to be fun. Otherwise they wouldn't call it "work".

In contrast to their industrial-strength cousins, personal computers crept into the home as game machines. These early machines were able to play only a limited number of pre-programmed selections, but only a small amount of effort was required to get the machine to operate and the personal enjoyment factor was large. After all, games are supposed to be fun. Otherwise they wouldn't call it a "game", they'd call it "work".

These machines came with special facilities for TV hookups and with joysticks for control. They were fun and easy to use. Now they're growing up. Indeed, the small

helpless creature we call the modern personal computer has as much computing power as the monster machine of a few years ago. But now the machine is highly portable; it will easily fit on a table top or chest of drawers.

CHEST OVER DRAWERS COMPUTER

This new device is being called upon to do everything from balancing the budget to washing the dog. It is therefore important that we understand what these devices are capable of before we transplant the bureaucratic errors of the past into the warmth of our living room.

Unfortunately, most personal computers are flirting with the same disaster that faces business and industrial computers. Just as the old machines were not very personal, so too, these personal clones contain many anti-social elements. In particular, most of the new machines use the same languages and operating systems that the digital dinosaurs fed upon. This is one of **our** objections to the computer culture.

THINKING ABOUT [TLC] LOGO

The traditional computer languages—like FORTRAN, COBOL, BASIC, and Pascal—carry the assumption that a computer is a device that calculates with numbers. Such a notion has been useful and profitable in science and business; mathematics and engineering allow scientists to reduce much of the physical world to discussions involving numerical relationships. The business and financial world glory in their magic numbers; even an individual's name may be folded, spindled, and mutilated into a collection of numbers.

So, valuable as they are, numbers are hardly the basis for a personal computing language. Clearly, few human activities have anything at all to do with numbers. We breathe, walk, run, ride bicycles, talk, and eat—all without worrying about numbers. And, in fact, many elements of

OMIGAWD! THE NUMBER 2 IS OUT TO GET ME!

our daily lives that do involve numbers have been introduced into our world simply for the convenience of computer-related data gathering. Much of this activity is resented—by all of us—because it is unnecessary and unnatural.

Fortunately the picture is not all bleak. Human-oriented languages are coming—languages that are related to the way humans think, work, and play. Traditional machine-oriented languages would require that these real-world situations be reduced to numerical relationships before anything resembling computation could proceed. Traditional languages expect to deal with The Real World in precise, unambiguous fashion; they are boring, but predictably so because their means for expressing ideas is so weak. Human-oriented languages, in contrast, allow us to express the situations to computers in terms more closely related to the way humans tend to deal with The Real World: fuzzily, spontaneously, piecemeal, and perhaps inconsistently; but creatively!

What features of human languages are important? One big win is our ability to use a single word to express a whole collection of ideas. For example, when we say "car", you think of a whole collection of ideas. You recognize a "car" as a means of

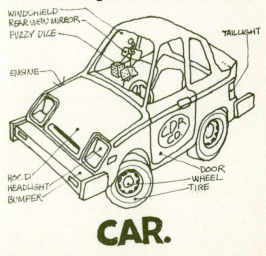

WINDSHIELD
REAR VIEW MIRROR
FUZZY DICE
TAILLIGHT
ENGINE
HOOD
HEADLIGHT
BUMPER
DOOR
WHEEL
TIRE

CAR.

transportation; this vision involves the function or purpose of a car, not its physical properties. However, you may also think of a car as a collection of component parts—wheels, engine, chassis, and so on. Furthermore, specific cars may come to mind— perhaps the fugitive from the wrecking yard that occupies your garage. All these visions of "car-ness" may come flooding in, all in the same mental breath. Yet, very little of this information deals with numbers. We think of "car" as a collection of all these properties, objects, and relationships between objects. Think about it for a moment. Aren't relationships between objects critical to the way we

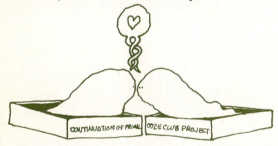

organize information? Indeed, we maintain our sanity in the complexity of the real world by covering up details and only focusing on the essentials of the current situation. Our mind's eye saves us from mental clutter just as our physical eyes suppress visual clutter. When we look at a scene, we only "see" a small bit. We focus on the important parts and ignore the rest.

When we decide to pick up a pencil, we don't think about it; we just do it. We don't watch the motion of our hand; and we don't think about how our arm feels as we position it to pick up the pencil. And we don't calculate distances using complex mathematics. We use common sense, seat-of-the-pants rules of thumb. Think about it; but notice that it takes an effort to slow down our minds to think about even these simple actions.

But now let's go deeper—to think about how we think. How do we organize information to solve even simple tasks like picking up a pencil? What if the pencil is across the room? —in a desk?—guarded by a tiger? So instead of listening to our bodies, we want to listen to our minds, trying to uncover the tricks that we use in thinking about problems, in discovering solutions, and in rejecting false leads.

What connection does all this have with personal computers and their languages? If we are to design effective tools for personal computers, we must take into account how humans organize and communicate information. It means common sense is still the best rule when we are thinking about what makes a "friendly" language. And common sense has little to do with numbers. Common sense is the art of making the difficult look easy, so that must be the goal of an effective personal language.

How do we transform this discussion of objects and relationships into anything resembling a language for computers? Let's take a specific example: let's sit down and think about a chair.

Rather than thinking about a chair as a collection of numbers representing the height of the legs, dimensions of the seat, and height of the back, we think about the notion of "chair" as an object that has certain properties. A primary property is the purpose of the chair; that is, a chair can be sat in to rest our weary bones. Less important properties might be its color, age, architecture, and who owns it. If pressed for details, we might begin to describe its parts and their relationships (four legs, attached to the seat, etc). It may not be clear yet that we can actually compute with chairs in the same way that we can compute with numbers, but at least the change of perspective should be refreshing.

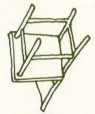

How can we represent objects? Well, in the next section—**Eye Object**—we show how to represent graphical objects we call

"turtles" by representing certain of their properties, such as shape, color, and position on the screen. That is, a turtle is represented by representing its properties. Of course, one particularly helpful property of such a collection of fuzz is that it has a classification. That is, it's a turtle, or it's a car.

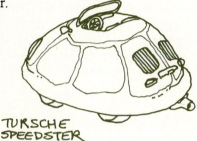

TURSCHE SPEEDSTER

The mind gets quite uncomfortable when faced with an unknown object; there seems to be a built-in urge to put everything in a category. So one property of a collection of objects that represents a turtle is that it **is** a turtle. Practically speaking, we need a way of telling the difference between a turtle and number. It doesn't make sense to ask a number to change color, nor is it appropriate to add the number 5 to a turtle.

Fortunately, there are some particularly attractive things we can do with Logo turtles. We can draw pictures and do animation, for example. But the general scheme for representing any kind of object follows the same pattern: to represent an object, represent its properties. And how do we represent properties? Well, properties are objects too; so we use the same recipe to represent a property. Of course, at some level we stop this representation game, saying, "This object is primitive, you fool."

We run into this same kind of situation when we start trying to find the definition of a word in a dictionary; either the definition satisfies us, or we must look up some of the words in the definition. Rather than shouting at us when it's time to stop, a dictionary is more subtle. We'll suddenly find a circular definition: one that uses a word whose definition we're trying to discover. We have learned to live with circular dictionaries; we can learn to live with objects

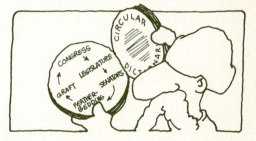

being represented by collections of properties, some of which are also objects that have to be represented. As we build up more clever systems that mimic human reasoning, we can expect to see more of such interrelated representations.

THINKING ABOUT [TLC] LOGO

Thus, a critical question is: how can we deal effectively with such complex interwoven collections of objects and properties. In the past a key to "effective dealing" has been shown to be the discovery of a good notation: that is, a notation that highlights the areas that are important for the topic under discussion. For example, the shift from Roman numerals (I, II, III, etc.) to Arabic numerals (1, 2, 3, etc.) opened the door to much of modern mathematics. More recently and closer to home, the introduction of high-level computer languages such as FORTRAN and COBOL made it much easier for professionals in engineering and business to specify the kind of computing they wanted done.

In engineering and the sciences, numbers and collections of numbers are used to represent mathematical relationships; in business, numbers and collections of alphabetic characters are used to represent facts and figures concerning individuals. We want to deal with objects, and thus need some way to represent them and describe relationships between them. What we need is a notation—a language—that will let us put these abstract relationships down in concrete terms. Whereas past notations have only had to deal with simple objects—numbers, characters, and well-defined collections of such— what we need is a notation for computing with, and thinking about, richly textured spaghetti-piles of interwoven objects.

Well, there has been a "FORTRAN-for-objects" language around for about twenty years. It is named Lisp (for LISt-Processing)

and is still the major language used for artificial intelligence research. Though Lisp has been an effective tool for the research community, it has not been particularly effective as an introductory language for learning about object-based notions. The Lisp language has a syntax that has been hard to teach to novices, and it tends to be run on expensive machines. Neither of these features made Lisp a candidate for Language-Of-The-Year. However, about fifteen years ago a Lisp dialect named Logo was developed. Besides introducing "turtle graphics"—the most visible feature of Logo—, the Logo developers included many of the features that made Lisp so valuable in the object-processing that occurs in artificial intelligence work. Some of the Lisp-like operations have been simplified, and the Lisp syntax has been replaced; all without doing great injustice to the simplicity, elegance, and expressibility of Lisp. These changes make Logo suitable for introducing some of the exciting applications of Lisp. Thus Logo has become something of a "BASIC-for-objects" language. We will use these Lisp-inspired list-processing facilities in the second part of the book.

We will use lists to implement objects, just like traditional languages use binary arithmetic to implement our more usual decimal arithmetic. In that regard, several machines have been designed and built to handle the notation of lists in hardware. More will come soon, and many will speak Japanese.

Back at a higher level, we must return to the question of notation for, and representation of, objects. The idea of an object is reasonably abstract. Perhaps the idea of pattern has a more concrete image. What is a pattern? Our dictionary says it's a "form or model proposed for imitation". The word "imitation" is reasonable. We can see if an object is a chair, for example, by seeing if it "imitates" or is similar to a pattern that we set up as the model of "chairness."

Essentially, we represent objects by patterns. If an object we come across matches a particular pattern then it belongs to a particular class of objects. Thus, a number is

recognized as a sequence or pattern of digits, perhaps decorated with a + or - sign in front. A turtle is represented as a sequence of properties too; this time the pattern is more complex because Logo turtles are more complex than numbers. Of course, by the time turtles and numbers get represented in the machine, they all look like the same old off-on switches, but that's not important. What **is** important is

that we can think about turtles as objects with which we can communicate.

And "communicate" is what we mean. For the next step is to develop a means for computing with turtles. Instead of demanding that our little turtle carry out our wishes without question, we want to suggest a different way—a more polite way—of dealing with the beast. We would rather think of the operations with turtle objects as the "sending of messages" to the turtle, and a turtle might just say "Buzz off, buster. I don't want to do what you re-

quest." Note the change of emphasis from computation to communication; this is important.

Think of each turtle-like object as a self-contained being that can make its own decisions about how to respond to messages. The being may handle the message itself; it may decide to pass the message to another being to handle; it may decide to reject the message totally. This style of message-passing supplies an elegant way of describing complex problems. You only have to describe the activity that each kind of being will perform and what the beings will do with messages that they don't understand. Thus we end up with a system of communicating beings rather than a society of slaves all being directed by the great computational know-it-all.

So, instead of coding our world as numbers for the machines, we can describe objects in terms we know and understand, and we can program computers to use these objects directly just as humans do. And instead of commanding our objects to perform for us, we will think about asking them to do things for us. We might even think about setting up a little self-governing society so that they can cooperate with each other to satisfy a request of ours. This idea of cooperating beings is a major change in attitude toward the machine and in the way we think about computation. The starting point is the realization that this change in perspective leads to personal languages—languages that will allow their users to present problems in more human-related terms. Logo—particularly TLC-Logo—is one of these newer languages.

Other languages that address these issues include Lisp, Smalltalk, and Prolog. We will say a bit more about these kindred spirits in Section IV. In this book we will be using TLC-Logo to illustrate the modern view of computing as communicating with objects by sending messages to them. Now, how far can we take these ideas of objects, communication, and messages? For example, can we apply these ideas to mimic the way humans think and reason in the real world?

For centuries, logic has been actively uncovering general rules that we seem to use in making sound judgements. For example, assume that we believe that whenever a certain situation is true, a second situation

must also be true. Furthermore, assume that we believe that the first situation **does** hold now. Then one rule of logic says that we must believe that the second situation also holds.

In more symbolic form:

We believe: Situation1 implies Situation2.
We believe: Situation1.
Therefore, logic says we must believe Situation2.

Furthermore, logic also tells us that if Situation2 is not true, then Situation1 must also not be true. For example,

We believe: The sun is shining implies it is daytime.
We believe: It is not daytime.
Therefore, the sun must not be shining.

These general rules, together with specific facts like:

Water boils at 212 degrees Fahrenheit.

If you run a red light, you'll probably get a ticket.

make up a good part of the information we use in carrying out intelligent behavior. Of course, the number of specific facts that a human knows is quite large, but the number of general logical rules that we use is quite small. What's interesting about this view of human information is that these rules and facts can be represented as patterns; that is, they are objects. Can we describe the way we use the logical rules and facts as computations with these objects and patterns?

Here are some informal examples:

(1) [[x + 0] == > x] might represent an algebraic simplification rule allowing us to simplify an expression like 2y + (4z + 0) to 2y + 4z.

(2) [[AND [IMPLIES S1 S2] S1] == > S2] might represent the first logical rule that we expressed a few paragraphs ago.

(3) Next, we might want to represent facts about the real world, classifying them according to their typical state (solid, liquid, or gas). An entry for water might contain the following:

THINKING ABOUT [TLC] LOGO

```
[Liquid [Name [Common Water]
        [Chemical H₂0]]
    [Boil [212° F]]
    [Freeze [32° F]] ]
```

(4) Even our discussion of traffic laws and the consequences of disobeying them could be represented:

```
[[ACTION [not[stop light]]]
        == > OUTCOME [ticket 61 %]]
```

So, in Section III we will write Logo programs to perform operations using facts and rules of logic. Do we then have an intelligent machine? No, we have a logical machine, capable of carrying out correct deductions. And what separates a logical deduction from an intelligent choice? A sense of purpose or direction, perhaps. And how much of what we call "purpose or direction" can we describe in terms of

PORPOISEFUL EXISTENCE

patterns, and computation, and communication? Such questions do not have nice, easy answers; but we can give some indications of what is possible.

In Chapter 7 we will show that it is possible to build a "smart" Logo system—a

Logo system that will be able to analyze its own behavior and make intelligent choices to recover from errors in a Logo program.

This intelligence includes the ability to correct the program, as well as continue the computation that had the error. A mind-reading program? Hardly. The "intelligence" is based on two very precise and important properties that languages should have.

- The programs are available in a form that the machine can manipulate. The machine will have to build new operations to solve new problems. One effective way to do this is to modify an existing program to handle a new situation. Of course, if we expect to build an error-correcting program, we have to modify the program that has the error. And how do we detect an error? That brings us to the second important property.

- The information about how we got to the error must be available in a form that the error-correcting program can use. This says that the program-running program leaves tracks around so that the error-detecting program can tell the error-correcting program what happened.

In the process of developing these ideas, we will have to analyze several levels of Logo. First, we have to become completely comfortable with the language itself. The **Eye Object** section will ask you to "play turtle" and submerge you totally in Turtles. Then we will "play computer", analyzing the way we could perform the computations if we were a computer. In this game we will discover that all computation —not just Turtle computing—is just "playing turtle." That is, all computation, no matter how complex, can be broken down into a couple of operations that are as simple and natural as those of turtle movement. Furthermore, the artistry and creativity that the Logo programmer uses in developing an elegant turtle picture corresponds to the intelligence component of the individual who applies these "computing rules." That is, just as there are "mindless, but correct" movements of the turtle, so too are there "mindless, but correct" applications of our rules of computation. However, we can show that a lot of what might be called purpose or direction, or artistry, can in fact be captured in programs.

It will take us most of the book to show how to build such an interconnected nest of Logo programs. It should be some consolation to realize that we do similar kinds of operations ourselves all the time in thinking, learning, and problem-solving.

Unfortunately, we don't think about how we think anymore. It's all second nature to us now.

To get a handle on these "thinking languages" we have to think about thinking—to "play brain." We have to pin down a few good ideas for organizing information and solving problems, and then try to work them into an effective language for programming a computer. For comparison, you might imagine what went on in the early days when counting and comparison

EARLY COMPUTER

gave rise to numbers and basic mathematics was born. Just as science and mathematics began to flourish when elegant mathematical ideas could be expressed in mathematical language, so too we are beginning to discover the need to invent good languages for describing the organization of thoughts, problem-solving, and intelligent behavior.

What are "thinking" ideas? We saw one earlier: the notion of everyday objects is a thinking idea. We think about a chair as a collection of information—some relating to its physical properties, and some related to its function as a receptacle for a posterior.

THINKING ABOUT [TLC] LOGO

Truly, a chair is a complex collection of ideas, yet we think about chairs without thinking about them. We take very complex collections of ideas for granted. Chairs come in all shapes and sizes, and next year will bring a new shape or two. If the shape is really bizarre, it'll take some convincing, but we'll accustom ourselves to the idea that this new object really is a chair because it fits the unspoken notion of "chair"

But how in the world can we expect to tell a computer what a chair is if we cannot

even give a precise description of it ourselves? Could we expect to come up with some magical mathematical formula for "chairness" and program that formula in Logo so that the number 18 comes out when we give the program a chair, and the wonderful phrase "it does not compute" is printed when we supply a boat, baby, or some other non-chair object?

No, we deal with the world in a very "sloppy" way, grouping similar objects together, and separating things that are different. But the importance of these similarities and differences change depending on the circumstances. We are capable of grouping complex objects (like chairs) into

collections, and are able to tell reasonably well whether or not some new object should be included in that collection. Decisions are made on the basis of properties that may change as time goes on.

Our ability to recognize similarities imposes order in chaos. It is the key to abstract thought—the ability to see that all chairs share a similarity of purpose is truly amazing. This ability to recognize similar objects can also be used to separate objects. As long as objects are not identical they will have differences, and in certain situations we may need to exploit the differences instead of the similarities. For example, when asked to set up a room for dinner, we would usually not consider using a rocking chair around the table; only in an emergency would we do so. Though all chairs are equal, some are more equal that others. Thus, there are specific properties of chairs that make them suitable for specific tasks. We are able to "mix-and-match" these similarities and differences at a very common-sense level, doing so with an ease that doesn't even begin to hint at the complexity of the operations our mind performs.

Unfortunately, we are too close to our minds; it requires great effort to think about how we think. This is because we play our minds like the virtuoso plays a musical instrument, thinking only of the desired effect, relying on the years of practice to carry out the details of execution. For example, beginning violinists will spend the majority of their time concentrating on the position of fingers and the angle of the bow. Hours of practice will be

SIMILARITIES & DIFFERENCES
"DITCH THE ROLLER, DEBBIE"

dedicated to making these motions "second nature". Only years later, when our student is a virtuoso, will she be able to concentrate on the mood and spirit of the music. When asked to analyze the performance our virtuoso can recount the details, and explain why and how the particular actions were done. Skills like driving a car or riding a bicycle have the same characteristics: the early phases concentrate on technique, only later do we become artists on wheels. But even then we could explain our driving techniques to others. It is much more difficult to analyze how you think.

Thinking is an acquired skill, like driving, riding, or playing an instrument. Unfortunately, the rules are learned so early in life that we have forgotten the practice periods. Even though we are still learning to think—still falling off our mental bicycle —we don't have the same kind of understanding that we do in the musical world. Unfortunately, we don't yet know how to teach thinking.

In the past, we have had some limited success by teaching specific subject areas that seem to contribute to "mind training;" Mathematics, Classics, and Physics come to

THINKING ABOUT [TLC] LOGO

mind. And of course, much of what we're talking about just involves **paying attention**; paying attention to our bodies, and paying attention to our minds. Again, these ideas are not innovations of modern computation; for example, acting techniques, based on Stanislavski's "Method," involve similar concerns to those raised in this book.

No, modern thought did not begin with the invention of the microprocessor. However, it **is** our belief that Computation offers the potential for a new discipline for mind-training: a discipline that will be closer to the actual topic—thought—than previous attempts. The personal computer will play a very important part in this new thought. The computer is a powerful tool and, as such, chances for misuse exist. As more and more powerful machines become available at the personal level, it becomes even more important that home users be aware of the potential applications their machines possess. The home computer is not just an electronic typewriter, a low-quality stereo, or a game machine; it has the potential to change the way the world thinks.

This book, then, has a much wider application than just learning to program in Logo. As we learn about Logo we should also learn about ourselves. We should try to pay attention to the thinking that we do, look for patterns—similarities and differences—in the way we approach problems. We should pay attention to thinking.

If we don't know how to teach thinking, do we know how to recognize it? Is thinking like "chair-ness", recognizable but indescribable? Of course, neither "chair-ness" nor thinking is totally indescribable; we can recognize intelligent acts as easily as we can recognize a lawn chair.

Let's lie back in our overstuffed green velvet chair and see what we can do about describing the process of thought. Well, a four-legged, straight-backed version of thinking is called problem-solving. That is, we have a specific goal we want to achieve—the problem; and we have a collection of techniques that may help us achieve that goal. The problem-solving process may involve:

- Planning what actions to take. Deciding to move a chair out of one room into another, involves making a plan, in our mind's eye, of how to get from one room to the next, moving from the original room to the final destination. This is a case of . . .

② BREAKING PROBLEM INTO SMALLER PIECES...

- Breaking the problem down into smaller pieces. Of course, even the best laid plans may go wrong. We may not be able to get the chair through a doorway, so we have to back up and try a different path. This is part of . . .

③ TRYING UNSUCCESSFULLY TO SOLVE THE PROBLEM...

- Trying to solve each of the smaller pieces. Obviously, if we can find a path from one room to the next, beginning at the origin and finishing at the storage room, then we have solved our problem. But of course, this is the real world and maybe there isn't any way to do it. Well, we never liked that chair anyway . . . .

④ FIND SHORTEST PATH...

⑤ WON'T FIT...

And how do we try to solve the smaller pieces? We apply the problem-solving process to each of the pieces. There is a characteristic optimism of human nature at work here, namely the belief that by breaking the problem into smaller pieces, the smaller pieces will indeed be simpler to solve. And furthermore, that the solutions to the smaller sub-problems can be combined to give us a solution to the large problem.

⑥ TRY ANOTHER PATH...

THINKING ABOUT [TLC] LOGO

The process of solving a problem by breaking it into sub-problems is quite complex. Yet we do things like this every day without—dare I say it?—without thinking about it. Yes, you are a virtuoso; you play your mental instrument very well. Much, much better than any computer equipped with the best of artificial intelligence software. Hey, how'd you get so smart?

⑦ DISASSEMBLE CHAIR...

⑧ THINK ABOUT IT

Of course, the bottom line on all of this—what separates these discussions from those that have occurred throughout history—is that these ideas can now be translated into actions. We can see the realization of the notions on machines. That's the exciting part of modern computing. And we can get to all of it from the lowly Logo turtle.

SECTION II: EYE OBJECT

What's an eye object? Well, there are at least two eyes to worry about. There's the mental eye—the mind's eye—that can visualize purple cows, talking turtles, and other abstract ideas. Then there's the physical eye, which has to be satisfied with the reality of brown cows, smelly turtles, and the hard, cruel facts of life. Of course, one person's abstract idea is another's reality. Hand-held computers are a reality to some of us, an abstraction to people twenty years ago, and beyond comprehension to a large percentage of the world's population. That's part of the intrigue of imagery and objects, and reality and abstraction.

Both the mind's eye and the physical eye "see" only a certain level of detail at any moment. When we "see" a physical chair, we probably ignore 99% of its detail. We only see the level of detail necessary to the current situation. If we're looking for a place to sit in a darkened theater, we want to make sure that the seat does not contain an object—like a person, a wad of gum, or a half-eaten hot dog. In this situation, we don't care about the shape of the chair (or the shape of the person, gum, or hot dog).

Similarly, our mind's eye is good at suppressing detail, imagining only the properties of the objects that we need at the moment. Of course, if more detail is required, our mind can dredge further into our mental stockpile of details. Our ability to change the focus of our physical and mental eyes is truly amazing. This ability to adapt—indeed, to understand that there is a **reason** to adapt—requires a sense of purpose. That sense of purpose is not

something we expect of a computer. Hmmm; is that a human prejudice, or fundamental difference between humanity and computers? We should probably try to answer this question before the computers do.

This section begins the search for answers. As with most puzzles, the key is to ask the right questions. Traditional computing has a tendency to ask the wrong questions:

- A computer is a series of light switches: Can a light switch think?

- A computer is a word-processor: Would you carry on a conversation with a word processor?

Languages like Logo are beginning to ask the right questions:

- A computer is a turtle: Would you take a turtle to lunch?

Of course, there's nothing special about turtles. Dogs, pigs, and ducks would work equally well. One important characteristic of this "barnyard" computation is that these creatures are good examples of visual objects. The creatures have properties like shape, color, and position. Another feature that attracts us is that these creatures **are** creatures; that is, they are beings that we can imagine having character and personality. It therefore makes more sense to think about conversations and communication with these animals. We will think about communicating with the creatures by sending them messages, rather than

viewing each as some obnoxious little machine. Furthermore, the messages will request that the creatures perform some motion that we can see on our screen.

First, we will build up our confidence in talking with these new friends. Then we will spend a chapter really putting the turtle through its paces. And in the final chapter of this section, we will open up the communication to a chorus of clamoring hatchbacks. In each of these adventures, we will be able to see the effects of our labors glowing on the screen. A picture is indeed worth a thousand words.

Humanity has used strong visual aids for a long time. We use maps to help visualize the path of a long trip. Yet what we see on the map is not a physical image of the actual path. At best we might have a topographical map—a map that indicates the heights of the land areas; but more than likely we have a map showing roads as little red worms on a field of uncooked pastry dough.

We may make drawings of a proposed house to help us imagine what it would be like to live in that house. Yet that house does not exist. We have pictures of the solar system, complete with the paths of the planets, even though no one has ever seen the system from the artist's viewpoint.

These examples show the power of visualization. Even very poor pictures frequently supply more information than pages of verbal description could provide. What happens when we move from physical objects to imagination? Do we think in words or in shapes? What does the mind's eye see?

Well, Albert Einstein had a tough time with words. He didn't talk until he was three and he had to work at putting words together into sentences when he wanted to speak or write. However, his mind's eye was wide open. He attributed his contributions to physics to a strong visual perception. He visualized the problems and their solutions in terms of shapes and images, rather than words and symbols.

Until recently, the written word has been the major way of spreading knowledge. The movie, the TV, and the video disc are starting to change that. We see the personal computer as yet another, more fundamental, component in the change. Even though the input language—Logo included—is still written, the graphical output offers a substantial advantage over the written word or piles of computer print-out.

If we could open up an encyclopedia to the discussion of the solar system and push a button that starts the planets moving around the sun we could gain a deeper understanding of planetary motion much more rapidly than if we had to build the visual images on paper or in our heads. We might find additional patterns involving the relative positions of the planets. We could, for example, discover how often the earth is in line with Jupiter and the sun. We want more than an animated encyclopedia, however. We want a tool to assist us in thinking about things that are not in an encyclopedia. We want to be able to communicate with our visual objects in our own personal way. Logo is an entry point to the new personal world of visual learning. Let's take a look.

CHAPTER 2
THE SHELL GAME

Meet the turtle. It's that little fellow sitting in the middle of your screen.

It isn't doing anything now except taking up space, but what can it do? Well, your turtle is a member of a rare species of Cheshire Chameleon; it can change its color and its shape. It can even make itself invisible.

Note to the gentle reader:
Since this book must apply to many different versions of TLC-Logo, we have to be

a bit vague about the shape, color, and versatility of the turtle. The best we can do is indicate general characteristics in this note, and strike a happy medium throughout the text.

Thus, on computers that support color, colors are indicated by numbers. Remembering which colors are associated with which numbers is an exercise best left to Logo. The solution is to define a word like blue to mean just that—the color blue. Logo uses make to associate objects—like numbers—with words that are more meaningful to us. If the number that indicates the color blue is 4, and you type the following:

make "blue 4

then you can type :blue instead of 4 whenever you want to refer to the color blue. We will use other words that we assume have already been defined with make. A complete list of these words appears in our Paint-by-Numbers section. If you expect to do a lot of Logo experiments, you may want to create an initialization file (called logo.log, for example) that makes your commonly used words. See your Logo user manual for details.

If your machine does not support color, don't read the preceding paragraphs. Similar variability will occur in the shape of the turtle—some turtles are arrows, some are sun dials, but in any case the default shape is displayed when the system comes alive. Furthermore, the number of shapes that the turtle can assume will vary from system to system.

The final area that we should mention is the screen size; since each set of hardware has different characterstics, your user manual should be consulted here.

We communicate with the turtle by sending it messages. For example, the ink message is used to ask the turtle to change

its color. The message:

ink :blue

will result in a blue turtle.

If the turtle doesn't look blue, get your system fixed or your eyes checked.

The "dots" character (:) decorating the word blue, specifies that the desired value for ink is the one that is associated with the

THE SHELL GAME

word blue. The word, ink, does not have "dots" in front because it is the request for an action ("change your ink color, please"). A word that does not have a decoration in front of it will always be interpreted by the turtle as a request.

Try a few other colors. The turtle will respond to every message you send, even if it doesn't understand it. If it receives a message that is incomplete—for example, if you request an ink change without specifying a color—it will let you know. If you send a message it doesn't know about, it will answer that it doesn't understand the meaning of the message.

We can also send messages that ask the turtle about itself. For example, the turtle knows what its current color is, and you can ask it by sending a slightly different form of the ink message:

ink ?

The ? is a value that Logo understands to mean "please tell me what the current value of the indicated property is". This time it responds with the number that corresponds to the color blue.

To make the turtle disappear we say:

turtle :hide

and to make it reappear we say:

turtle :show

where :hide and :show are also in our Paint-by-Numbers Section. And we can discover the current visibility of the turtle by:

turtle ?

To request a new shape for the turtle, we use shape, followed by a representation of a valid shape object. Shapes may be associated with words like "airplane" or "sun". For example:

shape :airplane
shape :sun

To get the arrow shape back enter:

shape :arrow

And of course the current shape may be discovered by

shape ?

So, a turtle has properties of color, shape, and visibility. In addition, a turtle has a position—its location on your screen—and a heading—the direction it is facing. The initial heading is straight up (or north); the initial position is the center of the screen. Now, let's get the turtle to move.

The l message asks the turtle to turn to the left some small amount. If you send

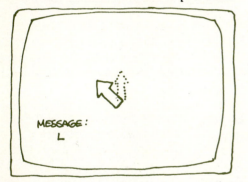

MESSAGE:
L

eight l messages, the turtle will turn all the way around, and back to the direction in which it started.

Try l l l l l l l l .

If the turtle's shape is an arrow, you will see the pointy end of the arrow change accordingly. So l can be used to change the heading of the hatchback. Pirouettes are wonderful, but what about getting off the dime? One way to do this is the f message. f causes the turtle to move forward in the direction it is facing. If you try it, you will discover another property of our friend: it draws lines as it moves.

The turtle is equipped with a pen that may be in one of two states: down or up. If the pen is down the turtle will leave a trail marking its journey. The color of the trail is determined by the color of the turtle. If the pen is up, the turtle will move without leaving a trail. The pen message allows you to examine or request a change in the pen state. That is:

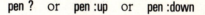

pen ?   or   pen :up   or   pen :down

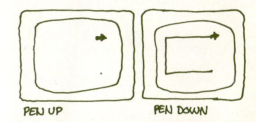

PEN UP   PEN DOWN

The type of trail left by the turtle is determined by its tile property. If the tile is a line tile, the turtle will draw lines as it moves. If the tile is a shape tile, the turtle will lay down rectangular tiles of the specified shape. The tile property is changed by the tile message. For example:

tile :sun   or   tile :heart

will result (assuming that the pen is down) in the turtle leaving a trail of suns or hearts behind it as it toddles around, while:

tile :line

will result in the turtle drawing lines as it moves.

Several tile shapes are predefined in your Logo system. It is also possible to make up your own tile shapes and name them. See your Logo manual for details on how to do this.

A turtle that is laying down tiles is called a tiling turtle or simply a "tiler". A turtle that is drawing lines as it moves is called a "toiler".

Given a specific sequence of messages that change its heading and position, the turtle will trace a path on the screen. For example, the sequence:

f l l f l l f l l f l l

will trace the sides of a square in either toiling or tiling mode.

The following sequence of messages:

tile :heart
f l l f l l f l l f l l

will draw a square whose borders are heart-shaped tiles. If we then send the messages:

tile :sun
f l l f l l f l l f l l

the heart-shaped tiles will be replaced by sun-shaped tiles.

So we have now discovered that the turtle has at least the following properties:

A shape
A color
A visibility state
A position
A heading
A pen state
A tile

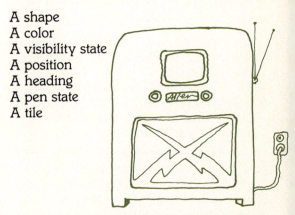

INVISIBLE PEN UP TOILING TURTLE

You can examine any of these properties by using ? with the appropriate message, and you can change any of these properties by supplying new values.

VISIBLE PEN DOWN TILING TURTLE

When the turtle first appears on the screen, its properties are as follows:

The shape of the turtle is an arrow.
The color of the turtle is black.
The turtle is visible.
The position of the turtle is the middle of the screen.
The heading is straight up (or North).
The pen is down.
The tile is a line tile.

Turtle Penmanship

Well, now you know what a turtle is. However, the description is about as exciting as the description of the physical characteristics of a chair or a musical instrument. Such descriptions never capture the total realm of possibilities that an object possesses. The physical description of a violin tells us nothing about the emotional power of the instrument in the hands of a virtuoso. Similarly, the realistic description of our chair doesn't hint at the imaginative power of that instrument in the hands of an eager mind. It took us several years to learn that chairs can be used to build forts

and precarious towers that may, at any instant, fall over and smash our mother's favorite vase. So, be patient. We will continue to pick and poke at the turtle to expose its potential applications.

Let's take another look at the infamous sequence:

f l l f l l f l l f l l

It consists of repeating the pattern f l l four times. This pattern draws a square. If we change the pattern by replacing each f by a sequence of the same number of f's, for example:

f f l l f f l l f f l l f f l l

we will get squares of increasing size.

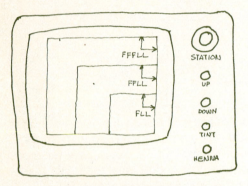

Try to imagine the drawing process by pretending that you are the turtle, standing at the lower right edge of the screen.

Now, let's change the original f l l pattern by adding or removing l's from the end. For example, try to visualize the turtle's interpretation of repeating the pattern f l several times. We get the picture! If the turtle turns only half as much we get twice the number of sides—an eight-sided figure. If we send other patterns of the form f l . . . l we get other figures. For example, f f l l l repeated over and over again will result in another eight-sided figure, an eight-pointed star. The additional f just makes it larger.

Adding even more l's to our pattern results in additional figures. Repeating the pattern f l l l l causes the turtle to march back and forth on the same line segment. Repeating f l l l l l l l l causes the turtle to march off the screen. This last effect occurs because our pattern asks the turtle to go forward and then turn completely around.

Repeating the pattern with f followed by five, six, or seven l's results in figures we have already seen: an eight-pointed star, a square, and an octagon. The only difference is in how the turtle draws the figure. These last figures are drawn as if we made right turns rather than left turns.

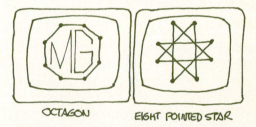

OCTAGON   EIGHT POINTED STAR

No new figures will be drawn by increasing the number of l's. For example, a sequence of nine l's following an f will produce the same figure as a single l since a sequence of eight l's is equivalent to rotating one complete turn. But this is the same as not turning at all. A sequence of 93 l's is the same as a sequence of five l's since each group of eight is the same as doing nothing at all; if we group them in blocks of eight we will have turned the twirling tortoise around eleven times with five left over.

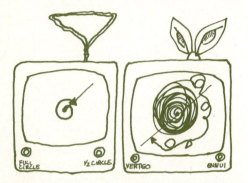

The turtle is a far better tool for visualizing this problem than dragging out a ruler and protractor, a device used to measure and draw angles (can **you** say "protractor"?). The message patterns are quickly and easily analyzed. The turtle is tracing a pattern. Our minds seem to work this way, too—always visualizing patterns. But our minds do more; they relate new patterns to old ones. The f l l message pattern repeated four times by the turtle tickles the mind in a way that brings up other images: the mathematical concept of a square, a window, a bad shape for a wheel, or—gack!—your seventh grade math teacher.

Our purpose is to expose the turtle's power and use it to look at some models of thinking. As we said earlier, we are after your mind.

Before we do any more of this business we will look at ways to improve our communication with the turtle.

It Moves, It Moves

Entering long sequences of messages can get very boring. What we need are ways to streamline our message-sending labors. For example, the square was constructed by repeating a certain pattern (f l l) four times. When we ask someone to repeat this sequence of actions four times we don't say: "do f and then do l and then do l and then do f and then do l and then do l and then do f and then do l and then do l and then do f and then do l and then do l." They'd lock us up for sure. Rather, we would say something like: "Repeat the following action four times: do f and then do l and then do l."

THE SHELL GAME

We want to get our message across in a nice compact form. TLC-Logo has a similar shorthand form when we want to send the same sequence more than once. It's called a **repeat** and it looks like this:

repeat 4 [f l l]

Whenever we send a **repeat** request we always need to provide two other pieces of information: (1) the number of times a pattern is to be repeated and (2) the collection of messages to be repeated. The collection of messages is enclosed in square brackets, and the resulting bracketed billet-doux is called a list. When the turtle receives a **repeat** message it just performs the contents of the list the specified number of times.

Notice that we could simplify the **repeat** example a bit more, saying:

"repeat the message, f followed by l twice, four times."

repeat 4 [f repeat 2 [l]]

Our turtle is certainly no great conversationalist. With the limited vocabulary of f and l, combined with **repeat**, it won't get asked to many parties. But we can turn the

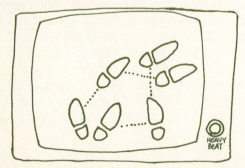

wallflower into the life of the party with a short course in surveying.

First, we'll let our friend know that f means "go forward 10 steps"; then we'll give the turtle a new message that will allow it to go forward any number of steps, and then watch out world!

The new message is named **fd** (forward). For example, **fd 32** asks the turtle to move forward 32 steps in the direction it is currently headed. There is also a message named **bk** (back) that requests the turtle move backwards a specific number of steps. We can use the **fd** message to draw windows of any size. For example:

repeat 4 [fd 25 l l]

is a request for the turtle to draw a square with sides 25 steps long.

Since we're building up our vocabulary, here are some other messages: to move the turtle north, south, east, or west, use **n**, **s**, **e**, or **w**, respectively. Like **fd**, each of them requires a number that says how far to step in that particular direction. However, they differ from **fd** in that they always go in the specified direction, ignoring the heading of the turtle. For example, we could draw a square using these messages:

n 25 w 25 s 25 e 25

However, this **n w s e** sequence will always draw a square that has a north-south orientation, that is, vertical sides and horizontal top and bottom, and will always leave the turtle in the southeast corner. In

contrast, if the turtle is facing a direction other than north when we send
repeat 4 [fd 25 l l], we would still trace a square, but now with a different orientation. The repeat 4 [fd 25 l l] captures the essence of squareness more completely than the n w s e sequence.

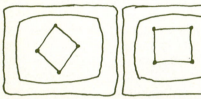

EXOTIC FLL POSITION EXCITING NSEW POSITION

Since we're talking about aesthetics, let's look at fd 25 and repeat 25 [fd 1]. The overall effect of the two messages is the same: the turtle moves from one position to another. The visual effect is quite different, however, because the time the turtle needs to take one large step is the same as it needs to take one small step. In the first case the turtle arrives at the destination almost instantly, but it takes the turtle about 25 times as long to stroll to its destination using the second message.

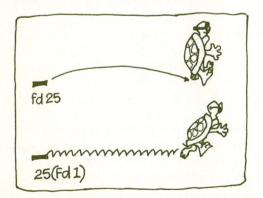

fd 25

25(Fd 1)

Actually, it is a very fast stroll. We can slow it down by using a delay after each step, as in repeat 25 [fd 1 delay 10]. The turtle will pause briefly after each step. If you want to decrease the speed of the turtle even more, simply increase the size of the delay, as in:

repeat 25 [fd 1 delay 20]

We can use this technique to create an animated object—a moving turtle. The first thing we want to do is to get the pen up so that no lines are drawn, then start the turtle moving in small steps. For example, the sequence:

```
home
pen :up
l l
bk :xmax/2
repeat :xmax [fd 1 delay 10]
```

requests that the turtle move to the right hand edge of the screen and then march quickly to the left hand edge of the screen.

home requests the turtle to return to its home position, i.e., the middle of the screen, facing north. l l requests the turtle to turn toward the left edge of the screen. (You've probably discovered by now that two l's will make the turtle do a quarter turn to the left; 4 l's request an about face; 6 l's cause a ¾ spin to the left (same as a ¼ turn to the right, but you knew that already); and 8 l's bring about a perfect pirouette. Finally, we use :xmax, as a name for the number of steps it takes to go all the way across the screen.

THE SHELL GAME

Since airplanes and suns are objects that typically move through the sky, we might want to change the shape of the turtle to one of those objects prior to sending the **repeat** message. Behold, the secrets of the

video games are unveiled! Moving objects are just shapes that are displayed at one position and then moved to the next position. Exploding airplanes can be accomplished by changing shapes. For example, try sending the following **shape** messages after sending the turtle across the screen:

```
shape :explode1 delay 10
shape :explode2 delay 10 shape :void
```

Assuming that we have defined the shapes :explode1, :explode2, and :void, the exploding turtle can be accomplished by changing the shape of the turtle without moving it. As another example, if we use two different shapes of a man—one shape depicting a man with his right arm up and his left arm down (:wave1), and another depicting a man with the left arm up and

the right arm down (:wave2)—we can create a frantically waving man by sending the message:

```
repeat 100 [shape :wave1 delay 10
            shape :wave2 delay 10]
```

HO, HUM

The **delays** are there to slow down the shape changes enough to obtain the desired visual effect.

We can combine these two forms of animation—changing shapes at the same position and moving a single shape from one position to another—to obtain an even more complex type of animation. To get a moving and waving man, try:

```
home
pen :up | | bk :xmax/2
repeat :xmax [shape :wave1 delay 10
              shape :wave2 delay 10 fd 1]
```

The role of the turtle has changed. Rather than an object with uninteresting properties like shape, position, heading and pen state, and simple line drawing capabilities, it has taken on the roles of entirely different types of objects. It's like a child —being home on a rainy day—suddenly realizing that Dad's favorite chair would make a great foundation for the Empire State Building; . . . then tables and lamps take on new meanings.

Your own creative instincts have changed how you view things. The chair and the turtle haven't changed. You have added new properties and new uses to objects that were already well defined. You wanted to build a copy of the Empire State Building and your mind gave you the best available building materials that it could imagine. Watch out, King Kong, here we come!

City Limits

Let's not get carried away with this monkey business. Let's go back to the wonderful world of turtles and messages. Notice that messages like f, fd, bk, n, and s are used to move the turtle around relative to its current position, while the l message is used to turn the turtle relative to its current heading. It's like giving the directions:

make one quarter turn to the right and walk 25 miles, then turn to your left one quarter turn and walk ten miles and wait for further instructions. Of course we know that directions may also be given more explicitly, if the receivers knows their way around town. Directions like "Go to the jailhouse and bail out Dad" work out much better in such cases. Well, the turtle knows its way around Turtle Town.

We need a way to identify each point in the world of Turtle Town. Since this is a two-dimensional town, we can view the town as a grid, assigning a pair of numbers to each landmark. We'll represent each such point as a list [first.point second.point] where the first.point indicates its horizontal (across) position in the town and the second.point indicates the vertical (up-down) position in the town.

Imagine that the screen is split into four equal parts by two lines: one splitting the screen into top and bottom halves (called the x-axis), and the other splitting the

screen into left and right halves (called the y-axis). The four parts are then the top-right (called the "first quadrant" by mathematicians; sounds like Star Trek, doesn't it?), the top-left (second quadrant), bottom-left (third quadrant), and bottom-right

THE SHELL GAME

(fourth quadrant). Now that we've just about O.D.'d on jargon we can get down to the business of . . . what was it? . . . oh, yeah, how to find our way around Turtle Town.

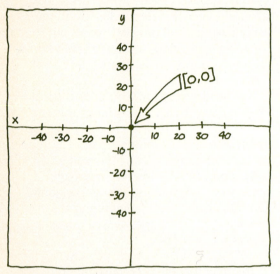

The center of the screen, where the lines cross, is the point [0 0]. This point has special meaning for our turtle friend; it is home. We can imagine that each of the lines is marked in turtle steps, and each mark is numbered. On the x-axis, numbers go up to the right and down to the left; on the y-axis, numbers go up as you go up on the screen, and down as you go down (clever, eh?). Since the center of the screen is [0 0], if we go to the left of center, or below it on the screen, we have to use negative numbers.

To find the pair of numbers representing a point, we see how far across the screen it is using the x-axis, and we find its vertical position using the y-axis. We agree that

whenever describing points by a pair of numbers, we always give the x-coordinate (position across) first, and then the y-coordinate. Notice that the point [30 40] (approximate location of Duckopolis) is not the same as [40 30] (Acme Cattery).

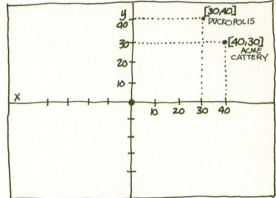

Since computers don't agree on how many points there should be on the screen, we assume that there are :xmax points across, and :ymax points vertically on the screen. Since the 0 point is in the center of each axis: the highest x-coordinate will be :xmax/2, call it :x.half; and the highest y-coordinate will be :ymax/2, call it :y.half. We can then claim that the corners of the screen are at the points [x.half y.half], [-x.half y.half], [-x.half -y.half], and [x.half -y.half], going counterclockwise from the upper right corner.

Armed with this information, the position of the turtle can always be described by a pair of numbers. This pair of numbers is used as the value of the position property—named pos—of the turtle. Whenever the turtle moves to another location, the

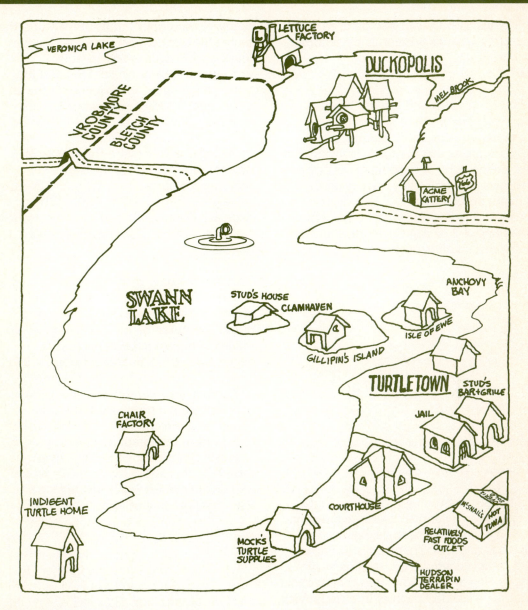

value changes to reflect this position. Messages like fd and bk move the turtle to new points on the screen without explicitly saying which point to move to. The pos

message allows us to ask the turtle to move to a specific point on the screen:

pos [25 59]

The **pos** message can also be used to ask the turtle what its position is by sending:

pos ?

We can also set and test the heading of the turtle. The heading of a turtle is measured in degrees. A heading of zero degrees means that the turtle is facing due east (to the right), a heading of 90 degrees indicates that the turtle is facing north (straight up), a heading of 180 degrees means it is facing due west (to the left), and a heading of 270 degrees implies it is is facing due south (straight down).

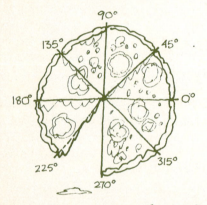

ANCHOVY PIZZA COMPASS (MEDIUM)

That is, the heading is an angle that is measured in a counterclockwise direction, beginning from the zero degree heading, which is due east. There are 360 degrees in a complete revolution, starting at zero and ending at 359. Now, you may wonder why there are 360 degrees in a circle. Well, we did too; we have spent a considerable amount of time, energy, and imagination discovering the true story. It is well known that Henry VIII's anatomy is the origin of

many of our current units of measure: the inch—the distance between the first two joints on his right index finger; the foot—the length of his left foot; and the yard—the length from his nose to the end of his right middle finger when his arm was fully outstretched. Well, in 1547 he decreed that the "V" made between his inch-finger and his yard-finger was 36 degrees, and was to be the standard measure for pizza slices. Why 36? Because he reigned from 1509 to 1547. Why degrees? Because the court pizza concession was run by C. DeGrease. But we digress . . .

So far, the only message we have that changes the heading is l; it is a special case of the lt (left) message. The lt message requires a number be included, requesting the turtle to turn left that number of degrees. Thus l is an abbreviation for lt 45.

Another way to request a change in heading is the rt (right) message. It is similar to lt, except that the turtle is asked to turn right instead of left. Both of these requests change the turtle's heading, relative to its current heading. We would also like to ask the turtle just to face a certain direction. Just as **pos** is used to set the

RT 270   RT. 66

position, we have a message, **hd**, to manipulate the heading of the turtle. The **hd** message is a request to either set the heading to a specific direction or to ask the turtle its current heading. The message:

hd 180

asks the turtle to face due west.

And we can discover which way the turtle is facing by:

hd ?

Another way to specify the turtle's heading directly is to have it face some other point in Turtle Town. The **face** message accomplishes this task. For example, **face [0 0]** will change the turtle's heading so that it faces the center of the screen.

Junk Mail Computing

Well, so now we know some of the details of Logo: how to communicate with the turtle, and how to draw some interesting pictures. It's amusing, but hardly a challenge to the local video arcade. There must be more to Logo than this! Indeed, let's rip away the superficial exterior, and examine the superficial interior. We can find some endearing principles behind the turtle tracks. Can we find any enduring principles? We have several of those, too. In particular, our notion of sending messages to turtles—though a little strange, even for California—contains some important lessons.

Each message has two components:

1. An indicator that tells what we kind of operation we want the turtle to perform (turn left, go forward, deal with a property);

2. A specific value for the turtle in conjunction with that indicator. The ?-valentines ask the turtle what its current value for a property is. Others ask the turtle to change the value of a property; some requests may require that the turtle move about to fulfill the request.

They're all messages, and it's up to the turtle to respond to them if it so desires. Fortunately our turtle is polite and patient, and will respond in a courteous fashion if the request makes sense.

If, for example, we say **fd 10** we are saying to the turtle "Hey, tortoise, we want you to go forward, and the distance we want you to go is 10 turtle steps." We can string messages together as in:

fd 10 rt 90

and the turtle is smart enough to figure out the two requests. (We don't mess around with stupid turtles.) The turtle is also smart enough to understand abbreviations, like:

repeat 4 [f l l]

for:

f l l f l l f l l f l l

This ability to abbreviate—to understand slang—shows that at least someone's playing attention; however the way an individual joins the IQ club is by demonstrating the ability to take existing concepts and group them together in novel ways.

And that individual's language demonstrates its expressive power and subtlety by allowing those new ideas to be expressed by new words—thus extending the heretofore mentioned individual's language. Indeed. Where would we be without words like "computer", "automobile", and "pontification"? Where would we be without pontification? Just think about all the unemployed dictionary publishers. Anyway, we'd like that same ability for our turtle language: the ability to define new words.

For example, we would like to expand the TLC-Logo vocabulary by having it

associate the pattern **repeat 4 [fd 10 lt 90]** with a name that indicates what it does. Well, what does it do? It builds a square, each of

whose sides is ten turtle units. Wouldn't it seem useful, therefore, to name this **square10**? Ok, how about:

```
to square10
  repeat 4 [fd 10 lt 90]
end
```

The **to** message informs the turtle what the new word is and what collection of

messages should be associated with it. The end message indicates the end of the definition.

That's all there is to making a definition. Using the new word is equally easy. Just use it, as in:

```
square10 rt 90 fd 15 square10
```

and we could capture this collection as yet another word:

```
to boxes
  square10 rt 90 fd 15 square 10
end
```

and use it: repeat 4 [boxes]

So, we can define new messages in terms of messages the turtle already knows. Logo keeps track of these new messages in a message dictionary. When adding a new entry to the dictionary two pieces of information are needed: the name of the message and what it means. The words describing the new message must be words that the turtle either already knows or can find in its dictionary. Gee, with power like this, we can conquer the world.

For example we could specify bigger and better squares, like:

```
to square20
  repeat 4 [fd 20 lt 90]
end
```

But a square is a square regardless of the length of its sides. What we'd really like is one message named square, say, that allows

us to specify what the length of each side should be, in the same way that we can specify a distance each time we use fd. To define a message that will require more than just its name when we use it, we need some way to indicate that additional information must be provided. Also, we need to indicate how that additional information is to be used in the definition.

The problem we face is like that of creating a form letter that leaves spaces for the name of the victim. When it comes time to send the message we fill in the name of the victim in all the appropriate places. For example:

Dear :victim,

It has come to our attention that you, :victim, have come into a large sum of money and that you, :victim, would like to be relieved of the awesome responsibilty of keeping it. Please contact . . . . .

Slovenly yours,

Chicken Cacciatore

where we have written :*victim* to indicate where substitutions are to occur.

THE SHELL GAME

This form letter filler is exactly what we need to describe our computational concept. Therefore we have called this the Junk Mail Model of Computation. In Junk Mail Computing—called JMC—we can embellish our simple to definitions with these dot-ified names. Thus a general, universal, and all-purpose square maker can be named **square** and defined as:

```
to square :side
  repeat 4 [fd :side lt 90]
end
```

When it comes time to actually make a square of size 10, for example, we will write

```
square 10
```

and the right thing will happen. That is, the turtle will find the name **square** in the message dictionary and will notice that it

needs a value to substitute in the victim slot **:side**. Fortunately for us (and the turtle), we have supplied a number, **10**, for if nothing is provided to fill in the slot then

the definition won't make sense to the turtle. And we don't want to mess with an angry turtle.

Before going on to more exciting turtle functions we should think a bit more about JMC and how our armored friend might perform the operations. So here is a more detailed discussion:

When the turtle retreats inside its shell after receiving the message:

```
square 10
```

1. It rummages through its list of known message indicators, looking for **square**.

2. It finds that the **square** recipe is a form letter.

3. Since **square :side** is defined as **repeat 4 [fd :side lt 90]**, it substitutes 10 for **:side** and replaces the problem of **square 10** with:

```
repeat 4 [fd 10 lt 90]
```

4. It busily goes to work on this problem and in short order has flopped around the screen as expected.

This is all there is to Junk Mail Computing:

I. The request is a message that is "obvious"—like f, l, or rt **90**. These are the primitive operations that the turtle is born with and they just get done—no fuss, no muss.

II. The request uses a defined word. The beast looks up the word, sees if it requires some values for victims and, if so, either complains if they are not given, or substitutes them into the definition if they are supplied. The turtle then tries to satisfy the requests in the new sequence of messages. Each of these requests will, itself, be a case of **I** or **II**.

Here's a more tricky example:

```
to growsquares :size
   square :size
   rt 20
   growsquares :size + 5
end
```

growsquares is our name, and growsquares 10 is our game.

It's not immediately clear what pattern this message will give us. We can be either theoretical or experimental tortoise torturers:

1. A theoretician would ponder growsquares 10—perhaps proving a few theorems—until the true nature of the turtle droppings became apparent.

2. On the other hand, a hacker's eyes would glaze over at even the suggestion of pondering. "Just do it!", he would shriek. And so we do.

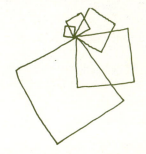

Here's how to view the JMC calculation of growsquares 10:

growsquares 10 is

square 10
rt 20
growsquares 10 + 5

but that says: "First knock off a size 10 square." That involves performing repeat 4 [fd 10 rt 90]; that is:

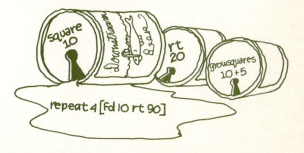

THE SHELL GAME

Of course, while we're performing the **repeat** we must remember to turn right **20** degrees and then **growsquares 10+5** after the square is completed. So we do, and finally we meet up with:

growsquares 10+5

We can simplify the expression 10+5 to 15, and so we can reduce:

growsquares 10+5 to growsquares 15

Of course, our toiler will begrudgingly respond, reducing the request to:

square 15
rt 20
growsquares 15+5

Get the message? Each gentle hint will be handled in exactly the same way. First, a substitution; then the execution of the resulting expressions, carrying out the requests in the order we find them in the JMC letter.

We have over-simplified one piece of the JMC computation in all our simplifying and substituting; namely our sly replacement of 10+5 by 15. This kind of arithmetic computation is a special case of JMC, but so commonplace that we overlook it. To make it more clear, consider the following TLC-Logo functions:

```
to sum.of.squares :x :y
  (sq :x) + (sq :y)
end
```

and:

```
to sq :x
  :x * :x
end
```

Inside **sum.of.squares** we used parentheses to specify the order in which the operations

were to be carried out. Without parentheses sq :x + sq :y would have been interpreted as:

sq (:x + sq :y)—not what was desired.

Logo tends to collect arguments with functions in a left-to-right order, the exception being infix operators like + and =. It's best to parenthesize any experession that's not totally clear. Basically, if it's not clear for you to read, then beware. However, the important point here is to show the evaluation of a complex experession:

fd sqrt sum.of.squares 3 4, where sqrt is the
        square root function.

To begin, we work on the expression sum.of.squares 3 4 and substitute 3 for :x and 4 for :y getting (sq 3) + (sq 4). So the above expression reduces to:

fd sqrt ((sq 3) + (sq 4))
> and similarly, sq 3 is 3*3, so we reduce to:

fd sqrt ((3*3) + sq 4)
> Now 3*3 can be reduced to 9, giving:

fd sqrt (9 + sq 4)
> similarly, we reduce sq 4 to 4*4 and then to 16, giving:

fd sqrt (9 + 16)
> which finally results in 25 as the value of sum.of.squares 3 4

Now we can apply the sqrt function, getting 5; and finally we can perform:

fd 5

Thus arithmetic computations can be handled by JMC in exactly the same way as turtle movement. The interesting thing about this last exercise is that such computation is the same kind of thing that many of us suffered through in high school algebra—the evaluation of "functional notation." That is, Logo definitions like sum.of.squares and sq represent mathematical functions that we might have seen in school as:

> "Let *f(x,y)* = *x*∗*x* + *y*∗*y*. What's the value of *f(3,4)*?"

Now we see that TLC-Logo can do this evaluation for us. Furthermore, as the sqrt usage showed, we can feed the results of one computation—sum.of.squares 3 4—directly

into another—sqrt. This ability to directly use results as values for further computation is called "functional composition." Such composition has not been demonstrated before because most of the turtle functions we've used were performed to move the turtle, not compute a meaningful value. Turtle functions like fd or rt give value "nothing.

This ability to compose Logo functions gives the language expressive elegance and simplicity. Without it, we would have to write such cretinous things as:

make "x sum.of.squares 3 4
make "y sqrt :x
fd :y

Basically, a fate too horrible to contemplate; but never fear, TLC-Logo and functional composition save us from such disaster. As we proceed, we will see this facility again and again, . . . but we digress.

THE SHELL GAME

To tie up loose ends, we should relate JMC to other kinds of computing. In particular, the notion of "victims" is identical to the mathematical idea of "arguments to a function", and to the programming term called "formal parameters". Furthermore, the technique replacing victims with values is closely related to the idea of "function evaluation" in mathematics, and "interpretation" in programming. Thus, in the future we will talk about "arguments (or parameters) to functions" rather than "victims", and "evaluation" or "value of . . ." as the result of performing JMC on a Logo expression.

We will come back later to poke the JMC model in more depth, but for now we will appeal to your good-natured common sense when it comes to carrying out to messages. Keep it in the back of your mind —or wherever you keep such things—that we can always go back to the JMC model to see what's going on.

Greasy Turtles

A few years ago—about 2400, to be precise—in early Greece, Pythagoras proved

the Pythagorean Theorem. We'd like to use our turtle knowledge to establish that result now. To do so we need the following:

1. Some idea of what the theorem states:

Let x and y be the sides of a right triangle, and let h be the length of the hypotenuse, then $x*x + y*y = h*h$. So, for example, we could define a right.triangle program by:

```
to right.triangle :x :y my :t.pos
  fd :x
  make "t.pos pos ?
  bk :x
  rt 90
  fd :y
  face :t.pos
  fd sqrt sum.of.squares :x :y
end
```

where my :t.pos declares that t.pos is a scratchpad name to be used inside right.triangle and no one else can play with it. And, where we have—just by accident, of course—already supplied the definition for sum.of.squares

2. Some idea of how to prove it:

What we'll actually do is show it graphically.

3. A collection of TLC-Logo functions to use in the computation:

We need to know how to draw squares;
we need to know how to draw triangles.

Well, we can already draw squares.

Triangles we have already handled too, but we used the Greek's result in the construction. So, below is an alternative, done more in the style that we'd expect with a straight-edge.

```
to triangle :x :y my :t.pos
  fd :x
  make "t.pos pos ? ; save the current position
  bk :x
  rt 90
  fd :y         ; make the other side of the triangle
  pos :t.pos    ; now draw a line to the saved point
end
```

The point of this demonstration was to link geometric discussions with numeric arguments by showing a construction that verified the Pythagorean Theorem. Well, here it is:

```
to demo :x :y
  triangle :x :y
  fd :x rt 180
  triangle :x :y
  rt 90 fd :x lt 90 bk (:x - :y)
  triangle :x :y
  rt 90 fd (:x + :y) rt 90 bk :y
  triangle :x :y
end
```

How does this help? Perform demo and find the three squares of sides :x, :y, and :h. We have to show that the area inside the :x-square plus the area inside the :y-square, equals the area inside the :h-square. Sneaky Greeks—that's why a number multiplied by itself is called its "square." Anyway, now convince yourself that the area **inside** the squares :x and :y but **outside** the :h-square, is equal to the area that is **inside** the :h-square but **outside** both :x- and :y-squares. Now don't complain that it's too hard! All Pythagoras had to work with was a sharp pointed stick and a sandbox.

And he owned cats, not turtles.

Notes to the Turtle

A simpler example: assume that we want to create a **square**-like program that will decorate the perimeter of the square with a tile shape of our choice. The definition will have two arguments: one for the size of the square, and the other for the tile shape to use. Here it is:

```
to tile.square :size :tileshape
  pen :down
  tile :tileshape
  repeat 4 [fd :side l l]
end
```

Now, if we type:

```
tile.square 40 :block,
```

we will get a tile-bordered square that is forty turtle trots on a side. The :block tile is a solid square shape. We must remember that the number that immediately follows the message name tile.square will always be used for the length of a side, while the second number will always refer to the shape of the tile to be used. To request a square tiled with hearts, we enter:

```
tile.square 40 :heart
```

The length of a side is always in turtle steps. Since a block or a heart might in fact be larger than one turtle step on a side, we

will not necessarily get forty hearts on a side; we'll get just enough hearts to make forty turtle steps. Thus, the message tile.square 40 :heart results in the same size square as tile.square 40 :shape for any value of :shape.

When we were messing around with message patterns involving f's and l's, we discovered that the number of f's determined the size of a turtle drawing while the number of l's determined the shape. Our shapes were limited because the l message does a left turn of a prescribed amount (45 degrees). Let's experiment with other turning angles. That is, if we repeat the message pattern fd :n lt :a over and over, where :n and :a are arguments to be supplied by the mad scientist, we can obtain all kinds of creations. To do this, we define a draw.pattern message as follows:

```
to draw.pattern :n :a
  fd :n
  lt :a
  draw.pattern :n :a
end
```

The first argument, :n, has the same effect as it did in the square message: it will control the size of the figure. The second argument—angle :a—will determine the shape. If we send,

```
draw.pattern 40 30
```

the turtle will look up the form, do a fd 40, a lt 30 and then get another copy of the form using the same arguments (40 and 30). This new copy will request that the turtle do another fd 40, another lt 30 and get yet another form , ... The turtle will continue this behavior forever, unless you press CTL-G (that is, hold down the CTL or CTRL or CONTROL key while you hit G), or in desperation, pull the plug. Some interesting results occur if you use draw.pattern with angles of 72, 144, 118.

Instead of punishing the same victims over and over again, let's change one of the arguments each time we ask the turtle to look up a new form. For example:

```
to new.pattern :n :a
  fd :n
  lt :a
  new.pattern :n+5 :a
end
```

Now, if we request:

new.pattern 5 90

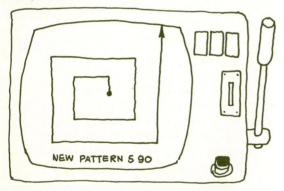

NEW PATTERN 5 90

the tiny toiler will stamp out a fd 5, and a lt 90, before looking up a new copy of new.pattern with arguments of 5+5 and 90. This new copy requests the turtle to stomp out a fd 10, a lt 90, and to get another copy of new.pattern with 10+5 and 90; eventually the turtle will stomp off the screen.

The turtle can add degrees as well as numbers. So, let's try changing the angle each time.

```
to mystery.pattern :n :a
  fd :n
  lt :a
  mystery.pattern :n :a+10
end
```

Try mystery.pattern with 5 for :n and 3 for :a. Visualize what the turtle will do. Do the same thing with 5 and 5.

By letting mystery.pattern call mystery.pattern, call mystery.pattern . . ., we can create some rather elegant pictures; however, it's rather bad form to bury our buddy's nose in the perimeter of the screen. In the next chapter we'll see a sure-fire way of protecting his proboscis; here we'll show how to control his cavorting and to make non-ending animated features. For example,

```
to fly
  shape :eastair
  pen :up
  pos [-:x.half 0]
  hd 0
  repeat :xmax [fd 1 delay 10]
  fly
end
```

Setting up the turtle to play airplane consists of taking its pen away, giving it an airplane shape, and putting it in a reasonable place from which to launch itself. The fly message sets the shape and pen state every time the fly form is sent.

THE SHELL GAME

Let's make the flight a round trip, and do the launch preparation only once by defining the following messages:

```
to launch
  pen :up
  pos [-:x.half 0]
  hd 0
  zip
end

to zip
  shape :eastair
  repeat :xmax [fd 1 delay 10]
  shape :westair
  repeat :xmax [bk 1 delay 10]
  zip
end
```

Now the turtle puts on the airplane costume only once; zip will scoot it across the screen from left to right, change its shape to an airplane looking left instead of right—airplanes don't fly backwards—and

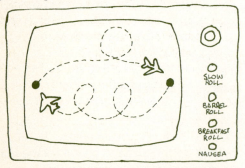

scoot it back. For a change of pace, suppose we want to make solid colored blocks on the screen. One way to accomplish this would be to drop block tiles along the border of a square, and then fill in the

center by tiling smaller and smaller squares inside the first one.

```
to blockout :size
  shape :block
  square :size
  blockout :size-1
end
```

This message tiles in our square as desired, but then the turtle freaks out and starts tiling in the opposite direction, creating a larger and larger block until it falls off the edge of the world.

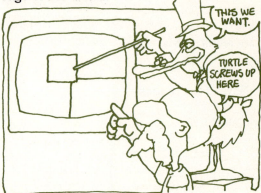

For example, blockout 4 results in:

```
square 4
blockout 4-1, which results in
    square 3
    blockout 3-1, which produces
        square 2
        blockout 2-1
            square 1
            blockout 1-1
                square 0
                blockout 0-1
                    square -1
                    blockout -1-1
```

or, summarizing the turtles activities:

square 4
square 3
square 2
square 1
square 0
square -1
square -2
square -3

. . .

A square with a negative number is drawn by moving forward negative steps, which means the turtle merrily goes a-tiling—backwards. Of course, eventually it will tile itself away. Our **blockout** message gives us more than we asked for. We'll visit **blockout** again later, and see that we **can** get it to do what we intended.

So that's the situation on turtle programming. We've seen our little buddy grow from a tongue-tied terrapin, to an accomplished conversationalist all in one easy lesson. In the next exciting chapter we send our little buddy to dancing school.

CHAPTER 3
LOGO MOTION: EXERCISING YOUR TURTLE

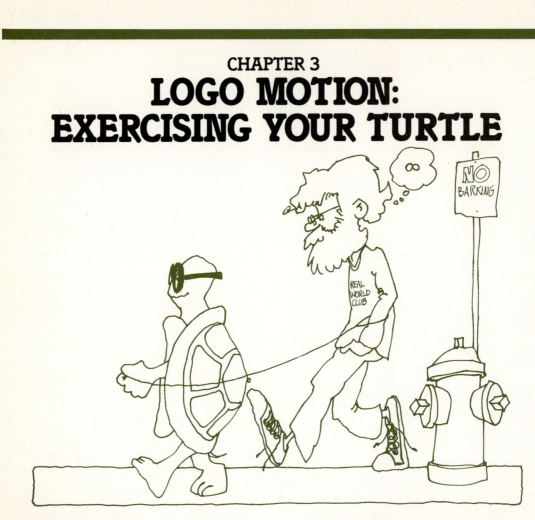

Decisions, Decisions

Now that you know all about the properties of a turtle and have had some practice walking it around Turtle Town, we can get on to the industrial strength stuff. This will expose some of the turtle's mystical mind-clouding capabilities that are best discussed in serious company after the lightweights have gone back to watching reruns of test-patterns.

We are going to examine the "thinking" processes of the calculating creature. Rather than just "playing turtle", we will ask you to think like a turtle—well, would you believe, bark like a duck?

Since we're on the subject of turtle brains, we should point out several rather anti-social attitudes that our little fellow demonstrated in the last chapter. In particular, **draw.pattern** wound up retracing the same old trails after awhile, while others, like blockout, proceeded to march the turtle off the screen. How tacky.

Of course our turtle had the best of intentions in blockout; it was supposed to fill in squares to make building blocks, that could be used as parts of larger pictures. For ex-

ample, a house can be built out of a triangular block and a square block, with other blocks for doors, windows, and

chimney. We want to fix up blockout so that it will paint the square and then stop. Enough's enough.

Just to refresh your dynamic memory, here is what the turtle was doing in the blockout message. The turtle, gone mad, started moving backwards when the :size argument became negative and these backward tile trails became increasingly longer. Eventually, the turtle backed off the edge of the world after tiling a much larger area than we intended. We would like to have the turtle think about what it is doing, and stop blockout when the step size turns negative.

We already know that the turtle is paying attention a bit; it can tell us what its color is, where it is, and in what direction it is heading. That is, it is able to examine the state of its own world. But that's only half

half the battle: if someone walked up to you and said "My frob is grebbon" you wouldn't know how to react to that information unless you knew that frobs should **never** grebbon (panic and run for cover!), or grebbon will drive up the price of pork bellies (good news unless you're a pig). That is, we have to be able to evaluate the information we receive and then change

because (or in spite) of that evaluation. So too, our armored colleague needs ways to test the fickle waters of reality to see if it's "sink or swim."

One of the most common tortoise tests is the old "tell me if these two things are equal" trick. In TLC-Logo we write this as:

:thing1 = :thing2.

For example, if the current ink is green and we ask:

(ink ?) = :blue

the turtle will recognize this as the question "Is the current color of the ink blue?". Our friend will resist the temptation to respond "Check your eyes, buddy", and will politely but firmly respond:

false

notifying us that green isn't blue.

We saw in the last chapter that turtles can do arithmetic. So, for example, if we type:

3 + 2 = 5

the turtle will tell us that this is a true claim by responding with the word **true**. Hey, this guy's no dummy.

We can also compare the relative size of numbers. For example, < is the "less than" relation in TLC-Logo. So if we enter:

3 < 1

asking if 3 is less than 1, the turtle will respond:

false

Turtle tests need not be restricted to numbers. For example, assume that the

turtle had just been sent home and we typed:

(pos ?) = [0 0]

this time the turtle will get the pos ? message, returning [0 0] since it was at home, and then check the equality of this point with the point [0 0]. It responds with true.

Furthermore, a variable may appear as part of a claim. For example:

:x = 4

will give true if the value of :x is 4, and will give false otherwise. This use of variables in testing is the key to halting the turtle at the right time in blockout. The turtle can look at the current distance (:size) in the definition of blockout and make sure it is greater than zero. We can set up the claim "The value of size is greater than zero" as:

:size > 0

and the turtle will respond with either true or false.

So we can collect and evaluate information. Since this is not a bureaucratic turtle, it must be able to make decisions and take action. To express this desire in TLC-Logo, we follow a claim with iftrue and/or iffalse messages.

iftrue [what-to-do-if-claim-is-true]

iffalse [what-to-do-if-claim-is-false]

For example:

(:wishes = :horses)
iftrue [beggar :ride]
iffalse [lt :out fd :poor.house]

The turtle's response to the iftrue-iffalse messages depends on the success or failure of the preceding claim. If the claim is true, the turtle will be asked to respond to the iftrue message-collection you supply. If the claim is false, the iftrue-collection is ignored and dropped in the dead letter file. For example, if we type:

(3 + 2 = 5)
iftrue [square10]

the turtle will evaluate the **square10** message because the claim immediately preceding it is indeed true. If we type:

(3 + 2 = 6)
iftrue [square10]

the turtle will trash the **square10** message and prepare itself for our next exciting request.

The **iffalse** message works in a similar way. Thus, if we follow up a false claim with an **iffalse** message, then the truthful turtle will respond to the **iffalse**-collection. For example:

(3 + 2 = 6)
iffalse [square10]

will require our honest turtle to scribble a square. If we type:

(3 + 2 = 5)
iftrue [something :else]
iffalse [square10]

the only ethical thing the turtle can do is **something :else** and ignore the **square10** request.

So, to summarize the situation: A claim is an expression that is either true or false. A claim that is followed by an **iftrue** or an **iffalse** message is called a conditional message. The conditional message allows the turtle to examine the state of the world and decide what to do based on the information it has at its disposal.

Turtle Construction Co. Inc.

And behold, we now have at our finger tips all we need to solve the problem of filling a square without sending the turtle into reverse tiling mode: we use a conditional message that compares the **:size** with zero; if it's greater than zero, then we want to continue tiling. Otherwise, do nothing—it's time to stop. So finally, we define a new, improved, solid-state **blockout** as follows:

```
to blockout :size
   (:size > 0)
   iftrue [square :size
          blockout :size-1]
end
```

blockout asks the turtle to pass judgement on the claim :size > 0. If the verdict is true, the turtle will draw the square and then do the blockout form with a :size that is one smaller. If the verdict on :size > 0 is false,

then the iftrue messages will be ignored. Since there is nothing more to do, the turtle just returns the final judgement and waits for the Post Office to deliver a new message.

So we can build some nice square blocks. Rectangular and triangular blocks would also be useful for Beginning Arts-and-Crafts. Well, we can tile a rectangle

similarly to the way we tiled a square. That is, simply start at one corner and tile smaller and smaller rectangles until the area is completely filled in.

Let's call the rectangular block filler, rec.block. It will need two pieces of information as arguments: one for the length and one for the width of the rectangle. Thus:

```
to rec.block :length :width
   ? ? ?
end
```

where the question marks indicate that we haven't really figured out what should go there yet. In blockout, we quit tiling if :size was less than or equal to zero. That worked because a square has only one size for all its sides, but a rectangle has sides of different sizes. So now we want to quit tiling if either the length or width of the rectangle is less than or equal to zero. Or, to put it another way, we want to keep tiling if both the length and width are greater than zero.

We're in luck. We can ask the turtle to ponder a clammy collection of claims by asking, "Are all of the claims in the following collection true?" If any of the claims in the collection is false, the turtle should declare that the big claim (the claim that they are all true) is false. If all the claims in the collection are true, our fair-minded friend should give a rousing **true** to the super class-action claim.

The Logo word to request a verdict on all members of a colossal claim is—appropriately—named **all**. We're in good hands with **all**, for now we can fill in the question marks in **rec.block**. The claims we want to make are that the following both hold:

:length > 0
:width > 0

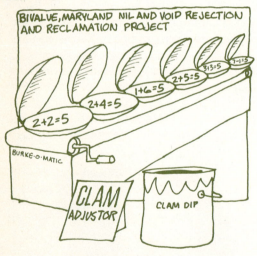

(A DISCLAMER)

and we include our claims in a list by surrounding them with square parentheses. Thus, the claim on which to pass judgement is:

all [:length > 0 :width > 0]

If it's false, we don't want to do anything. If it is guilty as charged then we want to tile a rectangle and then block out a smaller rectangle. Putting it all together, we want to replace the question marks by:

all [:length > 0 :width > 0]
iftrue [rectangle :length :width
        rec.block :length-1 :width-1]

We still haven't told the turtle how to **rectangle**. This little subproblem is solved by asking the turtle to draw two sides of a rectangle and then repeat them:

```
to rectangle :long :wide
  repeat 2 [fd :long rt 90 fd :wide rt 90]
end
```

The master builder still needs a triangular block. To keep things from getting any more clamorous than they have been, we will stick to triumvirates with equal

sides. That means, to make a triangle we turn the same amount after drawing each side. So:

```
to triangle :size
   repeat 3 [fd :size rt 120]
end
```

ought to do the job.

Now to fill in the middle part. This task is more like **blockout** than **rec.block** because all sides are the same:

```
to tri.block :size
   :size > 0
   iftrue [triangle :size tri.block :size-1]
end
```

Finally, let's try building a house. We start with a large blue square:

```
tile :block
ink :blue
blockout 25
```

Next is the roof. Our convex carpenter is sitting at the lower left-hand corner of the living part of the house—hardly the place to put the roof! So we move the turtle up to the top of the house and nail on a red triangle:

```
fd 25
ink :red
tri.block 25
```

Galloping Galapagos!!

Bleagh! A triangle is a triangle is a triangle, but a roofer with a sense of humor is a pain in the neck. So we'd better get our heading straight. We need to point the turtle towards the peak of the roof. Let's get rid of the misplaced roof by coloring it the same color as the screen:

```
ink paper ?
tri.block 25
```

The **paper ?** part of the message returns the background color of the screen, which is then used in the ink request. The **tri.block** message will then trace over the misplaced triangle. By painting it the same color as the screen, we effectively erase it. Pretty sneaky.

Now, let's put the roof on right.

```
rt 30
ink :red
tri.block 25
```

In order to get into the house, let's make a green door. We will remember to get the turtle in the right place this time:

```
pen :up
lt 30      ;because that points the turtle straight up
bk 25      ;now, it's at the left end of the foundation
rt 90      ;we're almost there
fd 9       ;doors are never in the middle of a house
lt 90           ;we're ready!!
pen :down       ;it won't show if we don't
ink :green
rec.block 15 7   ;do it!!
```

So much for Carpentry 1A. Now let's consider a slight variation of blockout:

```
to mystery :size
  :size > 0
  iftrue [mystery :size-1 square :size]
end
```

Though not obvious, perhaps you can see that mystery asks the turtle to strut its stuff from the inside, out; while blockout says to tile a square first, and then do the stuff in the block form. The differences between the two definitions can be clarified by examining detailed versions of the turtle's JMC travels—as we shall now illustrate:

Graphical Mystery Tour

Let's follow the actions of the turtle as it reacts to the following message:

```
mystery 3
```

To begin the Junk Mail Computation, the turtle will search its dictionary for the word mystery. Finding the definition, it fills in the

actual victim, 3, for :size, and then winds its way through the words contained in the filled-out form.

```
3 > 0
iftrue [mystery 3-1 square 3]
```

It sees the claim 3 > 0 and reduces it to true. Since the next message is an iftrue, it is left with the following message pattern to handle:

```
mystery 3-1    square 3
```

The turtle simplifies the 3-1 to 2:

```
mystery 2    square 3
```

Another mystery form is filled in to replace mystery 2:

```
2 > 0
iftrue [mystery 2-1 square 2]
square 3
```

Once again, since the claim is true, the turtle must act on the messages contained in the iftrue message. It now must handle:

```
mystery 2-1    square 2    square 3
```

Simplifying the 2-1 calculation, the turtle is left with:

mystery 1   square 2   square 3

We go through the substitution process again, which results in:

1 > 0
iftrue [mystery 1-1 square 1]
square 2
square 3

This simplifies to:

mystery 0   square 1   square 2   square 3

Gasp! Again, we fill out a new mystery form:

0 > 0
iftrue [mystery 0-1 square 0]
square 1
square 2
square 3

The turtle recognizes that 0 > 0 is false —about time! The iftrue part is ignored, and we are left with just:

square 1   square 2   square 3

The mystery message is no longer present and the turtle dispenses with the whole thing after tiling squares with sides of length 1, 2, and 3, in that order.

If we carefully followed the JMC expansion of blockout 3 (we'll leave that painstaking—or giving—process to you), we would find that it would result in:

square 3   square 2   square 1

That is, blockout 3 will tile a square 3, and then request a blockout 2, which asks the turtle to do a square 2 and blockout 1, and so on. The difference, then, is the order in which the squares are done. Anyone who has tried to walk through a closed door understands that the order in which actions are attempted can make a difference.

The Cheshire Turtle

What kind of antics must we put the turtle through to produce a chessboard on the screen? Well, we want to describe a turtle request that will lay down eight rows of squares, where each row contains eight squares. Furthermore, no two squares whose sides touch can have the same color. We won't always want a regulation chessboard. We might at times like a seven-squared board or a ten-squared board. We want the freedom to choose the colors. Thus, we want to define a new function, named chessboard, that expects to be given the colors for the squares and the number of squares on a side. What kind of turtle is best suited to the job? A toiler would come in with two buckets of paint and agonizingly paint one square using the paint in one

bucket, move over, and paint the next square with the color in the other bucket, without slopping over onto the square it just finished.

We'd rather propose a tiling turtle with two sacks of tiles, each sack containing tiles of one color. Our interior decorator will lay down tiles, first from one sack then the other, one row at a time so as not to step in the glue. When a row is finished, the toughened tiler will move down and do the next row, and so on, until the job is done. Now, we need to write down the recipe for doing this. Where shall we start? Let's say we choose the names "c1" and "c2" for the tile colors, and the name "n" for the number of tiles on a side. Our first communication will be:

"Make a row of n tiles across, alternating the colors c1 and c2."

Now we can proceed in one of two directions. We could stop and explain in detail how to tile a row, thickening the plot. Or, we could describe the next step in the tortuous task, and complete the recioe for row tiling at a later time. We opt for the latter, continuing with:

"After completing a row of tiles, move down and get ready to tile a row in the other direction right underneath the last one you did."

Finally, we say:

"The job will be finished when you have completed n rows of tiles."

The grand plan to accomplish the job is expressed in Logo by:

repeat :num [makerow :c1 :c2 :num downrow]

where :c1 and :c2 are the words used to refer to the two colors and the word :num is used to refer to the number of tiles on one side of the chessboard. **makerow**, which is coming soon, will ask the turtle to lay down tiles of alternate colors in whatever direction the turtle happens to be headed, while downrow will set up the turtle's heading and position so it can tile the next row down.

Before we set the tireless terrapin to work, we need to tell it where we want it to start, what kind of tile to use, and what color tile to use for the first tile. We need a "get ready to tile" message that sets up the

FILLMORE'S TILE SHOP

turtle with the desired tile shape, a starting position, and an initial heading to start the tiling. The color to use on the first tile will be the first one mentioned. chessboard can then be defined by:

```
to chessboard :c1 :c2 :num
  getready
  ink :c1
  repeat :num [makerow :c1 :c2 :num downrow]
end
```

getready will select a solid colored tile, plop the turtle down in the center of the screen, set the heading so the turtle is facing east, and set the pen down. Here's the definition:

```
to getready
  tile :block
  pen :up
  home
  hd 0
  pen :down
end
```

We need to define makerow so the turtle will install the correct number of alternating tiles in a row. Try this:

"Throw down a tile, change ink, and make a row of n-1 tiles."

Throwing down a tile is accomplished by sending the message fd :tile.width. This assumes that the turtle is headed either horizontally to the left or horizontally to the right when the message is sent. It also assumes that we have already used make to tell the turtle what the value of :tile.width should be. (This number will be different on different computers.)

Changing ink requires that we know what two colors are available and what the current ink color is. The colors are named :c1 and :c2. Since we can inquire about its current color, we can request an ink change by saying "If the current ink color is the same as :c1 then please change ink to :c2; otherwise, change to :c1." We can handle the ink switch with the following:

```
to changeink :c1 :c2
   (ink ?) = :c1
   iftrue [ink :c2]
   iffalse [ink :c1]
end
```

Now, back to thinking about makerow. We want to have our tiler lay down :n tiles. What do we do if the value associated with :n is less than one? Don't do anything. If :n is at least one we want to cement a tile and make a row of :n-1 tiles right beside it. Aha! makerow can be defined by:

```
to makerow :c1 :c2 :n
   :n > 0
   iftrue [fd :tile.width
          changeink :c1 :c2
          makerow :c1 :c2 :n-1]
end
```

Notice that each time we send a new makerow message, the value for :n is one less than the time before; thus, we can be certain that eventually :n > 0 will be false, and we will be done. Before we had conditional messages we were unable to stop—as our first version of blockout demonstrated. In general, it is considered good form to be sure your program stops. Either the program is "straight-line" code, an application of repeat, or it should use a conditional message that checks some stopping conditions—we don't want to wear out the poor turtle.

The one remaining thing we need to complete our chessboard message is a definition of downrow. downrow must turn the turtle around and move it down one row into position for tiling the next row. We don't

care what the turtle's current heading is; we can do an about face by turning right 180 degrees. To move it down, we just move south a distance of :tile.length (we assume that :tile.length has been defined with a make message); again, we don't care what the current heading is, the s message will not affect it.

One more thing: note that after laying down the appropriate number of tiles in one row, the turtle is out of the area to be tiled. After doing the about face and moving down a row, we need to move it over one tile before we actually start laying down tiles again for the next row.

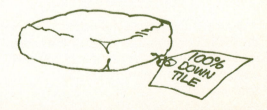

Here is the long awaited definition:

```
to downrow
  pen :up
  rt 180
  s :tile.length
  fd :tile.width
  pen :down
end
```

First, we lift the pen off the screen because we want to move the turtle without tiling. We move the turtle into position, and then put the pen back down. A question that we haven't examined—a possible bug—is: Is the color of the turtle set correctly? That is, will the next row start with the appropriate color? Well, the answer is yes! Why? Because back in **makerow** we see that the color changes after laying every tile. Since the last tile laid is just above the next tile to be laid, we can be confident that we will start out the next row with the right color.

Winter Wanderings

For our next trick, we have the turtle get into the snowflake business. Drawing flaky pictures can be done by a simple repetitive process called line fracturing.

The first thing we need to do is draw a line that we can fracture. So grab your turtle (make sure it has an eraser) and do it:

Now, split the line by erasing the middle third of it, and then draw a tepee whose

sides are the same length as the piece you just erased:

Now we have four lines. Do it again for each of the four lines. Now we have sixteen lines.

Guess what? Do it again for each of the sixteen lines. Now we have sixty-four.

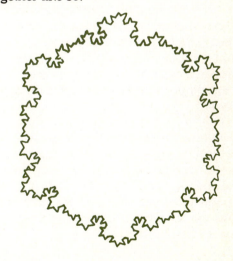

This doesn't look like a snowflake. But it does look like part of the outside edge of a snowflake. Hmmm, let's put several of these pieces together. Six copies are pasted together like so:

Now, we have something to rave about.

To ask the turtle to draw snowflakes like this we need to think about it a little more. Let's start with the general shape of the snowflake, ignoring the flaky edge for a moment. Before fracturing each side, we have a six-sided figure called a hexagon. (Hex means the number six in Greek.) To have the turtle draw a hexagon we would send the message pattern fd :x rt 60 a total of six times.

Instead of sending the message fd :x, which draws a line, we want to have the turtle draw the flaky part of the snowflake. So we start with the following message definition:

```
to hexaflake :x
  repeat 6 [flake :x rt 60]
end
```

where flake is a function that draws the flaky part. We are making the assumption that the turtle will draw one of the six flaky parts and will wind up in the same place it would if it had just done a fd :x. This assumption is reasonable as long as we always supply a value for :x that is divisible by three.

Now how do we draw the flaky part? First we should decide just how flaky we want it. Since no two snowflakes are the same and we don't know the effect of all the possibilities yet, let's write the definition so that we can draw snowflakes with different levels of flakiness.

That is, one level of flakiness will be the simple tepee (the four-line figure), the second level of flakiness will be the sixteen-line figure, and so on. Thus:

```
to hexaflake :level :x
  repeat 6 [flake :level :x rt 60]
end
```

flake will now have two arguments to play with: the level of flakiness as well as the size of the flake.

A first level flake is drawn by taking a line of length :x, erasing the middle third, and drawing the sides of the tepee. Rather than waste time erasing, we will simply draw a line of length :x/3, draw the tepee sides, and another line of length :x/3. In Logo, we say:

fd :x/3 teepee fd :x/3

Drawing the tepee so that the turtle is set to receive the last fd message is done by the following message sequence:

lt 60 fd :x/3 rt 120 fd :x/3 lt 60

Putting it all together gives us:

fd :x/3
lt 60 fd :x/3 rt 120 fd :x/3 lt 60
fd :x/3

This last sequence of messages describes a fractured line made up of four smaller lines of length :x/3. To draw a second level flake, we simply fracture or flake each of these smaller lines. Since each smaller line is drawn by the four fd :x/3 messages, one way to get a second level flake is to substitute the sequence:

fd :x/9 lt 60 fd :x/9 rt 120 fd :x/9 lt 60 fd :x/9

for each fd :x/3 message in the first level flake. (Note: one-third of :x/3 is :x/9.)

That is, a second level flake is obtained by doing a first level flake on each of the line segments in a first level flake.

But this is the key to the whole problem! A third level flake is drawn by doing a first level flake job on each line in a second level flake and a fourth level flake is drawn by doing a first level flake on the lines of a third level flake, and a fifth level flake is . . . well, you get the idea.

The message flake 1 12 is the first level flake message and flake 2 12 is the second level flake message for fracturing a line of length 12. Before asking the turtle to actually draw part of a flake, we need to check the level of flakiness required. If the level of flakiness is 1, then we send the sequence:

fd :x/3
lt 60 fd :x/3
rt 120
fd :x/3 lt 60
fd :x/3

and if the flakiness is a higher level we send:

flake :level-1 :x/3
lt 60 flake :level-1 :x/3
rt 120
flake :level-1 :x/3 lt 60
flake :level-1 :x/3.

That is, each line of length :x/3 is replaced by doing a :level-1 flake on that line. Our definition of flake becomes:

```
to flake :level :x
   :level < = 1
   iftrue [fd :x/3
           lt 60 fd :x/3
           rt 120
           fd :x/3 lt 60
           fd :x/3]
   iffalse [flake :level-1 :x/3
           lt 60 flake :level-1 :x/3
           rt 120
           flake :level-1 :x/3 lt 60
           flake :level-1 :x/3]
end
```

flake :l :n, where :l is an integer value that specifies the level of flakiness and :n is a number that specifies the length of the line, can replace any occurrence fd :n whenever we want to replace a straight line by a flaked line. This works since the turtle will end up with the same position and heading after completing a flake :l :n as it would if it had done a fd :n (as long as :n can be divided by three :l times and still be a whole number).

For example, we can modify square so that each side has been flaked:

```
to square.flake :x
  repeat 4 [flake 3 :x rt 90]
end
```

provided that :x can be divided evenly by 27.

We can generalize the dandruff drawing even further: any multi-sided figure can be flaked!

```
to anyflake :level :x :sides
  repeat :sides [flake :level :x rt 360/:sides]
end
```

Note that the angle turned after drawing a flaked side of our multi-sided figure is determined by dividing one complete turn by the number of sides in the figure. This way we can be sure that we have made a complete revolution by the time we have repeated :sides smaller turns, that is, :sides * 360/:sides = 360.

To draw a four-sided figure we turn 90 degrees (360/4), and to draw a triangle we turn 120 degrees (360/3).

THE COMPLEAT REVOLUTION

Dots, Dots, and more Dots

Remember the coloring book that had dot-to-dot drawings with numbered dots? The game was to connect the dots in the order specified by the numbers and reveal the picture trapped by the numbers. It was good therapy for tired minds, and by now the terrapin has a tuckered thinker. So let's teach the game to the turtle.

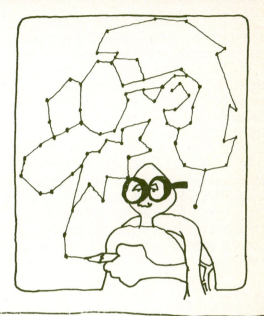

The key to the dot-to-dot game is the **pos** function. Recall that **pos**, followed by a list of two numbers will set the turtle at that specified point; **pos** followed by **?** supplies a list of the two numbers that represent the current position of the turtle.

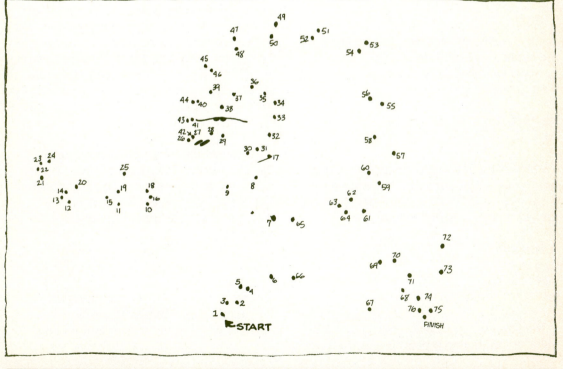

For example, assuming that the pen is down and the turtle is at the position [40 30], then we can draw a square with:

```
pos [40 10]
pos [60 10]
pos [60 30]
pos [40 30]
```

What we need for a dot-to-dot game is a collection of dots with numbers next to them, then we can use the turtle to connect them. First, let's create the dots and their number-tags on the screen. We'll set up our doddering dotter as a toiling turtle with the pen up:

```
tile :line
pen :up
```

Whether you want the turtle visible or not is a matter of taste. Regardless, the dots are created by moving the turtle to the position we want a dot, and then sending it a dot message. For example:

```
pos [10 20]
dot
```

Since we will want to create lots of dots, let's define a new function that takes a point as an argument, moves the turtle to the point and does the dotting:

```
to dot.at :loc
  pos :loc
  dot
end
```

Note that we need only specify one argument. Even though a point is specified by a pair of numbers, the pair is regarded as one object —a collection of two numbers. Any collection of things inside square brackets is regarded as a single object. To dot the four corners of a square we can simply use dot.at at each of the four corners. For example:

```
dot.at [40 10]
dot.at [60 10]
dot.at [60 30]
dot.at [40 30]
```

will do the job. So far, so good.

We still need to put a number tag on each point so that we know in what order to connect them. Luckily for us we have several options available here. The turtle can lay down tiles with numbers on them. However, tiled tags are annoying when we get to numbers that require cementing more than one tile in place. It requires a bit of care to define a Logo function that will get the digits out of a number, get the correct tile, and place it in the correct place on the screen.

So what's the alternative? Fortunately, the TLC turtle knows how to print words, numbers, and strings at its current position. The tp message—short for turtleprint—does this. For example, if the turtle is at [20 30], then:

```
tp 47
```

will print the number 47 beginning at [20 30]. The turtle won't change its position as a result of printing the message; it will just reach out with its pen and print the characters.

The turtle will print any word we ask it to, including numbers, regular English words, or garbage words like Ribbit. To print a number we just type it in, to print any other kind of word we type a quote character (") and then the characters that make up the word, and to print out arbitrary strings we just enclose the string in single quote (') characters. For example:

tp "Malicious

will print the nickname of a well-known duck, and:

tp 'Malicious Melvin'

will print the complete name of the aforementioned unaffable animal.

Back to dots. Since every dot that we make on the screen will have a number tag on it, we might as well include tagging in

the **dot.at** definition. But where should the number be printed? We need to be careful not to write the number on top of the dot,

so we want the turtle to move over before beginning its printing task. Let's call the complete definition **dot.n.tag**. It will have two arguments to deal with: the location of the dot and the number tag to be printed alongside the dot. Here it is:

```
to dot.n.tag :loc :tagnum
  pos :loc
  dot
  e :dot.width
  tp :tagnum
end
```

The first two lines put the dot at the location of the :loc argument, while the second two tag the point, placing the number just east of the dot. So, to create the pattern of dots used to draw the square we could send the following messages:

```
dot.n.tag [40 10] 1
dot.n.tag [60 10] 2
dot.n.tag [60 30] 3
dot.n.tag [40 30] 4
```

We can create our dots pictures, complete with tags, for any set of points we choose; but we want to streamline the way it gets done, letting the turtle handle all this drudgery for us. The new definition, named

dotmaker, will take a collection of points and generate a dot.n.tag request for each point in the collection. The first point in the collection will be tagged with the number 1 and successive points will be tagged with successive numbers. So dotmaker will have two arguments: a list of points, called :points, and a number, called :num, with which to tag the first point. We need to define dotmaker so that the message:

dotmaker [[40 10] [60 10] [60 30] [40 30]] 1

will accomplish the same thing as sending the four dot.n.tag messages listed above.

We want to grab the first point in the list, dot it, and tag it with :num. We can grab the first point in the list using the first operation and use that as the first argument in a dot.n.tag:

dot.n.tag first :points :num

That takes care of the first point. Now for the rest. To dot and tag the rest of the points we simply supply another dotmaker form with different arguments. The first argument in the new form will be the first argument in the current form with the first point removed. We accomplish this by asking the turtle to construct the list as follows:

"Get a pair of square brackets and make a copy of everything but the first thing in the list of points and stuff it between the square brackets in the same order as the original list of points."

The way we tell the turtle to do this is to say:

bf :points

The bf stands for "butfirst". For example, if the list associated with :points is:

[[40 10] [60 10] [60 30] [40 30]]

then bf :points will have the turtle construct the following list:

[[60 10] [60 30] [40 30]]

Now, the second point in the original list is the first point in this new list. Thus, the numeric argument in the new form should be one larger than the numeric argument in the current form because we want dotmaker to tag it with 2. Here's the result:

dotmaker bf :list :num + 1

Putting these pieces together gives us a definition of dotmaker:

```
to dotmaker :list :num
  dot.n.tag first :list :num
  dotmaker bf :list :num + 1
end
```

This will tag all the points by dot.n.tag-ing consecutive elements in :list. Now, :list—like all good things—must come to an end. Unfortunately, our dotmaker is unable to put on the brakes. To see what's happening and to see how to fix it, we examine what the turtle is doing when we just send:

```
dotmaker [[40 10] [60 10]] 1
```

Using the Junk Mail Computation rules for handling forms, the turtle replaces the original dotmaker request by:

```
dot.n.tag first [[40 10] [60 10]] 1
dotmaker bf [[40 10] [60 10]] 1 + 1
```

The turtle grabs the first point in the list and simplifies the above to:

```
dot.n.tag [40 10] 1
dotmaker bf [[40 10] [60 10]] 1 + 1
```

The turtle performs the dot.n.tag [40 10] 1, dotting the first point and tagging it with the number 1. It then looks at:

```
dotmaker bf [[40 10] [60 10]] 1 + 1
```

and simplifies it to:

```
dotmaker [[60 10]] 2 which it JMC's to:
```

```
dot.n.tag first [[60 10]] 2
dotmaker bf [[60 10]] 2 + 1
```

Our tortoise plods on, simplifying the above to:

```
dot.n.tag [60 10] 2
dotmaker bf [[60 10]] 2 + 1
```

The predictable beast dots the point [60 10], tags it with the number 2, and replaces the dotmaker message with:

```
dotmaker [] 3      and JMCs it to:
```

```
dot.n.tag first [] 3
dotmaker bf [] 3 + 1
```

Now we've got a problem: the turtle would like to simplify first [], but unfortunately there is nothing in the list to grab. The turtle complains, dispenses with the whole business, and replies with a nasty message. Our points did get dotted and tagged. However, this is hardly the polite way to treat a turtle.

We've seen this kind of a situation before. In **mystery** we square danced until the size of the square became zero; here we want to stop our dotting and tagging when there aren't any more points left in the list. So, when the list is empty, the turtle should be sent off to a well-earned rest. We can define a function named **empty** to tell if a list **is** empty:

```
to empty :l
  :l = []
end
```

We can use **empty** as follows:

```
to dotmaker :list :num
  (empty :l)
  ifalse [dot.n.tag first :list :num
          dotmaker bf :list :num + 1]
end
```

So if **empty :l** is false, then there are more dots to drop and tag, otherwise we bail out. And speaking of bailing out, it's time to pass on to other dotty topics. As we do, we want to mention again the connection between the behavior of **dotmaker** and **mystery**: both have to know how to stop; **mystery** counts down the square size to zero, while **dotmaker** counts down a list 'til it's empty. These techniques are powerful ways of controlling a computation, and are highly suggestive of the way **we** solve problems by reducing complex problems to simple problems.

Speaking of reducing the complex to the simple, we can frequently decode mysterious dot-to-dot figures into simple combinations of less mysterious dot-to-dotings. For example, cast your eyes upon the following lowly circle:

We could hack it into two pieces as follows:

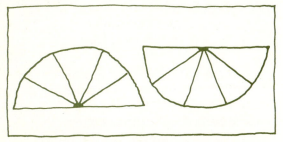

A less apparent trashing is the following:

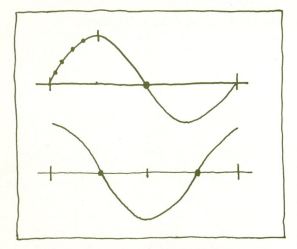

Now how in the world did we get that? We hacked the pizza into half-slices —eighteen degrees. We made a list of the second coordinates of points on the edge;

[0 .31 .59 .81 .95 1 .95 .81 .59 .31 0 -.31 -.59 -.81 -.95 -1 -.95 -.81 -.59 -.31 0]

we make a list of the first coordinates;

[1 .95 .81 .59 .31 0 -.31 -.59 -.81 -.95 -1 -.95 -.81 -.59 -.31 0 .31 .59 .81 .95 1]

and we plotted them using the following fine fractured-figures function:

```
to plot :l :n
  (empty :l)
  iffalse [pos list [:n first :l]
          dot
          plot bf :l :n + 1]
end
```

where :n is the minimal horizontal coordinate. And if we want to get our circle back we'd plug the two lists into:

```
to dots :l1 :l2
  (empty :l)
  iffalse [pos list [(first :l1) (first :l2)]
          dot
          dots bf :l1 bf :l2]
end
```

As a simpler example, look at our old dot square:

[[40 10] [60 10] [60 30] [40 30]]

If we write the points as two lists:

[40 60 60 40] and [10 10 30 30]

then dots [40 60 60 40] [10 10 30 30] gets us the square again.

"Wonderful, but **why** in the world should we do such a bizarre thing?" you ask. Two points:

1. Many physical systems that you have around the house—like bed springs, water dripping in the dirty dishwater, planets, and pendula—move in pat-

terns that are closely related (mathematically) to the behavior of our two-component dot-to-dot decomposition. If we can crack the motion code of an object, we can mathematically predict its movement.

2. Much of traditional mathematics —graphing, functions, even calculus and physics—can be discussed from this dotty position. For example, the two component curves that make up the circle are the *sine* and *cosine* functions. These functions arise in trigonometry, surveying, and of course physics. Using a tool like TLC-Logo, we can—in the privacy of our own home—graphically explore the mysteries of mathematics that may have eluded us in school.

Let's explore the second point a bit. First, plot can be replaced by dots if we define:

```
to line :n :m
  (:n < = 0)
  iffalse [fput :m
          line (:n - 1) (:m + 1)]
  iftrue [ [] ]
end
```

and notice that:

```
(plot :l -(length :l - 1)/2)
  is the same as (dots :l line (length :l)
                          -(length :l - 1)/2
```

Again, a giant yawn? Well, watch as we do some mathematics. Let's create a line:

make "id line 11 -5   creates a list:

[-5 -4 -3 -2 -1 0 1 2 3 4 5]   and:

plot :id −5 will give us an awesome:

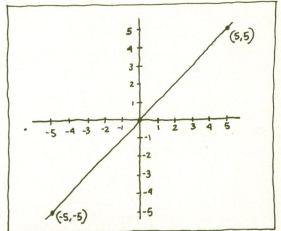

This is the graph of the function *f(x)* = *x* from *x* = *-5* to *x* = *5*. You remember good old Gack—your seventh grade math teacher—trying to beat that into your head, don't you? Now watch this:

```
to v.mul :l1 :l2
  (empty :l1)
  iffalse [fput (first :l1)*(first :l2)
          v.mul bf :l1 bf :l2]
  iftrue [ [] ]
end
```

This function will take two lists of numbers and manufacture a new list, each of whose elements is the product of the corresponding elements in the initial two lists. Now try:

```
plot v.mul :id :id -5
```

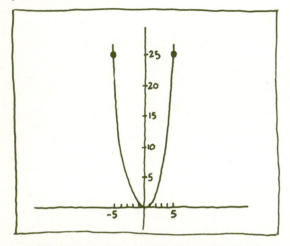

What you see is an approximation to the "parabola" *f(x)* = *x∗x* plotted in the range from *x* = *-5* to *x* = *5*.

This scheme of graphical exploration with functions can be extended into the domain of higher mathematics, demonstrating the concepts in differential and integral calculus. As the complexity of applications increases the delicacy of the implementation will also increase. Finer resolution will require that we increase the number of points in the list. For example:

```
make "y line 25 -12
```

Also, we might consider different implementations of the point lists. TLC-Logo supplies a "vector object" whose storage and access efficiencies may benefit larger applications. For example:

$<$ $<$40 60 60 40$>$ $>$ represents a vector of four elements in TLC-Logo.

Given vector objects, we can define a complete suite of vector-based functions using TLC-Logo. Such is the power of our programming tool—from kindergarten to calculus in one swell foop.

Putting the Turtle in its Place

By this time you probably think pretty highly of our turtle's abilities. Well, he's not

a bad little buddy—as little buddies go. We'd just like to put things in perspective before the little guy gets so smug that we can't stand him. Let's just see what kind of limitations our super turtle has.

We've been making a big deal out of the notion of objects and our desire to compute with them. How good an "object computer" is our turtle? Numbers are objects, and the turtle seems to be pretty versatile in dealing with numbers. We can perform operations on numbers—like addition and multiplication—that generate new numbers. We can compare two numbers to see if they are equal or not. We can send numbers to to-definitions as values to be used within the form-letter definition; and we can return numbers as values from to-definitions.

For example, we've seen:

```
to sum.of.squares :x :y
   (:x*:x) + (:y*:y)
end
```

expects two numbers as inputs and produces a number as value.

We have seen the beginnings of the same flexibility when dealing with lists as objects. For example:

```
to xpos :p
   first :p
end
```

defines xpos to respond with the screen-column of the point :p. This function takes a list as input and returns a number as value. We will see many more list examples in the second half of this book; definitions that return lists as values will be particularly important.

But let's peek further into the turtle's shell: we've had reasonable success in defining Logo programs to display a square, color it, rotate it, and mark it with a "B". It would therefore seem that a square is an object too. It's an idea that is as definable as the notions of number and list. So aren't squares really Logo objects too? Not really; squares never exist within Logo, they only exist as the result of the display operation. Since we have not kept any internal representation for these squares, the turtle has no understanding that a square has been drawn. It's like performing a connect-the-dots exercise and not recognizing what picture has been drawn. It's much like using a joystick to drag the turtle around the screen to draw a square. Ignoring the problems of getting the lines straight and the corners turned to the right angle, there again would be a lack of understanding—now, within the system rather than within the dot-to-dot maker—that a square has been drawn.

Here's another perspective on the problem: Suppose you went to Japan, knowing absolutely no Japanese. You'd have to hire

an interpreter, and any conversations you had would go through the interpreter. The interpreter would tell you what questions were asked and you would give the translator your response in English. The translator would phrase your answer in Japanese. You would be able to hear the questions and the answers in both languages, and thus have some chance of learning some words in Japanese.

Assume instead, that the translator knew enough about you to make up the answers. But instead of answering the question, the interpreter would tell you the Japanese sounds to make. That is, your translator would understand the Japanese question and would formulate an answer for it in Japanese; all you would do is say the right sounds. You'd simply be mimicking the sounds that your companion told you to

say. Operating this way, you'd have absolutely no hope of learning the language.

This mimicking of language corresponds to the process of drawing the square-like object with the joystick. That is, there is no real sense of what kind of object the user was trying to draw. Was it really supposed to be a square? Perhaps it was to be a rectangle whose width and length were just very close; perhaps it was supposed to be a parallelogram with equal sides, but corners that are not quite right angles. Since there is no record of what the movements were meant to be, we cannot be sure.

However, a Logo recipe makes clear what glop was supposed to be cooked up:

repeat 2 [fd 20 rt 90 fd 21 rt 90],   and
repeat 2 [fd 20 rt 91 fd 20 rt 89]

give two forms of "almost" square, while

repeat 4 [fd 20 lt 90]

describes a square. No mind-reading is required—or desired.

What is the essence of squareness?

—and no smart remarks, please! What characteristics of objectness are inherent in a square?

I. The figure has four sides. That's a start, but lot's of non-square figures have four sides.

II. All those sides are of equal length. That's better, but a rhombus would also fit this description.

III. All intersecting sides meet at a right angle. Gotcha!

These three conditions are sufficient to describe a square object to a reasonably sympathetic reader. That is, we assume that terms like "side", "intersection", and "right angle" are understood.

What would it mean for a language to have squares as objects? Well, some useful operations would include:

square :n   construct a new square of side :n. For example, we might assume that this square is sprouted with the sides horizontal and vertical, and the upper left-hand corner at the home position. This corner of the square is called the root, and will be used as the point of reference for the operations on the square.

print :sq   we would have to know how to print (or display) a square object, just like we now have to know how to print numbers or display turtles.

Of course we'd like more than one square to play with, so we have a question of how to refer to any particular square. There are several options available to us. We'll illustrate some of the possibilities using a sample operation we'll call **grow**. In all of our possibilities, **grow** will expect to receive an integer :n that will tell how much to increase the size of the selected square. Thus **grow 10** would increase the length of each side by 10 units. So here are three possibilities:

A. grow :n :sq   we think of **grow** as a Logo function that expects two inputs: a number :n and a square :sq and builds a new square, each of whose sides are :n units greater the the sides of :sq. This form of **grow** is like the operations in arithmetic or algebra; that is, when we say "add 5 to 6", we "build" a new number named 11.

B. ask :sq grow :n   asks the square :sq to grow larger by :n units, modifying the object named by :sq. You can think of **ask :sq grow 5** as consisting of two parts: (1) getting the attention of the object :sq, and (2) sending the message **grow 5** to the selected object. But if we're sending the message **grow 5**, why **ask :sq**, why not just say **:sq grow 5**?

Thus the third possibility:

C. :sq grow :n   since squares are so smart and smug, just send the message **grow :n** to :sq and be done with it.

Versions **A** and **C** represent two extremes of handling objects. Brand **A** is the most traditional, expecting the function **grow** to beat on the square **:sq**, while **:sq** sits there and takes it. Brand **C** represents the purest (or purist) form of message-passing—short of mind reading. For, in this case, squares are expected to be smart enough to handle all this message traffic themselves.

In the full-blown version of this view of computation, each object is a self-sufficient little entity that is either capable of handling a message or finding someone else who is. The most well-known advocate of view **C** and its classy society is a language named Smalltalk. We will say more about Smalltalk-like languages in Chapter 8. But back to squares . . .

Besides being compatible with the model of computing that Logo has followed, our quest for squareness suggests that position **B**—the middle-of-the-road—be utilized if we were to add square objects to TLC-Logo.

Some versions of TLC-Logo have a "class system" that will support this kind of computation directly, but we'll not get into that swamp here. Rather, we'll see how we

might build some of this stuff ourselves. What kind of messages, then, would make sense in our new square world?

grow :n   we already discussed this a bit. We can do shrinking by using negative values for :n. If the square is displayed it should be erased and the grown square redisplayed, using the root of the square as origin for the growth.

color :c   we should also allow colored squares. The color of the square is changed to :c. If the square is visible, the color message will change the color.

rotate :a   of course we should allow rotations of any squares. The rotation will be about the root of the square. If visible, erase and redisplay at the new angle.

pos :p   move the square so that its root is at position :p. This movement will happen without changing any other property of the square.

With this collection of primitive operations on squares, we can start to build up Logo-like operations. For example, we could give **to**-definitions that expected squares as arguments, and returned squares as values. Thus:

```
to conserve :sq
   ask :sq color :bland
   ask :sq pos :wedged
   ask :sq rotate :right
end
```

In this way, a square would become a "real" object rather than just another pretty face. The main idea that we're trying to get to through numbers and lists—and now, squares—is that to compute with objects we must have some way of:

- generating new objects,
- manipulating existing objects,
- defining new operations on objects

Alas, Logo's **square** does not meet these requirements. So we've humbled our tortoise somewhat; however, it does still have a surprise or two in store for us. The big surprise is in Chapter 6, where . . . well if we told you now, it wouldn't be a surprise would it? But we can let you in on one secret.

In particular, notice that squares have several of the same properties that our humble hatchback has; both have a color, can turn, and can move. The major differences so far are that squares can grow, and new squares can be built. Well, everyone knows that turtles grow; and we know that TLC-turtles can change their shape. Most everyone knows that the Easter bunny brings new turtles. Well, the TLC-bunny brings turtle eggs.

So, even though our buddy does have **some** limitations, it's a real first-class object in TLC-Logo. That means it can hatch more turtles and send them scurrying around the screen. Turtles are better than squares, anyday. So stay tuned: the next chapter will be filled with multitudes of tiny dancing tortoise toes.

CHAPTER 4
HERDING TURTLES

"Ya seen one, ya seen 'em all" doesn't apply to turtles; the more, the merrier. In fact, the more, the simpler. Just as **our** tasks can become more manageable when we have others helping, so too with turtle activity. We will see some mind-boggling graphical patterns that result from multiple turtles working independently of each other. And we will see some heartwarming examples of community spirit when we get gaggles of turtles working together in cooperative ventures. Of course, we're not going to be satisfied with just doodles on

the screen; we will continue to use turtling as an example of computing with objects.

When you tune in TLC-Logo, a turtle appears in the middle of your screen. This turtle is named Studs; we didn't mention

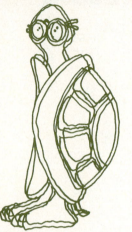

his name before because it didn't matter. With only one turtle, it was clear who was the recipient of the turtle messages—in the land of the blind, the one-eyed man is king. But now, Studs will hatch turtles, and those turtles can hatch more turtles, so names are needed.

We get Studs to hatch another turtle by sending him a **hatch** message along with the

name that we would like the new turtle to have. For example:

hatch "tillie

creates a new turtle named Tillie. Tillie will be a clone of Studs, inheriting all the current properties of Studs, except his name.

A clone can change its properties, however, without changing any of the properties of the cloner.

So, **hatch** does two things:

- It creates a turtle, and,
- It defines a new word that is used to reference that turtle.

Just as **make** is used to associate **4** with the word **blue**, **hatch** is used to associate a turtle with a name. And just like **make**, **hatch** will also return a value; the value of the **hatch** is the newly created turtle.

For example, whenever we type in :tillie, we mean the turtle that was created by the last hatch "tillie. If you hatch two Tillies by typing:

hatch "tillie
hatch "tillie

the second turtle is the one that is associated with the word tillie; the first one goes to turtle heaven. If you lose track of your turtle crew, the function tf (turtle family) will give you a list of your gang.

Messages are always directed to the turtle who's paying attention. When Studs is the only turtle, he responds to all turtle messages. You get a particular turtle's attention simply by asking for it. Thus:

ask :tillie

and now all love notes will be sent to Tillie. The value of the ask is the turtle that was in charge when the request was made; this way we can keep track of communication links between turtles. For example:

make "t1 ask :tillie

will change turtles to Tillie and t1 will remember who asked Tillie to dance.

If we want to ask Tillie to move forward ten steps immediately after being hatched, we can send the following tidings:

ask hatch "tillie
fd 10

hatch "tillie clones Tillie the turtle, passes the turtle to ask, which then gets the attention of Tillie. The subsequent fd 10 is then carried out by Tillie. The ask attention-getter is necessary because hatching a turtle is different from getting it to pay attention (of course, that's not news to anyone who has children).

As another example, consider the following sequence:

ask :studs
square 15
turtle :hide
hatch "tillie
pen :up
fd 5
ask :tillie
rt 90
shape :heart
bk 25

After requesting the attention of Studs, we send the **square**, **turtle**, **hatch**, **pen**, and **fd** messages to Studs. Then we ask Tillie to lay down a row of heart-shaped tiles while

Studs watches. If we then want Studs to counter with a run of diamonds we continue with:

```
ask :studs
pen :down
shape :diamond
fd 25
```

If one turtle is fun then four turtles should be four times as much fun. Let's have Studs clone some more:

```
pen :up hd 0
pos [0 60]
hatch "tillie
pos [60 60] rt 90
hatch "fred
pos [60 0] rt 90
hatch "lucy
pos [0 0] rt 90
```

This gives us the following arrangment of visible turtles:

tillie	fred
studs	lucy

with each turtle facing its clockwise neighbor, and ready to march around the breakfast table.

We can have each turtle construct a square by sending a **square** message to each one in turn:

```
ask :tillie square 20
ask :fred square 20
ask :lucy square 20
ask :studs square 20
```

We could also have each of our four friends draw only one side of its own square and then repeat the ritual three more times. This gives the visual impression that all four squares are being drawn simultaneously. A message form to perform this task is allsquare:

```
to allsquare :size
  repeat 4 [ask :tillie fd :size rt 90
            ask :fred fd :size rt 90
            ask :lucy fd :size rt 90
            ask :studs fd :size rt 90]
end
```

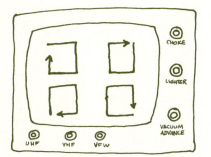

allsquare has the references to the four turtles we created stuffed inside its definition. This means we can use allsquare only with turtles with those names. But turtles are first-class citizens of Turtle Town and therefore potential victims of a form letter. So we should be able to create a new allsquare that contains arguments for four turtles and a size for the square.

```
to allsquare :t1 :t2 :t3 :t4 :size
  repeat 4 [ask :t1 fd :size rt 90
            ask :t2 fd :size rt 90
            ask :t3 fd :size rt 90
            ask :t4 fd :size rt 90]
end
```

Now we can apply allsquare to any able bodied turtles that happen to be walking around town. So, we can make Logo

ANONYMOUS TURTLE

definitions that use turtles as arguments; and previously defined turtle flogging functions can be modified to accept a turtle along with its other arguments.

For example, if we want to choose the turtle that draws a snowflake, we could define snowflake as follows:

```
to snowflake :turtle :level :size
  ask :turtle
  repeat 6 [flake :level :size rt 60]
end
```

where flake is defined in Chapter Three.

Furthermore, it may be convenient to define functions to act on specified turtles. Like:

```
to locate :turtle my :t1 :loc
  make "t1 (ask :turtle) ; switch to turtle and
                        ; save old value in t1
    make "loc pos ?     ; get the current position
    ask :t1             ; go back to previous turtle
    :loc                ; return the position of :turtle
end
```

This function reports the current position of the specified turtle while preserving the current turtle.

Or we could define a request for a victimized turtle to take one giant turtle toddle toward a specified point with:

```
to steptoward :turtle :point :dist
  ask :turtle
  face :point
  fd :dist
end
```

In this case, we have assumed that we don't need to remember which turtle requested that action.

We could combine steptoward and locate to have Studs take one giant step toward Tillie by:

```
steptoward :studs (locate :tillie) 5
```

Of course, there is no reason to limit the turtles to Studs and Tillie:

```
to toward :turtle1 :turtle2
  steptoward :turtle1 (locate :turtle2) 5
end
```

Now that we have our turtles lined up, let's go back to our four square turtles: Tillie, Fred, Lucy, and Studs. Assuming that each is facing its clockwise neighbor, let's have them start following their respective noses. We will start by having Studs take one giant turtle step toward Tillie:

```
toward :studs :tillie
```

Knowing that she is being stalked, Tillie takes one giant step toward Fred who, feeling the pressure, takes one giant step

toward Lucy, who decides to investigate what Studs is up to:

```
toward :tillie :fred
toward :fred :lucy
toward :lucy :studs
```

Sounds like a good soap-opera plot. Let's package up the whole idea with four turtle arguments:

```
to stalk :t1 :t2 :t3 :t4
   toward :t1 :t2
   toward :t2 :t3
   toward :t3 :t4
   toward :t4 :t1
   stalk :t1 :t2 :t3 :t4
end
```

and start things moving with:

```
stalk :studs :tillie :fred :lucy
```

If we continue this merry-go-round for a while, we discover that it isn't a merry-go-round at all. The motion of the four turtles is not that of a square or a circle. After the first round, Studs takes his second step into the square since Tillie is no longer on the corner. Tillie does the same because Fred is no longer in his corner, and the others follow the lead of Studs. On the third round Studs moves further into the dark interior of the square, stealthily stalking Tillie. The four turtles wind up spiralling into the center of the square, where they

find themselves chasing their own tails. We'll let our dervishes whirl while we press on.

Once we have seen the notions of multi-turtle messages, other applications come to mind. In particular, the chessboard problem of Chapter 2 can be done with two turtles, one for each color of tile; we can weave their paths between each other in several different and striking ways.

Animation is another example where multiple turtles work together to produce a visual sensation of action and motion. We did simple examples of animation in Chapter Two using a single turtle. We can also hatch two or more turtles next to each other, and give each of them a shape that is part of a more complex shape. For example, using the :head1 and :feet1 shapes for each of two turtles, with one directly above the other, provides a snapshot of a running

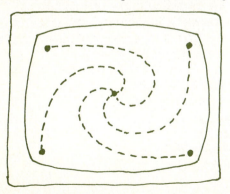

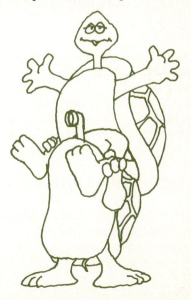

man. The messages that create the cooperative turtles and position them at a point of our choosing can be packaged in the following form:

```
to makeman :loc
  pen :up pos :loc hd 0
  hatch "upper
  s :tile.length      ; go south
  hatch "lower
end
```

At this point the two new turtles have whatever shape the hatching turtle has. We need to give each of them the appropriate shapes:

```
ask :upper    shape :head1
ask :lower    shape :feet1
```

How about moving the turtles together across the screen to get an animated feature? We can provide the shapes and move the man one position with the following form letter:

```
to poke
  ask :upper shape :head1
  ask :lower shape :feet1
  delay 10
  ask :upper fd 1
  ask :lower fd 1
end
```

makeman [0 20] followed by repeat :xmax [poke]

will move the two turtles across the screen together—with disappointing results. When we watch someone running, we see hands and legs moving. This creature appears to

be doing a trick on a skate board. What we need are a couple of different running positions that alternate as the turtles move across the screen.

We find our answer buried in shapes :head2 and :feet2. If we put these two shapes together as the upper and lower parts of the body, we see a figure that differs from :head1 and :feet1. We could create another form just like poke—say chop—with different shapes and then compute:

repeat :xmax [poke chop]

STEP BY STEP APPROACH TO PIGWALK

Since the only difference between the two forms is the shapes that are used, we define pokeman with the two shapes as arguments, and then use the same form with different tops and bottoms for the two different running positions:

```
to pokeman :head :feet
  ask :upper shape :head
  ask :lower shape :feet
  delay 10
  ask :upper fd 1
  ask :lower fd 1
end
```

The running man can be controlled by:

```
to trot :n
  repeat :n [pokeman :head1 :feet1
             pokeman :head2 :feet2]
end
```

The Worm Turns

We conclude our adventures into the Wild West by wandering into the wormy woods of Withering Wights. A giant worm named Willie wriggles through a forest; a deadly snipe lies hidden in the trees; and a vicious blink is lurking in our living room. Fortunately, our TV is on the blink; so we only have to deal with the worm and the snipe. We have a gun with which we can blast away at the worm, but it is useless against the snipe. Our only defense against the bird is to dodge when it comes flying out of its nest.

Without further ado we set the scene with the forest, the worm, and the gun. We will position the gun on the left edge of the screen, the worm on the right, and the forest between them.

The forest is created by hatching a tree-planting turtle, :watt, who lays down a tree-shaped tile (see :tree in the Paint-by-Numbers section) at each point in a list of points, :surewould. The general forestation operation is named forest; and the trees are planted by scatter.

```
to forest :ts
  hatch "watt
  ask :watt
  turtle :hide
  ink :green
  pen :up
  tile :ts
  scatter :surewould
end
```

HERDING TURTLES

```
to scatter :points
  empty :points
  iffalse [pos first :points
          dot
          scatter bf :points]
end
```

```
to init.worm
  ask :studs
  ink :red
  pen :up
  turtle :show
  hd 90
  shape :wormpart
  pos :worm hatch "wh
  s :tile.length hatch "b1
  s :tile.length hatch "b2
  s :tile.length hatch "b3
  s :tile.length hatch "wt
end
```

WORMAMBO

Now to the worm; five separate turtles named wh, b1, b2, b3, and wt make up the body parts of the worm and are related to each other as follows:

wh - the worm head segment
b1 - the worm body segment which follows wh
b2 - the worm body segment which follows b1
b3 - the worm body segment which follows b2
wt - the worm tail segment which follows b3

When our action begins, the worm is located vertically in consecutive tile positions begining at :worm:

The gun requires the use of two turtles, :gun and :bullet. The :bullet is visible only when the :gun has been fired, and is positioned to the immediate right of the gun. init.gun initializes these two turtles:

ARE YOU SURE THIS IS HOW THE 1812 OVERTURE GOES!

```
to init.gun
  ask :studs
    turtle :show
    shape :rtarrow
    pos list [:lt.edge 20]
    hd 0
  hatch "gun
    shape :slug
    pos list [(:lt.edge + :tile.width) 20]
    turtle :hide
  hatch "bullet
end
```

When Willie moves, all body segments must move together to keep the body segments next to each other. Moving the worm forward is done by fdwrm.

```
to fdwrm :d
  fwrd :wh :d
  fwrd :b1 :d
  fwrd :b2 :d
  fwrd :b3 :d
  fwrd :wt :d
end
```

where fwrd :tur :d moves turtle :tur forward :d units. Rather than asking each turtle making up the worm to do a fd :d, fwrd asks each turtle to move fd 1, :d-times. This way the turtles' movement is slowed down enough to give the desired visual effect:

```
to fwrd :tur :d
  ask :tur
  repeat :d [fd 1]
end
```

How about getting worms around corners? As the worm turns, the head will be moving in one direction while the tail will be moving at right angles to it. Each body part moving horizontally will have to move :tile.width units and each body part moving vertically will have to move :tile.length units if the worm is to remain in one piece. Let's just consider left turns for the moment. To make a left turn, we begin by asking :wh—worm head—to turn left 90 degrees and move forward a distance of :d1 where :d1 is tile.width if the new direction is horizontal and :d1 is tile.length if the new

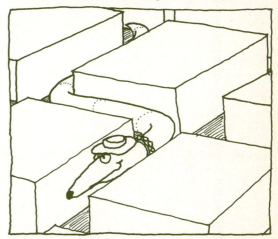

direction is vertical. The remaining worm pieces maintain their current headings and are moved forward :d2 steps where :d2 is either tile.length or tile.width (whichever :d1 isn't). Now, the worm's head is around the corner and it pulls :b1 around by moving its head forward a distance of :d1, turning :b1 90 degrees to the left, moving :b1 forward a distance of :d1 and moving the remaining parts forward a distance of :d2. The worm continues this process with its remaining parts until it has pulled its tail around the corner.

Right turns are exactly the same, except that we turn right rather than left. So we'll define the two turns in terms of one general turn—one good turn deserves another.

```
to ltwrm :d1 :d2        to rtwrm :d1 :d2
  mugwump :d1 :d2 "l      mugwump :d1 :d2 "r
end                     end
```

and where:

```
to mugwump :d1 :d2 :ect
  ask :wh   dir :ect
    fwrd :wh :d1    fwrd :b1 :d2    fwrd :b2 :d2
    fwrd :b3 :d2    fwrd :wt :d2

  fwrd :wh :d1
  ask :b1    dir :ect
    fwrd :b1 :d1    fwrd :b2 :d2    fwrd :b3 :d2
    fwrd :wt :d2

  fwrd :wh :d1    fwrd :b1 :d1
  ask :b2    dir :ect
    fwrd :b2 :d1    fwrd :b3 :d2    fwrd :wt :d2

  fwrd :wh :d1    fwrd :b1 :d1    fwrd :b2 :d1
  ask :b3 dir :ect
    fwrd :b3 :d1    fwrd :wt :d2

  ask :wt dir :ect
end
```

and finally:

```
to dir :coupe
  :coupe = "l
  iftrue [lt 90] iffalse [rt 90]
end
```

If the worm is headed north or south and we want it to make a left turn we call on ltwrm with :tile.width and :tile.length. If the worm is headed east or west and we want to do a left turn we say ltwrm :tile.length :tile.width. Similar logic applies for right turns.

This gives us a dozen legal worm actions:

Going . . .	Go To . . .	Logo . . .
North	North	fdwrm :t.l
South	South	fdwrm :t.l
West	West	fdwrm :t.w
East	East	fdwrm :t.w
North	West	ltwrm :t.w :t.l
North	East	rtwrm :t.w :t.l
South	West	rtwrm :t.w :t.l
South	East	ltwrm :t.w :t.l
West	North	rtwrm :t.l :t.w
West	South	ltwrm :t.l :t.w
East	North	ltwrm :t.l :t.w
East	South	rtwrm :t.l :t.w

where we've used :t.l and :t.w as abbreviations for :tile.length and :tile.width, respectively.

Ok, we've got trees, a gun, a bullet, and a worm named Willie—sounds like the Real American Dream. Now, on to a program that gives birth to the worm, loads the gun, plants the forest, and then moves the wriggly creature through the forest without running down any trees. The first part is easy; the next part requires some care.

We have to be careful about running into trees; we don't want to damage the future furniture. Since we know where the trees are, we can define the worm's dance to avoid them. And how should we describe the soft-shoe routine for the waltzing worm? A variation on the f-l language seems appropriate. All turns are 90 degrees here, and the size of the step depends on the current orientation of the worm, but directions like "Go north" (or east, south, or west) should be sufficiently descriptive. The worm should be smart enough to remember its direction and determine what to do with a new request. Our little **Going-Goto-Logo** table has all that information; if the move's not in the table, it's illegal.

We'll turn the tables into lists that carry the information on legal moves that can be made from each direction. We make four names—n, e, w, and s—be lists, each with a trio of elements. Each element of the trio contains a direction and the message required to move in that direction from the current direction. Thus:

```
make "n [[e rtwrm :tile.width :tile.length]
         [w ltwrm :tile.width :tile.length]
         [n fdwrm :tile.length]]

make "e [[e fdwrm :tile.width]
         [n ltwrm :tile.length :tile.width]
         [s rtwrm :tile.length :tile.width]]

make "w [[w fdwrm :tile.width]
         [n rtwrm :tile.length :tile.width]
         [s ltwrm :tile.length :tile.width]]

make "s [[w rtwrm :tile.width :tile.length]
         [e ltwrm :tile.width :tile.length]
         [s fdwrm :tile.length]]
```

Comparing the list elements with our table, we see that the first item is a member of the n e w s quartet, and bf of the item is a list that looks like the appropriate legal move.

Thus, first :s is [w rtwrm :tile.width :tile.length], and first of that is w, while bf of it is the list

[rtwrm :tile.width :tile.length].

We'll use these lists in the following fashion: Willie will select the list—n, e, w, or s—that corresponds to his current direction.

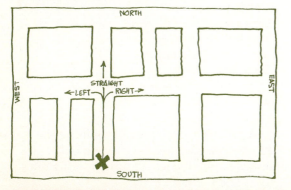

HERDING TURTLES

He will then select the element from the list that corresponds to the direction that he wants to go. If no such element exists, it's an error, and we take him fishing—the hard way. Given that an element exists, we use bf to get to the list that looks like a Logo expression; and then we run it, using the list as Logo code. We'll see more of run in Chapter 6; for now, here's how Willie's subconscious will use it, given a direction, :dir, and a list of possible moves, :moves:

```
to id :dir :moves
  empty :moves
  iftrue [throw "error ["willie.gone.fishing]]
  iffalse [:dir = first first :moves
          iftrue [run bf first :moves]
          iffalse [id :dir bf :moves]]
end
```

To help id make our segmented sorties smart, we need two pieces of information. We need to orient the worm in a specific direction, and we need to remember its position between moves. We will feed our worm a tape of moves like [n w w s e ...], and his brain, be will carry out the moves as follows:

```
to be :hornet2b
  ego :hornet2b "n
end
```

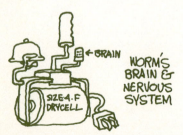

←BRAIN

WORM'S
BRAIN &
NERVOUS
SYSTEM

SIZE·4·F
DRYCELL

So we make sure that we start off pointing north.

```
to ego :tape :state
  (empty :tape)
  iffalse [ego bf :tape
              super.ego first :tape
                       :state]
  iftrue [:state]
end
```

super.ego will return the new state, as a present for the next call on ego.

```
to super.ego :vu :dejavu
  id :vu (thing :dejavu)
  :vu
end
```

thing is a Logo primitive that lets us get from the value of dejavu (which is a name) to the thing that name references. For example, if the value of dejavu is the symbol n, then thing :dejavu is the list of legal moves associated with n. That's what id wants to see. We'll see thing again in Chapter 6.

Finally, putting all the pieces together, here's Willie:

```
to worm
  init.worm
  init.gun
  cs      ; clear the screen
  forest :tree
  be [n w w s s w w w w n n w w]
end
```

Now for the violence. We will fire the gun by pressing the f key. If the bullet strikes a tree, it goes no farther. If it strikes the worm, the body part that it hits explodes. You will have to destroy all five body parts in order to win. The gun can be moved up (by pressing the u key) or down (by pressing the d) along the left hand edge of the screen. Keyboard control will be handled by rdcmd, a new function that we implant in Willie's super.ego:

```
to super.ego :vu :dejavu
  id :vu (thing :dejavu)
  rdcmd
  :vu
end
```

Now rdcmd requires some care because our program has to move the worm as well as check the keyboard. But we can't just use rl or rc because they will always wait until we type something and we wouldn't be able to move the worm. The key to rdcmd is a TLC-Logo function named rs (for read status). It checks if a key has been pressed. If we've seen a key, we use rc to get it and check it against 'd', 'u', and 'f'. If there's no key, we leave immediately.

```
to rdcmd
  rs
  iftrue [check.char rc]
end
```

where check.char checks for one of our three magical characters:

```
to check.char :c
  case lower :c
    [['f' fire]
     ['u' gun.up]
     ['d' gun.down]]
end
```

The TLC-Logo case expression compares the value of the first expression (:c) with the first objects in each of the following lists ('f', 'u', and 'd'); when it locates the first match it executes the rest of the list (fire, gun.up, or gun.down). We will have more to say about case in Chapter 6.

gun.up and gun.down move the gun up or down one tile provided that the gun will not fall off the screen, and the gun exists;

for a snipe attack may have destroyed it. The gun exists if the turtle :gun is visible. Something is on the screen if its y-position is less than :top and greater than :bottom, and its x-position is greater than :lt.edge and less than :rt.edge.

```
to gun.up
  (does.exist :gun)
  iftrue [(check.y :gun :top)
          iffalse [n :tile.length ask :bullet n :tile.length]]
end
```

where:

```
to does.exist :tur
  ask :tur
  (turtle ?) = :show
end
```

and:

```
to gun.down
  (does.exist :gun)
   iftrue [check.y :gun :bottom
           iffalse [s :tile.length ask :bullet s :tile.length]]
end
```

with:

```
to check.y :tur :y        to check.x :tur :x
  ask :tur                  ask :tur
  (last (pos ?)) = :y       (first (pos ?)) = :x
end                       end
```

   Finally, we get to the speeding bullet. If the gun still exists, fire will make :bullet visible and then move.bullet will complete the job. move.bullet expects a number that tells how far the bullet should go (provided that it doesn't hit anything).

```
to fire
  (does.exist :gun)
  iftrue [ask :bullet turtle :show move.bullet :rt.edge]
end
```

If the bullet hits a tree, :bullet is made invisible and repositioned at the gun. If the bullet hits the worm, that part of the worm explodes and disappears. What's left of the worm keeps moving. The interesting part of the moving bullet is contained in move.bullet and its companion, ahit. We move the bullet one tile position to the right and then call on ahit. If the tile under :bullet is a tree-tile or a worm-tile we know that we scored a hit, and we return the bullet to the

gun by calling on ret.bullet. Otherwise, we advance the bullet using move.bullet. Behold:

```
to move.bullet :cnt
   (:cnt < = 0)
   iftrue [ret.bullet]
   iffalse [fd :tile.width
           ahit
           iftrue [ret.bullet]
           iffalse [move.bullet (:cnt - 1)]]
end

to ret.bullet my :tmp
   ask :gun
   make "tmp fput (:lt.edge + tile.width)
                   bf (pos ?)
   ask :bullet
   pos :tmp
   turtle :hide
end
```

and:

```
to ahit
   ((under ?) = :tree)
   iffalse [((under ?) = :wormpart)
           iftrue [explode (pos ?) true]]
end
```

The Logo primitive function under will return the shape that is under the turtle. The explode operation uses pos.check to

discover which part Willie was hit and tastefully decorates our screen as it "deactivates" that segment of the worm.

```
to explode :postn
   check.pos :wh :postn
   check.pos :b1 :postn
   check.pos :b2 :postn
   check.pos :b3 :postn
   check.pos :wt :postn
end

to check.pos :tur :postn
   ask :tur
   (:postn = (pos ?))
     iftrue [splat :tur]
end

to splat :tur
   ask :bullet turtle :hide
   ask :tur
     shape :explode2
     delay 10
     shape :explode1
     delay 10
     turtle :hide
end
```

HERDING TURTLES

The last piece of the game is the snipe attack; that is accomplished by hatching a new turtle at :rt.edge opposite the current gun position, giving it the :bird shape, and flapping off toward the gun. If it encounters the worm, it flies over it; if it encounters a tree it flies north to get around it. If the snipe hits the gun, the gun will go splat; the encounter doesn't do a whole lot for the snipe, either. Furthermore, if the snipe runs into the top of the screen, it is transported south to a new location and tries again.

SNIPE

```
to attack my :n
  ask :gun
  make "n fput :rt.edge
              bf (pos ?)
  ask :studs
    hd 180
    shape :bird
    pos :n
    turtle :show
    hatch "snipe
    turtle :hide
  ask :snipe
    flap.n
    turtle :hide
end

to flap.n
  ((under ?) = :tree)
  iffalse [check.x :snipe :lt.edge
        iffalse [fd :tile.width flap.n]
        iftrue [check.pos :snipe (ask :gun pos ?)]]
  iftrue [check.y :snipe :top
        iffalse [n :tile.length flap.n]
        iftrue [s (rn :ymax) flap.n]]
end
```

And how do we incorporate our sniper into our morality play? A simple way is to include an attack in the command scanner, but to make the action unpredictable we will not attack everytime. We use the random number generator rn to generate a number between 0 and 9, and we attack if the number is greater than 6.

```
to rdcmd
  rs
  iftrue [check.char rc]
  ((rn 10) > 6)
  iftrue [attack]
end
```

A game of this complexity requires a good deal of thought. It must be built up in small chunks. We don't start with the top level procedure and work in a linear top-down fashion. Rather, we isolate specific subproblems such as creating the worm, the forest, and the gun, then develop the operations to move the worm one small step and to have it turn corners. The firing of the gun is another separate task. Interacting with the user is another task. Each task reduces the complexity of the main problem, and we proceed towards a completed solution, though apparently not in a structured fashion. But that's how people tend to solve problems: from partial solution to solution; from buggy solutions to better ones.

For example, note that while the worm is turning a corner, or the snipe is attacking we can't fire the gun because the Logo program is not looking for a key during these maneuvers. To cure this, we could add **rdcmd** calls at appropriate places in **mugwump** and **attack**. We could also spice up the interaction by considering each player—the worm, the snipe, the gun—as a separate entity, rather than as subjects under the control of one program. This strategy would use TLC-Logo's multi-processing facilities. Another modification would create a new worm brain, so that its journey through the woods will be more challenging. We must end our tour de forest here, but the possibilities for Willie boggle the mind.

And what has this exercise in gamesmanship brought us besides an exposure to how computer games are played and made? Well, though we have exposed

much of the groundwork of computer animation, we're after a more subtle philosophical game.

We're interested in an in-depth look at the principles of artificial intelligence. Part of the mystery of this topic stems from the notion that computers are only good at arithmetic. Well, video games clearly do more than hack and slash at dancing digits, and thus they give us a taste of how non-numerical computing can be done. Clearly, games are are still a long way from intelligent machines, but they're a long step from simple calculators.

We're almost ready to venture into the realm of intelligent non-numerical computing, so let's summarize what the first part of the book has done for us.

We began by looking at turtles as objects, as a collection of properties. We learned to communicate with turtles by sending messages and then we learned how to "teach" the turtle to associate message patterns with a word by drawing up a form letter which could include victim slots.

TURTLE [STUDS] VICTIM, ASK, HATCH, HIDE, COLOR, ETC.

TO
WHICH FIRST : CAME
IFTRUE [:CHICKEN]
IFFALSE [:EGG]

GOOD YOLK   BAD YOLK

HERDING TURTLES

We have examined the process a turtle goes through in carrying out a computation; this is the substitution and simplification mechanism of the Junk Mail Computation Model. We have seen that, in fact, the JMC Model is a version of the informal techniques we use in high school algebra.

We have seen that, besides numbers (as in algebra), shapes, colors, and lists representing points on the screen can be used as arguments to functions and returned as values of computations.

We have seen that turtles can also be used as arguments to functions, and have seen operations (**hatch** and **ask**, in particular) that return turtles as values. Thus, we can compute with turtle operations and messages as easily as we can with numbers.

So there are three key ideas:

• The discovery of computational objects

• The description of a computational model

• The application of pattern-matching to the model

These simple ideas are the basis for all computation.

This third point locates the "brains" that are applied in simple-minded form-filling of JMC. Simplification of an expression involves pattern-matching and replacement —that is, the recognition of a similarity and the replacement of a pattern with another pattern. For example, we can simplify $(2,345,678*89,749)*0$ to 0 by recognizing that the first expression is an instance of the pattern $x*0$, and then realizing that $x*0$ can be replaced by 0.

Our ability to recognize and manipulate patterns is one of our most powerful tools of thought. Somehow we reach into our store of facts and come up with objects that match a certain pattern.

In the next section, we explore some ways that we might represent these thought tools—patterns, facts, and matching—and ways of using these tools for drawing conclusions.

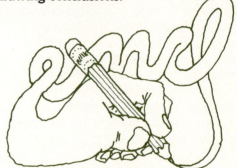

DRAWING A CONCLUSION

SECTION III: I, OBJECT

OK, folks, the show's over. No more pretty pictures for awhile. Now we're going to

PRETTY PITCHER

look behind the scenes. How do Logo programs work? How does Junk Mail Computing get done on your handy-dandy personal machine? And, deeper yet, is there anything that we can collect from these discussions of turtles and objects that will relate to how **we** solve problems? In the next three chapters, we'll iron out some of the details of these and other pressing problems.

The new wrinkle we introduce in these chapters is called list-processing. Just as the turtle was a convenient tool for building up complex and interesting shapes and animation, so too, list-processing notions are the right kind of clay for modelling mental shapes and motions. These shapes and movements make up part of the symphony we call "intelligence."

In Chapter 5, we'll give an overview and thumbnail description of a way we could organize our animal world. We'll have a highly illuminating discussion of turtles, ducks, chairs, and choppers. This will lead to the barnyard data base and will show how list-processing can help us keep track of our cast of characters.

In Chapter 6 we'll take a breather —highly appropriate after our barnyard field-trip. Here we'll sharpen our newly acquired list-processing skills on a variety of examples, ranging from plain vanilla definitions to major projects for the Turtle Construction Co.

Finally, in Chapter 7, we get back to the business of mental mining. By now we've had enough—in more than one way.

SECTION III: I, OBJECT

- We've had enough experience with the externals of Logo to be comfortable with reasonably complex Logo projects.

- We've had enough experience with the Junk Mail Model of Computing to be comfortable with the informal execution of Logo programs.

- We've had enough experience representing objects, patterns, and actions, as lists and list operations to be sure that the primeval object-ooze won't slip through our fingers when we explore more complex ideas.

Given all this, Chapter 7 orchestrates the components into:

- A representation of Logo objects in Logo. In particular, we can represent Logo definitions and expressions as lists.

- A set of Logo programs that act like the JMC Model when they operate on these representations, so we can describe Logo computations in Logo.

The elegance of the last movement is revealed as we show how rich the implementation model of JMC is: We can write a program that possesses the ability to examine and modify its own mental structures.

CHAPTER 5
BRAIN SURGERY

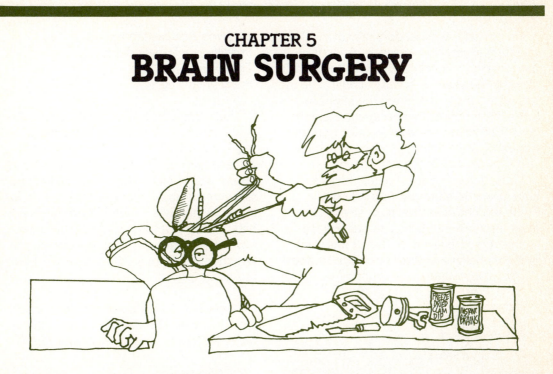

Well, so far we've had a reasonably interesting tour of turtle activity—amusing, but not something that would convince many of you to give up TV. The real excitement of Logo shows up when we analyze some of the ways we think about turtle activities.

For example, if we set Studs's color to green, we believe that he will remain green even while moving all around the screen. You might be able to convince yourself of this by experimenting with the turtle. Sure enough, the color remains constant, but perhaps we didn't move around long enough. Perhaps if we just made one more move, the color would change.

Assuming that there are no bugs in the programs, we all believe that Studs's color is not affected by movement. But is this kind of experiment or demonstration the best we can do in all cases? A further explanation like "just because" or "shut up!" seems appropriate in this case, but how can we give convincing arguments in general?

BRAIN SURGERY

Fortunately, we can do better than resorting to physical violence. A great monument to "just because" has been built up over the years. It is called Logic. The intent of logic is to pin down the slippery areas of mind-fuzz by specifying mental laws that seem to be the basis for human reasoning.

Thus, if you believe that all chickens have lips, and someone tells you that Clyde is a chicken, then logic says you must also believe that Clyde has lips. Of course, if you believe in Clyde's lips, you probably believe in the Easter Bunny, too.

BUNNY AND CLYDE

One of the powerful features of logical laws is that their validity doesn't depend on the particular facts (or non-facts) that appear in the discussion. It is only the **form** of the discussion that matters. Thus, these laws of reasoning can be applied in more general and less frivolous situations, like this one:

All female ducks lay eggs.
Priscilla is a female duck.
Therefore, Ergo, and Thus:
Priscilla lays eggs.

That's irrefutable logic. Such logic is the culmination of centuries of deep thinking—and strong drink. The strength of logic is that if you obey such laws in presenting your point of view, then you can beat your slow-witted opponents. Of course, it helps if you've had less to drink than they've had. We are not interested in whether or not our conclusions are true—but only in whether or not they follow logically from our assumptions.

Of course, there's nothing special about female ducks. The validity of the argument holds when we change the characters:

All pigs lay eggs.
Priscilla is a pig.
Therefore, Priscilla lays eggs.

This says that if we believe that all pigs lay eggs, and we believe that Priscilla is a pig, then we must also believe that Priscilla lays eggs.

In fact, we can translate such reasoning into a Logo program:

```
to lay.eggs? :x
  pig? :x
  iftrue [true]
  iffalse ['unknown']
end
```

Assuming that we have a way of testing for pig-ness, and assuming that we can tell Logo that Priscilla is a pig, we could type:

```
lay.eggs? :priscilla
```

and get true as an answer. Non-pig objects respond with unknown, since there may be other egg-layers that we haven't told Logo about.

And how would you define pig? and :priscilla so that pig? :priscilla responds true? That's a problem. Furthermore, if we insist

on believing that all turtles lay eggs too, the program would have to get messier:

```
to lay.eggs? :x
  pig? :x
  iftrue [true]
  iffalse [turtle? :x
          iftrue [true]
          iffalse ['unknown']]
end
```

then lay.eggs? :studs and lay.eggs? :priscilla would both respond with true.

This scheme is not unmanageable yet, but is rapidly becoming so. Each new piece of information requires the rewriting of lots of code. Being particularly lazy individuals, we'd like to add new information to our system without having to rewrite what it already knows. Just as Logo can compute with objects representing turtles, we'd like a language—call it LoBlo—that will let us compute with statements in Logic.

In the previous chapters, we had properties such as shape, position, and color defined for each and every turtle. In this chapter, we will be able to make statements that specify individual properties for the objects.

For example, in the past we looked at :studs as an object made up of all the properties and values we associate with turtles:

```
[turtle [name "studs]
    [shape :arrow]
    [color :black]
    [visibility.state :visible]
    [position [0 0]]
    [heading :north]
    [pen.state :down]
    [tile :line]]
```

Now we will be able to specify individual characteristics as needed. The difference is not in **what** we can say, but in **how** we say it. Instead of collecting all of our information about :studs in one place, we simply make statements about the properties we happen to be interested in at the time. We will have statements like:

Studs is a turtle.
The shape of Studs is an arrow.
The current position of Studs is [0,0].
Priscilla is a duck.
Signet is a bald duck.
Signet is the brother of Priscilla.

We will write such eternal truths as follows:

```
[turtle studs]
[shape studs arrow]
[position studs [0 0]]
[duck priscilla]
[bald signet] [duck signet]
[brother.of signet priscilla]
```

We write such statements in the form of a list whose first element is the name of a relationship (or property), and the elements that follow are the individuals whom we assert to be in that relationship (or possess that property).

So [brother.of signet priscilla] represents the assertion that

Signet is a brother of Priscilla.

We know you find these facts irresistible, so we're including a little cast of characters that will allow us to discuss turtles, ducks, and assorted odds and ends on the level of sophistication, subtlety, and seriousness that the subject demands.

The Ducks World
(Or, How To Get Your Ducks In Line)

Down on our farm we have a collection of turtles and ducks who have some varied personalities, and properties. The details follow:

• Malicious Melvin is a downright mean duck dude; he owns a Vespa Chopper in a joint venture with an addle-pated alligator named Mortimer.

• Studs Turtle is the hero of our cast; he's the sheriff and appropriately star-studded.

• The local psycho-practitioner is Signet Fraud; all he owns is a neurosis.

• Then we have Rigor Tortoise, who owns a Morris chair. We'll see more of Rigor's Morris.

• Of course, we also have Tillie Canoe, the industrious tiling turtle, who is particularly proud of her red "two"-shaped tile. Of course, she's infamous as Tillie Canoe the Tiler Two.

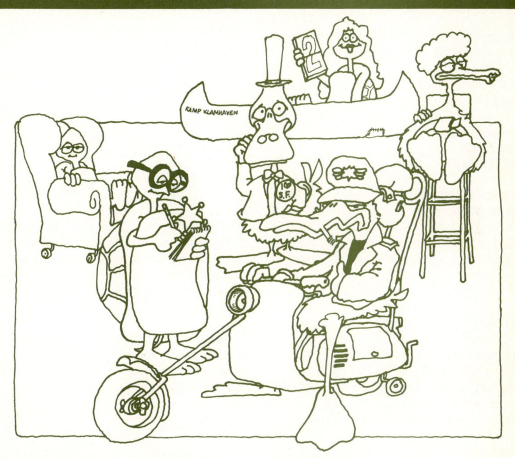

• And rounding out the cast is Pauline Pintail. She spends most of her time in her highchair, since she can't figure out how to reach the ground. Perhaps we can help her out of her perilous position?

At any rate, we can translate these relationships into LoBlo statements as follows:

[Owns Melvin Chopper] says Melvin owns a chopper.

[Partners Melvin Mortimer] gives us another Truth of the Universe, as does:

[Owns Signet Neurosis]   and,

[Owns Studs Star].   But,

[Owns Rigor Rigors.chair] [Type Rigors.chair Morris]

is a bit more interesting. These say that Rigor owns a specific kind of chair. We can use this ability to add detail to any description. We can specify as much (or as little) as we care to about the objects in the system, and we can add information at any time. Of course, any programs that we write will have to be able to find all the pertinent information about a given object, but that's getting ahead of ourselves.

Let's see what else we know about our friends.

[Owns Tillie Tillies.tile]
[Shape Tillies.tile Two]
[Color Tillies.tile Red]

[Owns Pauline Paulines.chair]
[Type Paulines.chair High]

Our LoBlo program cannot guess the species of our creatures, so we must also add:

[Duck Priscilla]   [Duck Melvin]
[Duck Signet]   [Duck Pauline]

and

[Turtle Studs]   [Turtle Rigor]   [Turtle Tillie]

We can also add family tree information, like:

[Brother.of Signet Pauline]

We can add more relationships, but let's see what all this work gets for us. If LoBlo is to be any good at all, we should be able to ask questions about our accumulated wisdom. Questions like:

"Is Pauline a duck?"   (Yes!)

or

"Who's a brother of Pauline?"   (Signet)

And Pauline might ask: "How do I get down from my highchair?" (Of course **we** know she's stuck forever. You don't get down from a chair; you get down from a duck!) Truly a case of the perilous puerility of Pauline. But we digress.

How are these mysteries to be revealed to a doubting world? How can a computer—a device that "only uses zero and one"—possibly deal with such questions?

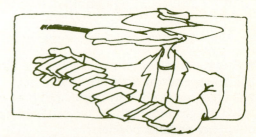

Well, watch our hands closely; at no time will our arms leave our sleeves. We will show you how to write such wondrous programs and, in fact, we will show how to build your own LoBlo in Logo.

As a first step, we have to represent the farmyard facts in LoBlo. Such a collection of facts is called a data base. We can represent such a data base in Logo in many different ways. Here, we will assume that the data base is simply a list of the facts about the individuals. This kind of representation

fits directly into Logo's list structures. In particular, we can directly represent lists of the form:

[duck chuck]   or   [likes chuck tillie]

We have already seen such lists in operation in dealing with a turtle's **pos** message. Recall that **pos ?** returns a list representing the location of the turtle on the screen. And we used **nth** to select a specific component of the list. The only other property of lists that you needed to know was that the order of the elements was important. For example, [30 40] is not the same list as [40 30].

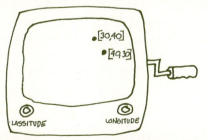

In Turtle Town, the point [30 40] represents the approximate position of Duckopolis,

while the point [40 30] is the location of the ACME Cattery (Get your kits on Rt 66).

The novelty of the new situation is that the elements of a data base list may be objects other than numbers. Names, like herman, fd, and zit, can be in lists like [midget herman], and [color zit yeech].

In a full-sized data base we would have to worry about efficient representation and storage of this data. However, our barnyard base will not require such mystical incantations from the folklore of computer science. We are more concerned with "what has to happen" than with "how to make it happen most efficiently."

And what has been accomplished by introducing such symbol-laden lists in place of nice numeric ones? We realize that we could replace names like Owns, and red, with nice mnemonic numbers like 44 or 9. Of course, lists with names make facts much easier to write and to understand and that ease carries over to the programs that answer questions. There are basically two kinds of questions:

1. Questions that will be satisfied by a yes-or-no answer, like:
   Is Priscilla a Duck?
   Does Priscilla own a chair?
   What is the meaning of life?

2. Questions that require us to exhibit a specific answer. Like:
   Who is Priscilla's brother?
   What color is Signet?
   How many angels can dance on the head of a pin?

Answers to the first kind of question are easy to describe, once we have described the questions. Behold, we will write questions as lists! Thus:

"Is Robert Wimple a midget?" becomes

is.true [midget robert.wimple], where is.true is defined as:

```
to is.true :pat
  (compare :pat :duck.world) = "no.match
  iftrue ['unknown']
  iffalse ['yes']
end
```

We compare the list (or pattern), :pat, with the list of facts, :duck.world, which represents all we know about the farm. Our Logo comparison program, named compare, expects two inputs:

- A coded question, and
- A list of elements in the data base with which to compare the question.

Thus:

```
to compare :q :db
  if you find a comparison say true
  if you can't find a comparison, say
  no.match
end
```

But how do you find out if a comparison exists? Well, if we gave you a photograph and our family album and asked you to tell us if the picture was already in it, you'd be able to do that without thinking about it. But if forced to explain your action, you'd probably say something like:

"Compare the picture with the first one in the book. If they're the same, quit with an appropriate response in the affirmative. If they're not the same, compare with the next picture. Keep this up, turning pages

when necessary, until either a matching picture is found or there are no more pictures to check. If the end of the book is reached, pout appropriately." Or:

```
to compare :q :db
  empty :db
    iftrue ["no.match]
    iffalse [match :q against the first element
             of :db,
             if that's not it, look in the rest of :db]
end
```

Now let's tackle the remaining piece: "match :q against the first element of :db, . . ."

There are two cases again:
• It matches! We quit a winner.

• The miserable thing fails, and we must compare :q with the rest of the pictures in the album.

Not suprisingly, TLC-Logo comes to the rescue with exactly the right tools. To get the first element of :db, compute first :db

For example,

first [[duck fred] [pig otto] [cow boyd]] is [duck fred]

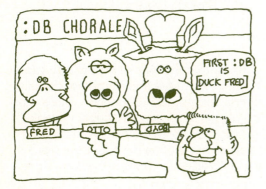

If the first element of the data base is not the one we want, we can compute bf :db, which gives us the rest of the data base.

For example,

bf [[duck fred] [pig otto] [cow boyd]] gives

[[pig otto] [cow boyd]]

With these tools in hand, we can add more detail to our incomparable compare program. Namely, we'll call a pattern-matching program—called match, amazingly enough—that will compare the coded question :pat1 with an element of the base, :pat2. match :pat1 :pat2 will respond with true if the two elements match, and will respond with "no.match if they don't. Thus:

```
to compare :q :db
  (empty :db)
    iftrue ["no.match]
    iffalse [(match :q first :db) = true
              iftrue [true]
              iffalse [compare :q
                               bf :db]]
end
```

Now we have to write match. It's similar to compare, except that we take two objects represented as lists and compare them element-by-element. Thus:

match [1 2 3] [1 2 3] gives true because all elements are equal;

match [has chicken wings] [has chicken lips] gives no.match because they disagree on the third element.

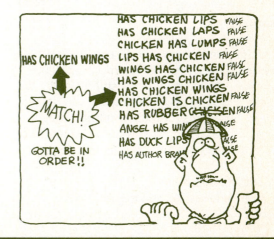

Matching is not so difficult after all:
• If both patterns are empty, then they match.

• If one is empty, but not the other, then no match is possible.

• If neither is empty, they must each have a first element; if the first elements are the same, match must check out the remainders of the patterns.

• If the first elements were not the same, then no match is possible.

Since there are so many possible tests, we use cond instead of a lot of nested iftrue and if-false expressions.

```
to match :pat1 :pat2
  cond [[(empty :pat1) (empty :pat2)
                  iftrue [true]
                  iffalse ["no.match]]
        [(empty :pat2) "no.match]
        [(first :pat1) = (first :pat2)
            match bf :pat1 bf :pat2]
        [true "no.match] ]
end
```

With is.true, compare, and match, we have almost all we need for a simple question-answering system. What's still missing? We need a way to add new facts to the data base. So here is a function named add.fact that will take one argument, a fact, and add it to the data base.

```
to add.fact :new.fact
  make "duck.world fput :new.fact :duck.world
end
```

Simplicity personified! Now let's bring back is.true and compare, so we can see all of these functions together on one page:

```
to is.true :pat
  (compare :pat :duck.world) = "no.match
    iftrue ['unknown']
    iffalse ['yes']
end
```

```
to compare :q :db
  (empty :db)
    iftrue ["no.match]
    iffalse [(match :q first :db) = true
                iftrue [true]
                iffalse [compare :q
                                 bf :db] ]
end
```

Notice that the :duck.world data base can be used by both is.true and by add.fact, but is not an argument to either function. In this context, **duck.world** is called a "global variable." You must be careful whenever you have global variables floating about your programs. If **anyone** changes the value of a

global variable, it is changed for **everyone**. Sometimes it is hard to track down the culprit when an undesirable change has been made.

In order to get things started we need to make duck.world an empty data base:

```
make "duck.world []
```

So, what've we done? We can now create a data base, add facts to it, and ask questions about what is in it. But the only kind of question we can ask is one that can be satisfied with a "yes" or "no" (actually "yes" or "unknown") answer. Suppose we want to ask "What color is the truck?" or "Who is Pauline's brother?"

First, we need to decide how to ask such a question. We can use the same form we used for facts, with a question mark standing for the missing information. Thus:

"What color is the truck?" becomes
    [color truck ?]
and "Who is Pauline's brother?" becomes
    [brother.of ? pauline]

Second, we need to decide how to answer such a question. Instead of simply checking if two objects are identical—a yes-or-no problem—match will have to supply an answer wherever there is a question mark.

We define a function find that will accept a pattern containing a question mark and, using compare and match, return a value for the question mark that makes the statement true.

```
to find :question
  compare :question :duck.world
end
```

So, we now expect compare to return either a matching value or no.match.

```
to compare :q :db my :val
  (empty :db)
    iftrue ["no.match]
    iffalse [make "val (match :q first :db)
             :val = "no.match
             iftrue [compare :q
                            bf :db]
             iffalse [:val]]
end
```

Crafty little devil, that compare! It just passed the buck to match. One new thing here is the my-parameter named :val. This will be used as scratch paper by compare. No one outside of compare will see what's in :val. :val's purpose is to capture the value of match :q first :db. We want to compute that value once, but want to use that value in two places:

• in the predicate test :val is compared with "no.match, and
• if the comparison fails, we want to return :val as the answer.

Let's see how match handles the new problem.

```
to match :pat1 :pat2
  cond [[(empty :pat1) (empty :pat2)
                      iftrue [true]
                      iffalse ["no.match]]
        [(empty :pat2) "no.match]
        [(first :pat1) = (first :pat2)
            match bf :pat1 bf :pat2]
        [all [(first :pat1 = "?)
            (match bf :pat1 bf :pat2) = true]
         first :pat2]
        [true "no.match] ]
end
```

We added one more possibility to the conditional in match: if we see a question mark in :pat1, then return the corresponding element of :pat2 if the rest of the patterns match exactly, otherwise return no.match. Thus, match can result in three kinds of answers:

- If the patterns match exactly, return true.
- If there is a question mark, supply the value that makes the patterns match.
- If no match is possible, return no.match.

This version of match will be able to answer the questions that require a single match, but what about situations like:

match [1 [cow ?] x ?] [1 [cow boyd] x boyd]

We would expect ? to match boyd.
But what do we do about requests like:

match [1 [cow ?] x ?] [1 [cow boyd] x 2]

We would like the luxury of specifying two options:

- There is no match since ? has to match two different symbols.

- There is a match with the first ? matching boyd, and the second ? matching 2.

But why would we want to have more than one question mark? Consider the following:

Crime in the Barnyard!

Someone smashed Tillie's two tile while she was snorkeling in Swann Lake. Our star-studded hero must solve the mystery. There are feathers scattered among the tile fragments. "Aha!" exclaims Studs, "A duck did this dastardly deed!" Searching the scene further he discovers chopper tracks among the wreckage. "The culprit is a duck who owns a chopper. Now who might that be?" asks Studs.

Our barnyard data base contains the answer, but we need to find someone that satisfies two facts at the same time:

[duck ?]   and   [owns ? chopper]

We can certainly define find so that it takes a list of conditions that must all be satisfied, but how can we be sure that it finds the same answer for both the question marks above? And what if we had even more information that might require two different answers. For example, suppose we know that the culprit has a partner. There might be lots of ducks who own choppers, but only one who also has a partner.

[duck ?] and [owns ?chopper] and [partners ? ?]

How do we know which question marks have to stand for the same individual, and which ones could be different? In Logo, we use different names for different individuals; we'll do the same in LoBlo. We put a question mark on the front of a name to show that we don't know what the value should be and we want match to supply one. We call these question-marked names "variables", since the values they have can vary. Thus:

match [1 [cow ?pat] x ?pat]   [1 [cow boyd] x 2] would give no.match, and

match [1 [cow ?poke] x ?pat]   [1 [cow boyd] x 2] would give [[?poke boyd] [?pat 2]], while

match [1 [cow ?pattie] x ?pattie]
        [1 [cow cake] x cake]
gives [[?pattie cake]].

Thus, the details of the dairy disaster can be phrased as:

[duck ?culprit]   and   [owns ?culprit chopper]   and [partners ?culprit ?friend]

We submit the question to find as follows:

find [[duck ?culprit] [owns ?culprit chopper]
    [partners ?culprit ?friend]]

Now we must redefine find so that it expects to be supplied a list of conditions to be satisfied, and returns a list of values for the question-marked names. We'll have it return a list of two-element lists (the variables and associated values) so we know which value goes with which variable (this kind of variable-value list is known as a "symbol table"). For example, a solution to the above problem would be [[?culprit Melvin] [?friend Mortimer]].

```
to find :conditions
  compare.lots :conditions :duck.world
end
```

Not much of a change. All we did was change the name of the argument from :question to :conditions and replace the call to compare with a call to a new function compare.lots, which will have to worry about getting lots of conditions satisfied.

Now compare.lots has some bookkeeping to do. It is not enough to just call compare lots of times; the answers have to be the same for every occurrence of the same name. Hmmmmm. That means we'll have to keep track of any answers already found,

and check them whenever looking for a match. We'll use a my variable to keep track of the table as we build it.

```
to compare.lots :conditions :db my :tbl
  make "tbl []
  repeat (length :conditions)
         [make "tbl compare first :conditions :db :tbl]
end
```

Well, true to our lazy style again, compare.lots passes off the hard work to compare. Compare the old compare (on page 124). We need to add an argument representing the symbol table. We need to add a condition to stop the comparison if the symbol table is no.match. If the data base is empty, then we can find no match; that part is okay. Otherwise, we let :val be the result of matching the question with the first element of the data base. Of course match will need to know about the symbol table too. If that match is unsuccessful, we compare the question with the rest of the data base; nothing new there. If the match was successful, we return :val. Nothing changes there! And now it looks like match gets all the dirty work! (Somebody has to do it.) Here is the "new" version of compare:

```
to compare :q :db :tbl my :val
  cond [[:tbl = "no.match "no.match]
        [(empty :db) "no.match]
        [true make "val (match :q first :db :tbl)
              :val = "no.match
                iftrue [compare :q
                                bf :db
                                :tbl]
                iffalse [ :val ]] ]
end
```

Now for our industrial strength matcher:

```
to match :pat1 :pat2 :tbl my :val
  cond [[(empty :pat1) (empty :pat2)
                   iftrue [:tbl]
                   iffalse ["no.match]]
        [(empty :pat2) "no.match]
        [true make "val match.first first :pat1
                             first :pat2
                             :tbl
             (:val = "no.match)
               iftrue ["no.match]
               iffalse [match bf :pat1
                              bf :pat2
                              :val ] ]
end
```

Well, apparently match has decided that it needs some help too. It passes the job of matching the first elements of the patterns on to match.first. Of course, if the match on the first elements is impossible, so is the match on the entire pattern.

It is no longer sufficient to return a single answer when one is found; there may be several variables in the pattern this time. match has to continue checking the rest of the given patterns, this time using the symbol table returned by match.first (which may have new information added to it). And how does match.first accomplish all this?

```
to match.first :item1 :item2 :tbl my :val
   cond [[:item1 = :item2 :tbl]
       [is.var :item1
           (in.table :item1 :tbl)
               iftrue [match.first lookup :item1 :tbl
                                           :item2
                                           :tbl]
               iffalse [include list [:item1 :item2]
                                           :tbl]
       [true "no.match] ]
end
```

What happened? The case that deals with a variable has changed quite a bit. Before, all we had to do was look for a question mark, and when we found one we were done. Now things are more complicated.

1. To see if we have a variable, we use a function is.var; it will have to see if the name it is given starts with a question mark.

2. If we have a variable, we have to check the symbol table to see if we already have a value for it.
   a If we do have a value, then we try to match that value with :item2.
   b If this variable is not yet in the symbol table, we include an entry

associating it with :item2 into the old table and return this new table.

All this complication occurs because we now allow several variables to appear in the list of conditions to be satisfied. We still have to define is.var, in.table, lookup, and include, before we could actually run our question-answerer.

But is.var is easy: to grab the first character of a word, we use string to turn the word into a string of characters and then use first to select the first one. is.var simply compares this with '?' to determine if a variable has been seen.

```
to is.var :x
   (first string :x) = '?'
end
```

Now **that** is elegance. Here, in match & Co. we have the basis for discussing a broad range of applications from data base management to artificial intelligence. All these applications share a common thread: the use of a pattern matching system to manipulate information.

Enough self-adulation. We still have to collect the matches we make as we proceed through the patterns, and we must check the previous matches each time we attempt to match two new items.

For example, it should not be possible to match:

[partners ?culprit ?culprit]   and
[partners Melvin Mortimer]

since if ?culprit is associated with Melvin, it cannot be matched with Mortimer, and vice versa. Our version of match works fine in this case. But what happens when we have more than one condition to be satisfied as in:

[[duck ?culprit] [owns ?culprit chopper]]

We need to find one value for ?culprit that will satisfy both conditions; but what do we do when the first match satisfying [duck ?culprit] does not satisfy the second condition?

We actually ignored that problem in the discussion of compare.lots. We defined it so that if the first successful match fails on a subsequent condition, we simply claimed there was no match. This is not really the answer we want. Although we can be sure that any match found by compare.lots is in fact a correct one, there may be several answers that compare.lots has overlooked. Let's see how it **should** work.

"Name a duck that owns a chopper" is translated into:

find [[duck ?x] [owns ?x chopper]]

First, we find a duck. (Say, Priscilla.) Next, we see if that duck owns a chopper. (She doesn't.)

Now what? We check out another duck. And how do we do that? That is, how do we indicate that we have already rejected Priscilla, and should analyze Signet, or some other duck? We must understand this problem if we expect to write a Logo pro-

gram to solve it; we cannot duck the issue. The solution? Like Hansel and Gretel, we need to leave bread crumbs to find our way through :duck.world. So at each step—each place that we apply the compare function—we must make a note of what we were trying to do, where we were in the process, and in particular, where we were in the data base.

One way to do this is to have compare return more information than just the symbol table. If we are successful, we need to know where we should start looking in the data base if we have to find a alternative answer for the same condition later.

This is the same kind of situation that we ourselves face in solving problems. A particular attempt may not work, so we have to back up and try another approach. We keep track of where we are and what we're doing in several different ways. If the problem is easy, no real reminders need to be

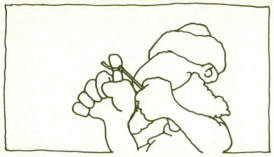

constructed, but if the situation is complex we'll find ourselves writing notes, tying strings on fingers (hopefully ours), and leaving more explicit clues that will help us through the maze.

This kind of bookkeeping will be done by compare.lots with compare acting as a co-conspirator. In addition to a list of conditions that remain to be satisfied, we need to specify where in the data base we'll begin to look for a solution. We'll bundle up some of this information as arguments to compare.lots:

1. :to.do is the list of conditions still to be satisfied.

2. :done is a list representing where we've been, each element of :done is, itself, a list made up of:
    a. a condition that has been satisfied;
    b. the part of the data base to use if we need to find another way to satisfy that condition.

3. :db is the data base to use on the next condition to be satisfied.

4. :tbl, as before, is the symbol table containing the values we've found so far in our quest to satisfy all the conditions. Its

structure is a little more complicated now, since we may need to be able to "undo" part of the matching accomplished so far. For example, when looking for a duck, we found Priscilla; but she did not own a chopper. To find someone that satisfies both conditions we have to "undo" the choice of Priscilla for ?culprit, so that we can find another duck who might in fact also own a chopper.

And how does compare.lots deal with all this complexity? Veeerrry carefully!

• If the list of conditions still to be satisfied is empty, then we are done; the answer is :tbl.

• If the data base, :db, is empty, then we've failed to find a match on the current condition given the current state of the symbol table. We back up and try to resatisfy the last successful condition, hoping that new values might make it possible to succeed on the goal we failed to satisfy. In order to "back up" we have to be able to undo any matches that were made the last time we satisfied the condition. If there is nothing to resatisfy, then no match is possible.

• Otherwise, we attempt to satisfy the first condition on our list of things :to.do, in the data base :db. Failing that attempt, we try to back up over our last success. If we succeed, then we proceed to work on the other conditions in our list of things to do. Voila!

```
to compare.lots :to.do :done :db :tbl my :pair
 cond [[empty :to.do :tbl]
       [empty :db (empty :done)
               iftrue ["no.match]
               iffalse [compare.lots fput first first :done
                                              :to.do
                               bf :done
                               bf first :done
                               bf :tbl]
       [true make "pair compare first :to.do
                               :db
                               fput [] :tbl
           (first :pair) = "no.match
           iftrue [(empty :done)
                   iftrue ["no.match]
                   iffalse [compare.lots fput first first :done
                                              :to.do
                                   bf :done
                                   bf first :done
                                   bf :tbl] ]
           iffalse [compare.lots bf :to.do
                           fput fput first :to.do
                                   bf :pair
                               :done
                           :duck.world
                           first :pair] ] ]
end
```

Now things are getting pretty complicated. Our new version of compare must send back not only a new table, but also where we were looking in the data base when we found the match (just in case we

have to come back and look for another answer later). The table itself has changed shape. It is now a list of separate symbol table components, each generated by the match on a single condition. Thus, when compare.lots calls compare, it sends the table along with an empty list on the front of it

for compare to fill in as needed. Actually, compare just passes it along to match, and match bows to match.first, who uses include to add to the table; so include is the only one that really has to worry about it. We'll define include in a minute, but first let's see our new version of compare.

```
to compare :q :db :tbl my :val
  cond [[:tbl = "no.match fput "no.match []]
        [(empty :db) fput "no.match []]
        [true make "val (match :q first :db :tbl)
             :val = "no.match
             iftrue [compare :q
                              bf :db
                             :tbl]
             iffalse [ fput :val bf :db]] ]
end
```

The structure of the table we set up is that of a list of tables, each of which is a list of variable-value pairs. For example:

```
[ [[?x Filmore] [?y Melvin]]
  [[?culprit Melvin] [?hero Studs] [?victim Tillie]]
  [[?z Priscilla]] ]
```

So now we're really going to exercise your ability to work with lists. A table is in fact represented as a list of lists of lists!!! Rather than trying to keep straight all the levels of lists in a symbol table, we'll think of it as a list of symbol table components, where each is a list of entries, and each entry is a list consisting of a variable and an associated value. First we'll see if a given variable is already in the table.

```
to in.table :var :tbl
  cond [[empty :tbl false]
        [empty first.comp :tbl
            in.table :var rest.comps :tbl]
        [:var = var.part first.entry first.comp :tbl
            true]
        [true in.table :var fput rest.entries first.comp :tbl
                    rest.comps :tbl]]
end
```

We need to define the selector functions that decompose a symbol table into its components, each component into its entries, and each entry into its variable and value parts.

```
to first.comp :tbl        to rest.comps :tlb
  first :tbl                 bf :tbl
end                       end


to first.entry :comp      to rest.entries :comp
  first :comp                bf :comp
end                       end


to var.part :entry        to value.part :entry
  first :entry              nth :entry 2
end                       end
```

And finally, here are lookup and include:

```
to lookup :var :tbl
  cond [[empty :tbl "not.there]
        [empty first.comp :tbl
            lookup :var rest.comps :tbl]
        [(var.part first.entry first.comp :tbl) = :var
            value.part first.entry first.comp :tbl]
        [true lookup :var fput rest.entries first.comp :tbl
                    rest.comps :tbl]]
end


to include :pair :tbl
  fput fput :pair
            first.comp :tbl
        :tbl]]
end
```

It wasn't easy, but we have now constructed a very powerful question-answering system. It can determine whether an entire sequence of conditions can be satisfied by facts in the data base. But we are not done yet!

Indeed, the world hungers for answers to questions like:

"Is Melvin a Duck?"

But soon—fickle world that it is—it will want to know the answers to more relevant questions like

"What is the meaning of life?"

Now, a major step toward that goal can be made by discovering the significance of the statement:

"Chickens have lips"

This statement is packed with information. For example, it says that if we have in our possession any chicken at all, then that chicken must have lips. It says that every chicken, until the end of time, will have lips. It says that if we're playing "animal" and are trying to guess a lipped animal, asking "Is it a chicken?" is a good move.

YUP-IT LOOKS LIKE A CHICKEN, QUACKS LIKE A CHICKEN, WADDLES LIKE A CHICKEN SO IT MUST BE A CHICKEN

We realize that chicken-hood questions are pretty silly, but ducks are serious business. So let's assume that:

- Fillmore is a mallard, and assume that we know that
- Mallard is a particular kind of duck.

Then, if we asked:
"Is there a duck named Fillmore?" most people would say "yes". But that simple answer involves a reasonably hefty piece of thinking:

MALLARD FILLMORE

- We check out the known ducks without success but then we find a rule that says:
- if you're looking for ducks, see if you have any mallards.

Indeed, Fillmore fits the bill. Now, can our Giant-E-Lectronic LoBlo Brain handle this kind of reasoning? Can we show how to represent these general rules, and then improve the matcher to use these rules? Would we go through all these pages just to say "no"? Not likely. So here's the scoop:

We'll have a facts base, and a rules base. The facts base is what we've been calling the data base. The rules base will contain representations of our rules. Each rule will be a list whose first element tells what kind of problem the rule might help solve:

[[duck ?x] IF [mallard ?x]]

says "if ya needa duck, see if ya gotta mallard." Not being chicken, we will handle tougher rules like:

[[brother.of ?x ?y] IF [male ?x]
                    [parents.of ?x ?u ?v]
                    [parents.of ?y ?u ?v]]

What's that say? It says if you want to see if a particular person is someone's brother, see if that person is male and both people have the same parents. We don't really need the word IF in the list, but it reminds us of an intuitive way to read the rule. We can also think AND between each of the conditions since we require that they must all be satisfied.

Guess what the following represents:

[[parents.of ?x ?y ?z] IF [mother.of ?x ?y]
                         [father.of ?x ?z]]

Well, the feathers are really flying now! The actual programs for matching rules and facts will get quite complex, but the basic idea remains very simple:

INTELLIGENT ART FOR THIS SPACE UNAVAILABLE

- First we describe our knowledge in terms of patterns:

Simple facts are represented by lists whose first elements name a relationship and the other elements name the objects that are related.

Rules are represented by lists of conditions, the first condition is true if the rest of the conditions can be satisfied. Each condition is the same form as a fact, except that it might contain variables.

- Then we describe the investigation of this knowledge base as a program that matches and manipulates patterns, but we **keep it simple**. We keep the general knowledge in rules that specify simple logical relationships.

We will only hint at how a pattern-matching system could be extended from a meek-and-mild fact retriever to a rough-and-ready de-duck-tive system. For example, if we were trying to find the brother of Dee we would phrase the request as:

[brother.of ?x Dee].

First, we could use our old compare & Co. to see if we had any facts in our fact base about the brothers of Dee. Assuming that we had no explicit fact in the base that told who Dee's brother is, the system would look into the rule base to see if we have any general rules about the brother.of relation. The system might pounce upon the rule:

[[brother.of ?x ?y] IF [male ?x] [parents.of ?x ?u ?v]
                      [parents.of ?y ?u ?v]],

matching ?y with **Dee**, as it sets up the sub-problems of

[male ?x], [parents.of ?x ?u ?v], and
[parents.of Dee ?u ?v].

Now if the system is **really** stupid, it might start to work on [male ?x], effectively searching the world's male population for Dee's brother. This may in fact work, but the only move that makes good sense is to limit the search by first trying the third case:

[parents.of Dee ?u ?v]

This approach should discover values for ?u and ?v—Jack and Jill for example. Then a clever system would try:

[parents.of ?x Jack Jill]

homing in on the kiddies of Jack and Jill. Of course, the system might say, Ha!

[parents.of Dee Jack Jill], and [male Dee] and we'd be presented with [brother.of Dee Dee].

See the system lose. But garbage-in-garbage-out, as they say. We should have

prevented this by strengthening our rule to:

[[brother.of ?x ?y] IF [male ?x] [parents.of ?x ?u ?v]
                      [parents.of ?y ?u ?v] [not.equal ?x ?y]]

Then our system might discover
   [brother.of Dum Dee].

There are several necessary changes to include rules. Some are obvious, while others are more subtle. For example, our pattern-matcher will have to change because the second pattern, not just the first, might contain variables (not an insurmountable problem, but certainly one we must consider). Another problem that you might not notice right away is that we might have to use the same rule more than once, and we want to be able to supply different answers each time. How do we tell the difference between ?x and ?x the next time around? An outline of the steps in our deductive question answerer follows:

Given a list of conditions to satisfy,

1. choose one to work on;
2. see if there is a fact that satisfies it (If so, skip to **7**);
3. see if there is a rule that applies (If not, skip to **9**);
4. make up new names for all the variables in the rule;
5. see if you can match the chosen condition with the conclusion of the rule (If not, go back to **3**);
6. replace the chosen condition with the conditions in the rule and go back to **1**;
7. if there are no more conditions, return the table of answers;

8. if there are more conditions, go back to **1**;

9. you can't satisfy this condition, so try to back up (that is, undo the last part of the table and try to resatisfy the last successful condition). If that is impossible, return `"no.match`.

Wow, we really have to watch where we stepped in this Chapter

NO BARE FEET
—COW BOYD

DO CHICKENS HAVE LIPS
BY JOHN ALLEN

THE MEANING OF LIFE

. . . but we should have damaged a few of your preconceptions about computing. There have been no numbers and no mathematics as you typically think of mathematics. Yet, we've woven an elegant basis for some very fancy computing. These simple systems consisting of facts and rules, represented by patterns, and driven by pattern-matchers are the basis for much of the work in artificial intelligence. Such rule-based systems have been quite successful in geology, medicine, and chemistry, for example.

At this level of complexity, systems have the capacity to surpass our ability to comprehend their behavior. The whole system becomes greater than the sum of its parts. As a result, such systems frequently include an "explanatory" component so that a human user may always ask how a conclusion was reached by the system. This kind of information forms the basis for taking "intelligent" systems one step further.

We will make that jump in Chapter 7, when we examine how we can build systems that examine and modify their own behavior. We are not willing to suggest that such programs "learn"; we are willing to demonstrate that such programs are starting points for programs that can examine their own "consciousness"—in other words, do introspection.

Before we get to this level, it will be valuable to gain some more experience with these new list-processing ideas. The next chapter serves that purpose.

CHAPTER 6
SHARPENING THE AXE

Chapter 5 was a motivational message, intimating how we could use lists and list computations to store and retrieve information in a data base. We also waved our hands about how such a fact-retriever could be turned into a deduction-maker, by searching for a rule whose conclusion matched the required condition. We then

expected the system either to satisfy the conditions for the application of the rule or, failing that, come up with an alternative rule. This process was applied until either the initial request was satisfied—the problem was solved—or, all possible matches failed—the request couldn't be fulfilled using the facts and rules of the base.

We will begin this chapter with some detailed discussions about the construction of list-functions, replacing the hand-waves about lists, facts, and rules with facts and rules about lists and hand-waves. We will stress the techniques that will carry over to the analysis and construction of other functions. In particular, if you examine the matching functions of the last chapter you'll see that they work by reducing a large question about matchability to a sequence of smaller questions about matchability. And—eternal optimists that we are—we expect that answers to the smaller questions can be combined into an answer to the larger quest. In the case of Logo functions, our hopes are fulfilled.

As we develop these example functions, we will also show a detailed execution of the JMC-model. For, behold, one of the functions we will describe for you is a Logo program that will carry out the steps of the JMC model. We will combine this gaggle of functions into a system that can be used to propel our machine through the sea of computations.

Going to Great length

Though length is pre-defined in TLC-Logo, consider how we might define such a function. Let's define a function called l.length—standing for list length—that will give us the length of a list. We know that

...GOING TO GREAT LENGTHS, LONG ISLAND

lists come in two flavors: empty, or non-empty. Therefore we have two cases to consider:

• The empty list—its l.length is zero.

• A non-empty list—its l.length is 1 greater than the l.length of the list with one element removed.

These conditions translate into the following TLC-Logo definition:

```
to l.length :x
  empty :x
  iftrue [0]
  iffalse [1 + l.length bf :x]
end
```

Let's look at how we could compute l.length [A]. First, substituting [A] for :x, we get:

```
empty [A]
  iftrue [0]
  iffalse [1 + l.length bf [A]]
```

We know that empty [A] is false. Thus:

```
false
  iftrue [0]
  iffalse [1 + l.length bf [A]]
```

But we know false iftrue [*a*] iffalse [*b*] will reduce to *b*. So we get:

```
1 + l.length bf [A]
```

Since we know that bf [*a b ... c*] is [*b ... c*], we can reduce the bf-expression to:

1 + l.length [].

Returning to the definition of l.length,

```
1 + (empty []
     iftrue [0]
     iffalse [1 + l.length bf []] )
```

then:

```
1 + (true
     iftrue [0]
     iffalse [1 + l.length bf [] ))
```

and verily, we roll along to:

1 + 0, finally resulting in a comforting 1.

This example, carried out in horrible detail, illustrates several points:

• This is clearly a task that humans should not do. It is long and tedious, but . . .

• It is a task that a machine can do. We used a collection of rules for simplifying expressions, and used a rule for substituting values for parameters. These are mechanical tasks; however, . . .

• Frequently there are choices of which of the above rules to apply. For example:

```
1 + (empty [A]
     iftrue [0]
     iffalse [1 + l.length bf [A]] )
```

could have been replaced with:

```
1 + (empty [A]
     iftrue [0]
     iffalse [1 + (empty bf [A]
                   iftrue [0]
                   iffalse [1 + l.length bf bf [A]] ))
```

instead of:

```
1 + (false
     iftrue [0]
     iffalse [1 + l.length bf [A]])
```

The substitutions and simplifications we picked were the "obvious" and "natural" ones . . . or were they? As in any situation where there are choices, we should try to understand the implications of each of our decisions.

The first question is: does it make any difference how we apply the rules? For if all paths lead to the same result, it's simply a question of which path is faster?

Well, it **does** make a difference in some cases. For example, given the pair of functions:

```
to flip.flop :x :n      to rabbit :s
 :n = 0                   fd :s rt 90 rabbit :s
 iftrue [1]              end
 iffalse [:x]
end
```

consider: flip.flop rabbit 1 0

Of course this is a silly computation, but who says computations have to make sense? If they did, we wouldn't have a computer industry. Regardless, we substitute into the definition of **flip.flop**, and get:

```
(0 = 0
 iftrue [1]
 iffalse [rabbit 1] )
```

and since **0 = 0** is true, this mess simplifies to **1**. But if we decide to expand the definition of **rabbit** first, we go from:

flip.flop rabbit 1 0   to:

flip.flop (fd 1 rt 90 rabbit 1) 0   and then to:

flip.flop (fd 1 rt 90 (fd 1 rt 90 rabbit 1)) 0

and on and on and . . . , but you get the idea. So we **do** have to make some rules about what is "natural" and "obvious". Here are our choices:

• In dealing with arguments, always reduce them as far as possible before tackling the definition. So, using this choice, **flip.flop rabbit 1 0** would never stop.

• Reduce conditional expressions as soon as possible, using rules like:

false iftrue [*a*] iffalse [*b*] becomes *b*

true iftrue [*a*] iffalse [*b*] becomes *a*

Applying these kinds of decisions to control the use of our rules, we can totally specify the order in which computations are performed.

So the order in which we perform computations can make a difference between a program that computes a value and a program that runs forever. It may have occurred to you to ask if it is possible to apply the rules to an expression so that we can compute two **different** values. That's a tough question to answer, but the answer is no. If we get any answer, it's a dependable one; it may not be the one we wanted, but it's dependably unexpected.

Just The Facts

Our next example comes from mathematics and illustrates our "making little ones out of big ones" technique on good, old-fashioned numbers. This example—the factorial function— can be defined by a pair of equations:

0! = 1
(n+1)! = (n+1)∗n! for *n* a non-negative integer
(*0, 1, 2 . . .*).

This definition has an immediate translation into TLC-Logo, as follows:

```
to fact :x
  :x = 0
  iftrue [1]
  iffalse [:x∗fact :x-1]
end
```

And to exercise our substitution and simplification rules, we look at the dreadful execution of fact 1 which, by substitution, gives:

```
1 = 0
iftrue [1]
iffalse [1∗fact 1-1]
```

which simplifies to:

```
false
iftrue [1]
iffalse [1∗fact 1-1]
```

and on to: 1∗fact 1-1,

and then: 1∗fact 0

Replacing fact 0, we get

```
1∗(0 = 0
  iftrue [1]
  iffalse [1∗fact 0-1] )
```

Simplification gives:

```
1∗(true
  iftrue [1]
  iffalse [1∗fact 0-1] )
```

once more gives: 1∗1

And, with a dull thud, we end up with 1.

Great Lengths, Indeed!

On the basis of the previous examples it would appear that we are determined to give computation a bad name: to compute is simply to belabor the obvious. But there are some lessons to be learned from simple examples. In particular, both of these examples demonstrate the techniques of computing a value by combining the results of computing the function for smaller values. This is an incredibly powerful idea. And it works! It works for very general kinds of objects, not just lists and numbers. The general principle recognizes that objects are either primitive objects (in these examples, the empty list or zero) or are built up by operations (here, fput-ing or adding one). Then if we wish to define a function that operates on such objects, we can do so by tearing the objects apart (by butfirst-ing or subtracting one). We will terminate this decomposition when we encounter a primitive object.

The key to using this technique—called definition by recursion—is to discover what object to decompose, and how to decompose it. The effect of a recursive

definition borders on the mystical, for at no step in the definition does anything really "significant" happen. However when the whole mechanism is put together, the result is a cathedral of computation.

Of course, the complexity of the definition will depend on the complexity of the problem and the complexity of the objects that are involved. However, the typical definition involves only a couple of cases:

• The object is primitive, and we're stuck. We have to do something.

• The object is composed of other objects. Pass the buck; make someone else do the

work and show how to use that labor to solve your problem.

Review the l.length and fact examples; look for the "buck passing", look for the work steps, and look for the combining steps. One other thing to notice is the importance of the order in which we apply our rules. For example, in the last phase of l.length [A], the expression bf [] appeared. We know that computation is undefined and will cause an error message if executed; yet the l.length computation terminated successfully because the bf [] appeared within a piece of a conditional expression that was not evaluated. A similar situation occurred in the evaluation of fact 1, and will also occur in the next section.

An Attack of Appendicitis

Here's a list-processing function of some merit. We call it append, and it is to receive two lists, generating a list that has the first list glued onto the front of the second. Thus:

append [1 2] [a s d]   gives   [1 2 a s d]

append [] [q u a c k]   gives   [q u a c k]

The first issue is to determine which argument should be decomposed. The first argument seems a likely candidate. Thus:

```
to append :x :y
  empty :x
  iftrue [:y]
  iffalse [ ? ? ? ]
end
```

A good start. Recalling our laziness motto, and noting that in the **iffalse** case, :x will have a first element, we ask:

If we have computed **append bf :x :y**—the old pass-the-buck trick, how can we get to **append :x :y**—the old combine-the-results trick?

Well, assuming :x is [1 2], and :y is [a s d], we want:

append :x :y = append [1 2] [a s d] = [1 2 a s d]

But first,   append bf :x :y = [2 a s d]

So [1 2 a s d] = fput 1 [2 a s d]
            = fput 1 append bf :x :y

and therein lies the clue:

fput first :x
    append bf :x :y = [1 2 a s d], and thus:

```
to append :x :y
  empty :x
  iftrue [:y]
  iffalse [fput first :x
            append bf :x :y]
end
```

Let's see how this definition handles **append [c] [a b]**. A substitution begins the process:

```
empty [c]
  iftrue [[a b]]
  iffalse [fput first [c]    append bf [c] [a b]]
```

After a couple of very tedious steps, we get:

fput first [c]   append bf [c] [a b],

which simplifies to: fput "c   append [] [a b]

where we have "quoted" the c to distinguish it from fput c … (which would indicate the function c.) Now a tastefully elegant substitution gives:

```
fput "c
    (empty [[]]
    iftrue [[a b]]
    iffalse [fput first [ [] ]
            append bf [ [] ] [a b]])
```

which, since **empty []** gives **true**, results in:

```
fput "c
    [a b]
```

and, yawn, to: [c a b]

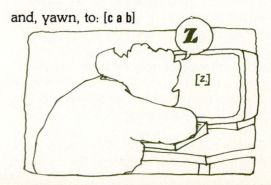

Notice that an undefined expression bf [] shows up but is never evaluated. Notice, too, that append differs from l.length and fact in that those functions just compute a value based on the existing objects, whereas append builds up a new object. The next example has this same kind of constructive property.

Lovely As a Tree

Our next example can actually be used! (Truly, this violates all the principles of example-hood: example programs should always be useless.) The function—named subst—can be employed in the JMC-Model computer that we will unveil in a few moments.

subst expects three arguments: :x—an arbitrary expression, :y—a symbol, and :z—a list. subst :x :y :z will compute a list that looks like :z except that every occurrence of :y in :z will have been replaced by :x.

For example:

subst 1 2 [2 [a 4 2] 3]   gives   [1 [a 4 1] 3],

subst 1 2 [a s d [4 5]]   gives   [a s d [4 5]],

subst [a s] 2 [1 2 3]   gives   [1 [a s] 3],

subst 1 2 2   gives 1, and subst 1 2 3   gives 3

The trick is to design subst so that it will search out each nook and cranny of the :z argument. This requires that subst visit all sublists of :z as well as visiting the elements

of :z. This gives us a clue about which object to operate on and how to dissect it: the patient is :z.

From our examples, we see that the primitive case involves a :z-value that cannot be decomposed further. This happens when :z is not a list. Then, there are two cases: :z equals :y, then substituting :x for :y in :z gives :x; or :z is not the same as :y, so the substitution causes no change in :z. These cases give us our starting point:

```
to subst :x :y :z
  not.list :z
  iftrue [:y = :z
        iftrue [:x]
        iffalse [:z]]
  iffalse [ ? ? ? ]
end
```

So we're now faced with the case that :z is a list. If so, it has a first-part and a bf-part. We're back to the age-old question: given the results of subst on the subparts of :z (pass the buck), how can we combine the results to make subst of :z (panhandle the spare change)? We can put the parts together with some fput glue:

```
to subst :x :y :z
  not.list :z
  iftrue [:y = :z
         iftrue [:x]
         iffalse [:z]]
  iffalse [fput subst :x :y first :z
           subst :x :y bf :z]
end
```

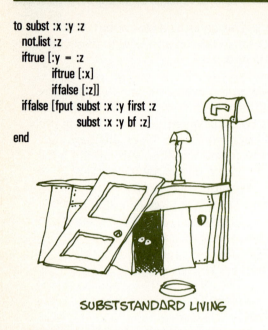

SUBSTSTANDARD LIVING

Wonderful, but how can we employ **subst** for the betterment of Junk Mail? **subst** will be used in the JMC model to replace :-ed names with specific values. So, for example:

subst [1 2] ":x [fput first :x append bf :x :y]

will give: [fput first [1 2] append bf [1 2] :y]

Note carefully: the thing we construct **is** a list; it just **looks** like an expression. Compare this observation to the occurrence of ":x instead of :x; the latter would reference the value of :x, whereas what we want is the symbol :x.

Paper and pencil calculations with our definition, the substitution rules, and the simplification rules, will show that the last **subst** computation generates:

```
fput "fput
  fput "first
    fput [1 2]
      fput "append
        fput "bf
          fput [1 2]
            fput ":y [ ]
```

before collapsing to the aforementioned list.

In the next section we combine all these ingredients: the list-processing, the JMC-Model, and the hints about deductive systems that we dropped around Chapter 5.

Getting Your Axe Together

We're now going to develop an interactive Logo system to carry out the substitution and simplification replacement rules. We'll perform this operation in three phases:

1. We give an overview of what the system does, and how it does it. We specify the user interface. How do we specify which operation we want to perform? How do we specify which expression we want to operate on?

2. We specify a Logo representation for the objects that make up the system.

3. Finally we introduce Logo functions that will implement the ideas.

Now for some specifics. What should the system do? Well it's mostly a bookkeeper, making sure that the request we specify—a substitution or a simplification—is legal. It should complain if we attempt an illegal move. The match routine will be responsible for checking the legality of each move. "Legality" is defined to be "equality". Each position in our game is defined by an equation like:

[append [1 2] [3 4] = fput first [1 2] append bf [1 2] [3 4]]

It is up to the legal move controller to assure that only equality-preserving operations are allowed. The system must also supply us with a way of referring to expressions—either new expressions that it creates, or expressions that we give it. We will design the system to recognize the following conventions:

A. The system will supply names for any new expressions it manufactures. These names will be numerals, beginning at 1. The system will also recognize names for system-level or user-defined rules, like D1, C4, or R87.

B. The system will respond to requests to substitute a Logo expression for a variable in an equation. The format is S followed by a trio:

S [*Logo expression*]   *variable*   *equation*

For example S [empty [a b]] :x 4 will replace every occurrence of :x in equation 4 with empty [a b].

C. The system will respond to requests to replace Logo expressions with equivalent Logo expressions. The format is:

R   *equation1*   *equation2*

where *equation1* is of the form [*f=g*]. The R command will generate a new equation that looks like *equation2* except every occurrence of *f* is replaced by *g*.

For example, if equation 6 is: [bf [3] = []],

then R 6 [append [3] [1 2] = fput 3 append bf [3] [1 2]]

gives: [append [3] [1 2] = fput 3 append [] [1 2]]

To use these interactive commands, we need some equations that indicate what things are equal to what other things—like [x + 0 = x]. These rules will contain patterns that indicate the pieces to select and match. Occurrences of ?x's indicate pattern matching like that of Chapter 5. Now we add a new match possibility, called a segment match, and written $x. Such an occurrence is an order to collect a sequence of elements. A $-variable may satisfy a match condition by collecting nothing. For example:

[2] and [?x $y] will match with ?x as 2 and $y, as [].

[1 2 3 4] and [1 $x 4] match with $x as [2 3], or:

[[A A] [A D D] A D D] and [?x [$y D] $y D] with ?x as [A A] and $y as [A D].

When we supply values for ?-variables, those values replace the instances of the variables. Thus, replacing x with [1 2] in [A B ?x] gives [A B [1 2]].

In contrast, segment values are "spliced" into the result. Thus, replacing $x with [1 2] in [A B $x] gives: [A B 1 2]

With this extended matcher, we can now indicate some of the rules we need:

Conditional Rules

C1 [false iftrue [$a] iffalse [$b] = $b]

C2 [true iftrue [$a] iffalse [$b] = $a]

. . .   . . .

Rules for Lists

R1 [empty [?x $y] = false]

R2 [empty [] = true]

R3 [first [?x $y] = ?x]

R4 [bf [?x $y] = [$y]]

R5 [fput ?x [$y] = [?x $y]]

. . .   . . .

Definitions of Logo functions

This section would include forms of all the to-definitions we reference. For example:

D1 [append ?x ?y = empty ?x
    iftrue [?y]
    iffalse [fput first ?x
        append bf ?x ?y]]

. . .   . . .

Rules for Logo Primitives

We have to include rules Logo primitives that the particular application might use—like arithmetic simplifications, turtle movement, or list manipulations. For example, the following rules capture some of the relationships between a list object and its components:

After this bath in terminology, it's time for an example. Again, we offer up append [c] [a b], this time illustrating some of steps of the system. In the following, lines beginning with ► indicate user input; lines beginning with ; are comments; the other lines are typed out by the system.

```
► S [[c]] ?x D1
1 [append [c] ?y = empty [c]
                iftrue [?y]
                iffalse [fput first [c]
                        append bf [c] ?y]]
```

; The system names the result equation 1

```
► S [[c]] [?x $y] R1
```

```
2 [empty [c] = false]
```

; Here the system verifies that [c] is non-empty before allowing 2 to be formed.

```
► R 2 1
3 [append [c] ?y = false
                iftrue [?y]
                iffalse [fput first [c]
                        append bf [c] ?y]]
```

; Notice that we can continue our "computation" even though no value has been designated for ?y.

```
► R C1 3
```

```
4 [append [c] ?y = fput first [c]
                append bf [c] ?y]
```

```
► S [[c]] [?x $y] R3
```

```
5 [first [c] = "c]
```

; The system has to know to quote the c

```
► R 5 4
```

```
6 [append [c] ?y = fput "c
                append bf [c] ?y]
```

```
► S [[a b]] ?y 6
```

```
7 [append [c] [a b] = fput "c
                append bf [c] [a b]]
```

. . . and on, and yawn.

Cute, but can we build such a system? Well the tedium of the preceding sample is definitely mechanical, and so is a candidate for programming. For starters, we'll have to specify a super-duper new matcher that will handle the segment variables, but that is just an amusing extension of the work we did in Chapter 5. But just because we can specify the parts for a concrete airplane, doesn't mean that it will fly. To

show that **this** system will fly, we need to describe implementations for the other pieces.

The first order of business is the representation of the objects. The objects in this system come in two flavors, as usual: primitive and non-primitive varieties.

SHARPENING THE AXE

PEKING DUCK

The Primitive Variety

These are the definitions. Each definition—like C1, . . . , D1, . . . R1 . . . above—is of the form *f = g*. They will be represented as lists:

[*the-name   the-f-part   the-g-part*].

As in: [C2
　　　 [true iftrue [$a] iffalse [$b]]
　　　 $a]

or　　[R1
　　　 [empty [?x $y]]
　　　 false]

The Non-Primitive Variety

These objects are the result of Substitutions or Replacements that were performed on existing objects.

A replacement object (like line 6 above) has a line number, and two parents—the primary expression (line 4) and the expression that was used as a replacement (line 5). So, again, we make a list:

[*expression-number the-f-part*
　　　　　　　　　 the-g-part
　　　　　　　　　 main-parent
　　　　　　　　　 sub-parent]

Thus line 6 would be represented as:
[6
 [append [c] ?y]
 [fput "c append bf [c] ?y]
 4
 5]

The other non-primitive type is the substitution object. It results from an existing object by replacing variables with expressions. Thus its list-representation will have the form:

[*expression-number   the-fpart   the-g-part*
　　　　　　　　　　 the-parent
　　　　　　　　　　 the-pattern the-substitution]

For example, line 2 would appear as:

[2　 [empty [c]]　　false
　　 R1
　　 [?x $y]　 [c]]

Notice that we can tell the difference between a primitive object, a substitution object, and a replacement object by looking at the length of the list that represents them. Thus:

```
to is.prim.obj :x          to is.subst.obj :x
  (length :x) = 3            (length :x) = 5
end                        end
```

```
to is.repl.obj :x
  (length :x) = 6
end
```

We can also define selection functions to retrieve the f- and g-parts of expressions.

```
to f.part :e          to g.part :e
  nth :e 2              nth :e 3
end                   end
```

And the name that graces any expression can be found by:

```
to moniker :e
  nth :e 1
end
```

Additional selector functions will be needed to grab the components of substitution and replacement objects, but that we'll leave to you. We'll also leave—in your capable hands—the design of the more enlightened subst function that can stuff segment values in equations. This is part of our credo of lazy programming: make someone else do it. This brings us to the control of the user's input, the maintenance

of the derived expressions, and the printing of the results.

Printing is easy; just reformat the f-part and g-part slightly, making a list with an = between them, and prefixing the mess with the equation number.

As with the data bases of Chapter 5, the maintenance problem can become quite troublesome in large systems. As with Chapter 5, will ignore the problems of efficient storage and retrieval, and just store the objects in a list. Then the following function will suffice for locating a specific object.

```
to find.obj :name :obj.list
  empty :obj.list
  iffalse [(moniker first :obj.list) = :name
       iftrue [first :obj.list]
       iffalse [find.obj :name bf :obj.list]]
end
```

The final piece involves listening to the user's tiny dancing fingers. This requires

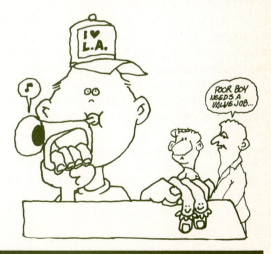

POOR BOY NEEDS A VALVE JOB...

the design of a "listen-loop", perhaps using rl (readline), to collect the command and dispatch to the appropriate command handler.

There are several pieces of this system that must still be filled in, but the general pattern should be coming clear. We'll leave the details to you. One thing about our representation that's worth a mention is that each expression "knows" the reason for its existence; it's either a primitive rule, a substitution, or a replacement. That says we could add a new command, W—a Why command, that would allow us to uncover the history of any equation in the system. Thus the system could answer questions about its own behavior. For example, we could type:

► W 6

and the system might respond:

Equation 6 is the result of a replacement in line 4 noticing that first [c] is just the symbol c.

Even though this system is controlled by the user, such an explanatory component becomes quite useful when we are dealing with very large collections of facts and rules. And when the system is able to make its own deductions, an explanatory component becomes an absolute necessity.

Of course, you might argue that the system isn't thinking, it is just responding to rules that were prescribed for it. But **we** never do **that**; do we?

Will you repeat that, please?

In our wanderings through the previous Logo landmarks, we have found repeated application for repeat. Many different tasks fell victim to the power of that mighty operation. Squares were child's play:

```
to square :side
  repeat 4 [fd :side rt 90]
end
```

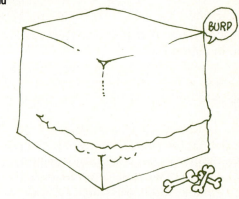

As useful as repeat was, we could do without it in this case by defining:

```
to square :side      to sq :n :m
  sq :side 0            :m = 4
end                    iffalse [fd :n rt 90 sq :n :m + 1]
                     end
```

Hmmm, so what happens if the second argument to sq is 4? Nothing special: the iffalse is not true, so it's ignored, and the value of the call on sq is the value of :m=4; that is: true.

Hmmm, hmmm, so repeat may not be so indispensible after all. In fact, can we always replace uses of repeat with other phrases in the Logo vocabulary? Of course, even if we **can**, it doesn't mean that we want to, anymore than we want to limit the way we can use natural language. Indeed, the more ways we have of expressing things, the better. The reason for analyzing repeat is not to **remove** it, but to **understand** it: what does it really mean. For example, in our square-translation, we return true, yet that's not true in the repeat-based case: the value there is "nothing. How do we know? Well, we can run the program. Big deal; how do we know that there aren't bugs in the system? Certainly we must be able to give more understandable and rational reasons for answers that this!

In natural language, we have dictionaries to explain the meaning of words, giving definitions of words in terms of other words. That's what we want to do in the next few sections: we'll analyze the meaning of several TLC-Logo words, showing their meaning in terms of other Logo words and phrases. And so our journey goes from programming to language; from entomology—the study of bugs—to etymology—the study of words; from the frying pan to the fire!

Purveyors of programming languages —TLC included—burden their readers with documents that "explain" the meaning of each and every construct of the language. Our worthy offering contains the following description of repeat:

"repeat *number* [*exp.1* ... *exp.n*]

The expressions in the list are evaluated left-to-right the specified number of times. The value of the repeat is the value of the last expression evaluated."

Wonderful. But a whole lot is left to the imagination—always a dangerous thing to do in computing.

• What happens if *number* is less than zero?

• What happens if *number* is not a number?

• Do we execute *exp.1* first *number*-times, then *exp.2*, that number of times, etc., or do we behave, and do what's "obviously" asked for?

As we have already seen, the "obvious" isn't always obvious. But if we're to be nice, we should at least give it a try. The first obvious question to answer is: "What is the value of repeat?" First, if *number* is initially less than one, we'll say that the value is "nothing; if *number* is non-numeric, it's an error; and finally, if all else is well, the value is the whatever *exp.n* last produced. We can combine all these requirements as follows:

```
to repeat :n :list
  rep1 :n :list "nothing
end

to rep1 :n :list :value
  :n < 1
  iftrue [:value]
  iffalse [execute all the expressions in :list
          and save the value of the last one as
          the new :value.
          Now execute rep1 with :n - 1, :list, and
          the new :value]
end
```

where we cover the non-numeric *number*-case by letting repeat choke at the < operation.

Now, we can simplify the fuzz a bit into:

```
to rep1 :n :list :value
  :n < 1
  iftrue [:value]
  iffalse [rep1 :n - 1
               :list
           (execute all the expressions in
            :list and save the value of the
            last one)]
end
```

Now we only have two pieces to finish off; but fortunately, one function will handle both problems for us. The secret lies with Logo's run function. To jog your memory, we've seen run in action before in Willie's brain. run takes a list of objects representing a list of Logo expressions, ex-

ecuting each expression, as it works from left-to-right through the list. The value returned by run is the value of the last expression in the list. This is exactly what we need.

As a simple example, consider:

```
run [fd 4 rt 90 'ok']
```

run will execute fd 4, follow it with a rt 90, and finally return the string 'ok' as value. Sounds pretty useless . . . until we realize that the argument can be any list at all—including one that we construct. Consider:

```
to schizo :dir :n :l
  run fput :dir fput :n :l
end
```

Then   schizo "fd 4 [track 29]

and   schizo "e 10 [rt 66]   will send the current turtle forward 4 or east 10, respectively,

QUIRK.

before executing the rest of the list. With run we can build up a list and then execute it as Logo instructions. With run we can conquer the world.

Meanwhile, back to the reality of rep1. All we need to do is slip :list to run, thus:

```
to rep1 :n :list :value
 :n < 1
 iftrue [:value]
 iffalse [rep1 :n - 1 :list (run :list)]
end
```

. . . and the magic all happens. If :n is less than one, we bail out with :value; if not, we compute a new value for :n—one less than the old value—and a new value for :value—the result of run :list, and try rep1 again. Each time we go through the process, the value of :n decreases by one and so will eventually be less than one, and we'll stop. What could be simpler? Well this is reality remember, so things usually go wrong; and run is no exception as the following senario illustrates.

Assume we want to use our new handy-dandy repeater to execute

repeat 4 [fd :n rt 90]

and assume that the current value of :n is 8. We expect to get a square, each of whose sides is of length 8. Well let's see what JMC will do.

repeat 4 [fd :n rt 90] expands to:

rep1 4 [fd :n rt 90] "nothing

but that expands to:

```
4 < 1
iftrue ["nothing]
iffalse [rep1 4-1 [fd :n rt 90] (run [fd :n rt 90])]
```

We've been through this kind of situation before:

4 < 1 is false and, thus we take the iffalse branch. We must now expand the three arguments to rep1. 4-1 gives 3, [fd :n rt 90] is a constant list, and the final argument asks run to evaluate that list.

The first thing we run into is fd; no problem. The next thing we see is :n; problem. What's the value of :n? We know the value is 8, but every known Logo will give 4! It gets that bizarre result because the last time :n collected a value was the call to rep1. Of course, the problem is that we don't want **that** value, we want the value **we** gave :n—which was 8.

The problem involves two issues: a "clash" of names—here, the system and

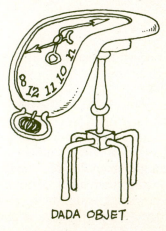

DADA OBJET

the user both gave values to :n—and second, the presence of objects that can suddenly turn from data objects into executable code—like the list [fd :n rt 90]. These two features combine to cause bugs and headaches.

The problem with rep1 seems like a clear and obvious bug that could be cured by substituting 8 for :n in the list before we started into the insides of the repeat. However, it is quite unacceptable for a system to go around arbitrarily replacing names—like :n in the list [fd :n rt 90]—with values, even if it "does the right thing." It's guaranteed to be the wrong thing to do elsewhere.

The short-term cure for the headache —called a "hack"—is to reserve some distinctive names to be used by definitions (like rep1) that will accept a list to be run at a later time. Thus:

```
to repeat :#%!n :#%!list
    rep1 :#%!n :#%!list "nothing
end
```

and

```
to rep1 :#%!n :#%!list :#%!value
  :#%!n < 1
  iftrue [:#%!value]
  iffalse [ rep1 :#%!n - 1 :#%!list (run :#%!list)]
end
```

The long-term solution requires some careful thought about the JMC models, about their implementation, about the nature of programs, about the representation of programs and, more generally,

about the distinctions between objects and representations. We will bring these issues into better focus in Chapter 7.

. . . and you thought Logo was child's play!

The case of a cond Artist

One problem with the iftrue-iffalse conditionals is that complex conditions turn into
    long nested
       conditional
           expressions
      (one test
        inside
           another test
             inside yet
              another test).
         Much like
        the mouse's tale, they
     are hard to
  read and hard to
     follow.

Because of such anti-social programming style, we introduced the cond expression:

```
cond [[test.1 action . . . action]
      [test.2 action . . . action]
          . . . ]
```

Such cond expressions straightened out the logic of the nested iftrue-iffalse-conditionals. Thus the above example would replace:

```
test.1
iftrue [action . . . action]
iffalse [test.2
        iftrue [action . . . action]
        iffalse [ . . . . . . ]
          . . . ]
```

NESTED CONDITIONAL EXPRESSIONS

As with **repeat**, we could define **cond** in TLC-Logo itself, but it would require some extra care. In particular, consider the following example:

```
cond [[:x = 4 fput 1 list [:x]]
     [test :x bk 10 e 4]
     [active :x axa :y maxa :x]]
```

and consider what the definition of **cond** might look like using the *%$#!* names:

```
to cond :%$#!list
    Get the first element of :%$#!list. It's of the
        form:    [test action ... action].
    Use run on the test part.
    If the result is false, ignore the actions and
        try cond on bf of :%$#!list.
    Otherwise, use run on [action ... action].
end
```

That's a pretty hefty description. A lot of it translates into a simple Logo description. The only thing we have to add to it is a test for an empty *:%$#!list*:

```
to cond :%$#!list my :%$#!element
    empty :%$#!list
    iftrue ["nothing]
    iffalse [make "%$#!element first :%$#!list
             run.test.part :%$#!element
             iffalse [cond bf :%$#!list]
             iftrue [run.action.part :%$#!element]]
end
```

Notice that, following our principle of lazy programming, we've left all the hard work for **run.test.part** and **run.action.part**. And hard work it is! How does **run.test.part** discover how much of the list *:%$#!element* to munch? In our example, the first test takes three elements—**:x**, **=**, and **4**—, the second test gobbles two—**test**, and **:x**; and how many does the third take, please? To discover that, we have to know how many parameters **active** needs. Not a trivial problem. To simplify the problem, we cheat and implement a simpler kind of **cond**:

```
cheap.cond [[[test.1] action ... action]
            [[test.2] action ... action]
                ... ]
```

Now it's easy to finish:

```
to cheap.cond :%$#!list my :%$#!test :%$#!actions
    empty :%$#!list
    iftrue ["nothing]
    iffalse [make "%$#!test first first :%$#!list
             make "%$#!actions bf first :%$#!list
             (run :%$#!test) = "false
             iftrue [cheap.cond bf :%$#!list]
             iffalse [run :%$#!actions]]
end
```

So, with the extra brackets, **cheap.cond** can be completed. While TLC-Logo's **cond** implementation is more complex internally, it can say "brackets? brackets? We don't need no stinkin' brackets!"

And what is the point of all this? It shows how we can define parts of Logo in Logo itself and, as a result, have a very precise description of what words like repeat and cond mean. The particular problem we ran into with cond shows that it may be difficult to give a simple description of **every** Logo operation, but even cheap.cond's definition is better than the ambiguous, but deathless, prose of traditional documentation.

Get Off My case!

Another control construct we've seen is case. It allows us to compare a single value with one of several possibilities. We used case in Willie's marksmanship exploits, as follows:

```
to check.char :c
  case :c [['f fire]
           ['u gun.up]
           ['d gun.down]]
end
```

The case allowed a clean presentation of the requested options and actions. Now, what can be done to make a clean presentation of all of the meanings of case? As with cond, we'll do that by supplying a definition in Logo. First, we give a more complete description of the general form of case:

```
case exp [[object actions]
          [object actions]
          . . .
          [object actions]]
```

where *exp* is evaluated and compared with the *object*s. As soon as a match is found, the associated *action*s are performed, and the remainder of the case components are ignored. The word "ow is recognized as a special *object* in a case; it stands for "otherwise" and will match anything. "ow can be used to make sure that at least one "arm" of the case has a match.

We can define case in TLC-Logo as follows:

```
to case :%$#thing :%$#caseload
  cond [[empty :%$#caseload :%$#thing]
        [:%$#thing = first first :%$#caseload
            run bf first :%$#caseload]
        ["ow = first first :%$#caseload
            run bf first :%$#caseload]
        [ow case :%$#thing bf :%$#caseload]]
end
```

That is a reasonably concise definition; no fuss, no muss. Notice that the problem we had with cond (versus cheap.cond) doesn't occur, because there is a single *object* to compare, rather than an expression to (find and) evaluate.

Well, with these three examples—repeat, case, and cond—you should be convinced that we can define lots of Logo in Logo itself. You could use that wondrous knowledge to add new operations, but the more important lesson is that these definitions show a power similar to that found in our natural languages: the ability to define the words of a language using that very same language.

Catching Our Breath

Time for a short breather before we go off to scale another monument. We'll start by taking a peek at nth—a pre-defined TLC-Logo function that selects an item in a list (or string, or vector).

On the surface, at least, nth is a pretty vanilla function: given a list, get the desired element. But the world can be cruel; someone, sometime, somewhere might walk up and say:

nth [duck turtle chair] 7

What's a person to do? It's not appropriate to just say 'buzz off, Bozo' and keep on computing; we should alert the system to the error and come to a dignified stop. Indeed, the system does this, and we'll now show you how to play hardball with errors just like the system does.

To do that, we'll define our own version of nth, called item. Just what kinds of errors should item watch for? It should at least make sure that the requested selection is greater than zero. Thus:

```
to item :list :num
    :num ▶ 0 ; if :num is non-numeric, ▶ will complain
    iftrue [item1 :list :num]
    iffalse [ ? ? ? ]
end
```

Ah! Those crufty little ?'s again; they always mean trouble. In this case, they introduce a TLC-Logo function named throw. throw will appear with two arguments:

- A symbol name
- A list of expressions

as in, throw "error ['Buzz off, Bozo'].

Now, what does such an expression do? Assume we replace the ?'s in item with the irreverent throw-expression we just introduced. Then if item is given a number less than zero, the computation will terminate immediately and return to the system with the value 'Buzz off, Bozo'. So for example:

fput item [duck turtle chair] 7 first [[pig] cow]

would never complete the fput or evaluate first [[pig] cow].

And how do such wondrous things happen? throw is actually half of a siamese twin; its alter ego is named catch, and it too is followed by two arguments of the same form as throw. A catch-throw combination is set up as follows:

• We begin by executing a catch *label* [*expressions*] This involves remembering the *label* for future reference, and then executing the *expressions* of the catch.

• If we come across a throw *label* [*expressions*] while executing some of the catch's *expressions*, we execute the throw's *expressions* and return that value as the value of the closest surrounding catch whose *label* matches the throw's *label*.

The idea is that the catch sets up a "safety-net" before beginning execution of its expressions; if the execution doesn't involve a use of throw, then the execution is completed normally, and the net is taken down. If a throw with a matching label is discovered, then the computation falls into the net. We can have many layers of catchers and the throws are trained to fall into the appropriate safety net.

Now, the system is prepared automatically to catch errors by recognizing throws whose label is "error. In this way, you can make your error detection system compatible with that of Logo. We used this feature in item, and will now use it again in completing item1:

```
to item1 :list :num
  cond [[empty :list
          throw "error ['not enough elements—item']]
         [:num = 1 first :list]
         [item1 bf :list :n-1]]
end
```

so we'll throw to "error if :num is larger than the length of the list :list.

The catch-throw pair can be used in more exotic applications than just error handling. The functions can be used to set up speedy communications between some innermost computation and a surrounding control system.

catch and throw are more complex and perhaps more difficult to understand than the other Logo functions. If we try—as in the previous sections—to give definitions of catch and throw in Logo, the source of this difficulty may become apparent.

```
to catch :lab :list.of.exprs
  save.somehow.catch :lab
  run :list.of.exprs
end
```

```
to throw :lab :list.of.exprs
  find.somehow.catch :lab
  run :list.of.exprs
end
```

The mystery lies within save.somehow.catch and find.somehow.catch. In particular, find.somehow has to reorganize the world so that when we finish run-ing the throw, we end up at the end of the catch, not the end of the throw. That's a very strange operation —like walking into a room, turning around and walking back out, only to find that the room you enter is not the one you just came from!

Few languages let users have the necessary ingredients to implement save.somehow.catch and find.somehow.catch, but just give catch and throw as primitives. These restrictions are imposed because these ingredients give access to the very subconscious of the computation. We will examine these subconscious urges in Chapter 7.

Without a leg to stand on

. . . that's the condition the "Logo's-only-for-kids" faction will have found themselves in by now. TLC-Logo is a heavy-duty operator. And as lead-in to our Logo sales pitch, notice that nth is length without a leg to stand on . . . and that's really going to great lengths to make a pun.

Indeed, length and nth are nice to have around, but we have seen that they are easily defined provided that we have first, bf, and conditional expressions. The important operations in list processing are the ones that dissect the list (first and bf), the ones that build new lists (fput, and list) and the ones that test lists (=, empty) for some condition. These basic operations are the primeval operations from which we can build up complex kinds of objects.

We have also seen that repeat is not an indespensible part of Logo. Given the representability of Logo programs as lists, and given run, we could define repeat, case, and cond in Logo. Logo is one of the few languages that allows the user to define new control operations. The key is a representation of programs as objects that can be manipulated by the language. List objects and run provide that facility in Logo.

A one, and a two, and a . . .

In the grand finale of Chapter 3 we talked computing with squares. There, we mentioned several properties that we might associate with square objects. The properties we mentioned included:

size,
position,
heading, and a
color

In addition, we will associate a name with each square so that we can tell one square from another. We must also indicate that this blob of information is a square object, for we may have many different kinds of objects in our system.

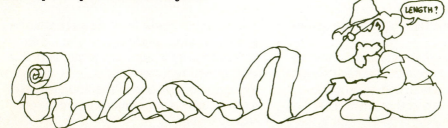

SHARPENING THE AXE

We also discussed some desired operations on squares:

square :name :size - creates a square of the designated size with the upper left corner at the center of the screen. The point at the upper left corner will be called the origin in the square and will be used to represent the location of the square. In addition, the square so created will be named :name, and will be accessible through that name.

grow :size - changes the size of a square

color :ink - changes the color of a square

rotate :angle - rotates the square about its origin

sqpos :pos - positions the origin of the square

All squares can share the same function for displaying themselves; but each square will have its own collection of properties—position, color, and so forth. Fortunately, Logo lists are a good vehicle for

keeping track of all these properties. So, when we create a square we manufacture a list containing the size, position, heading, color, and name; we also decorate the list with some information telling that it represents a square object. So, for example, when we say

square "hollywood 20

HOLLYWOOD SQUARE

we construct the list of properties:

[square 20 [0 0] 0 0 hollywood],

associate the list of properties with the word **hollywood**, and return the list. To display it, we'll place Studs at the origin of the square with a heading that matches the heading of the square and ask him to do a **repeat 4 [fd :size rt 90]** where :size has the value 20.

Instead of simply hacking a representation for squares together, we will define square-ness in a sequence of steps: first, a list that will represent our objects, and then we define operations to manipulate these representations. Operations come in four basic varieties:

1. We may specify functions to create new objects. These functions are called *constructors*, because they construct new objects. For example:

```
to make.square :size :org :head :color :name
  list ["square :size :org :head :color :name]
end
```

2. Another batch of object operations is the *selectors*. They are used to extract components from existing objects. Here are the square selectors:

```
to sq.size :sq        to sq.pos :sq
  nth :sq 2             nth :sq 3
end                   end


to sq.hd :sq          to sq.ink :sq
  nth :sq 4            nth :sq 5
end                   end


to sq.name :sq
  nth :sq 6
end
```

3. Some objects will need to have some of their properties modified—a turtle will change color, a square will change origin. Functions that change values are called *updaters*. In particular, we want updaters for the position and heading of squares.

```
to sq.update.pos :sq :loc   to sq.update.hd :sq :h
  set :sq 3 :loc              set :sq 4 :h
end                         end
```

4. Finally, we need a general object fondler—called a *recognizer*—that will tell us the type of an object. For example, we can define the square recognizer by:

```
to is.square :obj
  all [(type :obj)="list (first :obj)="square]
end
```

This suite of constructors, selectors, updaters, and recognizers gives us an elegant way to talk about squares. So, here's the definition of square:

```
to square :name :size
  make :name make.square :size [0 0] 0 ink ? :name
end
```

where the make makes sure that the newly created square can be referred to by its name. draw is defined as:

```
to draw :sq
  displaysq sq.size :sq
            sq.pos :sq
            sq.hd :sq
            sq.ink :sq
end
```

where displaysq is accomplished by:

```
to displaysq :size :loc :heading :color
  ask :studs
  pen :up
  pos :loc
  hd :heading
  pen :down
  ink :color
  repeat 4 [fd :size rt 90]
end
```

Squares have names so that we can send messages to particular ones. We will handle collections of squares like we handled herds of turtles. That is, there will be a current square that is paying attention, and we will use **sq.ask** to change to different square, just like **ask** is used to re-direct turtle talk. The current square is always available as the value **:cur**. The definition of **sq.ask** is:

```
to sq.ask :sq
   make "cur sq.name :sq
end
```

SQ.ASKING A CUR

We also want to define operations that change the position and heading of the current square as well as request the current values. Now, the value of **:cur** is the **name** of the current square, not the square itself. We need to get hold of the value associated with the name, and the TLC-Logo operation called **thing** will do this. That is:

```
thing :cur
```

will give us the square object that is indirectly referenced by **:cur**. For example, if the current value of **:cur** is "hollywood, then **thing :cur** gets the square named "hollywood.

Given **thing**, we can develop Logo functions to set-and-test the position and heading slots of the current square. These

functions—called **sqpos** and **sqhd**, respectively—will accept a ?-message and respond with the current position or heading

—respectively. If **sqpos** is respectfully sent a list, that list will be installed as the new position for the square. In this case we will erase the current picture of the square, change the square's postion to the new position, and draw the square. The definition of **sqpos** is:

```
to sqpos :loc my :sq
   make "sq thing :cur
   :loc = "?
   iftrue [sq.pos :sq]
   iffalse [erase :sq
           draw make sq.name :sq
                   sq.update.pos :sq :loc]
end
```

where **draw** was previously defined and **erase** is accomplished by drawing the square in its current location using the background color.

The definition of **sqhd** is similar:

```
to sqhd :angle my :sq
  make "sq thing :cur
  :angle = "?
  iftrue [sq.hd :sq]
  iffalse [erase :sq
        draw make sq.name :sq
                sq.update.hd :sq :angle]
end
```

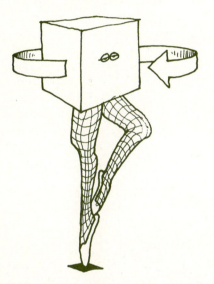

We are in good shape now to define the
rotate operation, that will expect an angle
telling how much to rotate, and it will ask
the current square to rotate itself about its
origin by the amount of that angle. But this
is just a matter of adding that angle to the
current heading of the square, and using
the sqhd operation to do the rest. Here it is:

```
to rotate :angle
  sqhd (sqhd ?) + :angle
end
```

These complex operations are much
easier to describe because of the careful
thinking that took place when we set up

the representation for squares. We can
build on that work now, defining complex
operations with very simple functions. For
example, we can spin the current square
around its origin with:

```
to spin
  rotate 20
  spin
end
```

To get things moving, just create a
square and start it up:

```
square "hollywood 20
sq.ask "hollywood
spin
```

Or we could define spinany, that expects the
angle of rotation to be supplied:

```
to spinany :angle
  rotate :angle
  spinany :angle
end
```

Once grow is defined—an exercise for the
reader—we could define a message that
causes the current square to grow as it
rotates:

```
to spin.n.grow :angle :size
  rotate :angle
  grow :size
  spin.n.grow :angle :size
end
```

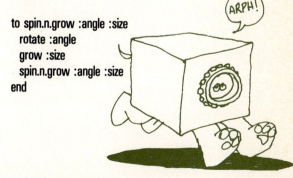

SHARPENING THE AXE

We'll let you put the rest of this square world together, defining grow and color, and anything else that strikes your fancy.

A Faun-ed Farewell

Oh, dear, it's time to close this chapter. But we've learned a lot more about objects, and their representations as lists. In particular, objects can be thought of from at least three different perspectives:

First, as abstract objects (squares, ducks, numbers, turtles and lists)—as objects to draw, objects that quack, objects to use in calculating sums and products, objects that crawl around on our TV screen, and objects that represent a collection of objects.

Second, the less abstract level that we can quantify—the representation of objects—as a collection of properties with which we might want to compute.

Finally, the most concrete level—representation of objects as Logo lists that we can use to build a real computational environment.

All of these levels interact to improve our understanding of thinking and computing.

CHAPTER 7
ON TOWARDS INTROSPECTION

Brain Surgery (Chapter 5) laid out the groundwork for a nifty question-answering system based on pattern-matching and logic. We gave you enough rope to hang yourself, without giving complete enough programs that you can hang us. This was done intentionally. Why? Because computing is not a think-by-numbers, drill-and-kill experience. You, gentle reader, are **supposed** to be learning the power of Logo as a language for describing abstract ideas (like turtles, and facts, and relationships, and deductions). And these abstract ideas, though perhaps fuzzy around the edges, have enough substance that we are able to actually compute with them—to build

models of them and their interactions in the machine and, by "computing" with them, find new relationships. Part of learning—part of making the abstract, concrete—is believing. The way to believe in computational ideas is to work with them, and thus we leave holes for you. TLC-Logo is Swiss cheese, not "imitation processed dairy substance."

We did it to you again in Sharpening the Axe (Chapter 6) where we demonstrated some of the techniques of deductive logic and axiom systems to analyze the ways of computation. Since these computational processes can tell us a lot about how artificially intelligent systems work—and indirectly, tell us a lot about how we think—we will go back into the murky swamp to analyze Logo computations using Logo itself.

This use of a language for self-analysis or self-explanation is actually no big deal; we do it all the time in natural language. Our dictionaries give explanations of words by using other words in that same language. We can do this kind of thing in Logo, defining l in terms of lt, and lt in terms of rt:

```
to l            to lt :n
  lt 45           rt 360 - :n
end             end
```

Sooner or later, though, we expect to develop a set of Logo operations that are sufficient to explain all the rest. This is an interesting characteristic of programming languages, not shared with natural languages. In human language we often have definitions that are circular, where the definition of one word will involve another word whose definition uses the first word.

Our ability to deal with circularity and even down-right inconsistency is something not shared by most computer languages.

A trick **we** use in dealing with our inconsistent reality—sorry, but consistent worlds and Easter bunnies are out—is to ignore the situation until we have no other option. At this point, we'll just make the best of a bad situation.

Keep two points in mind as we try to mimic this flexibility:

• Confrontation with inconsistency or incomplete information arises dynamically. That is, we don't go looking for trouble; we wait until it comes up and pokes us in the eye.

• Inconsistency or incompleteness is handled on a case-by-case basis, using the information we have available at the moment.

kludge—the reader—, thereby transmitting the information to the machine.

The humble programmer would never enter The Machine Room that contained this reader, but would pass the blessed card deck to the spirit world through a small opening. This world was ruled by the dreaded Machine Operator. If the machine or program failed, the Operator would present the programmer with The Dump. Dump was a proper description of the product—a listing of numbers, representing the contents of all of the machine's memory locations. This dump frequently had nothing to do with the source of the problem, but you never knew for sure until you looked. And what if the program worked? Work? Work? Surely, you jest.

Though these two points are obvious from a human/duck/turtle perspective, traditional computing languages have been hard-pressed to handle the idea. These languages expect that, before a computation is begun, all syntax has been sanitized, all program pieces are present, and that any anti-social behavior occurring during a computation will immediately terminate the program—if not the programmer. The root of these problems lies in the history of computing. In the ancient days of computing (thirty years ago!) the typical computer was very large, very expensive, and very unreliable. A machine installation would cover two floors of a large building: one floor held the machine, while the other floor held a humongous air-conditioning system. The electronic bean counter generated a lot of heat and, as a result, failed frequently. The typical input device was a punched-card reader. People were actually paid to drill little holes in rectangular pieces of cardboard, and the holes were then sensed by an electro-mechanical

SHIRLEY JESTING

It was most fortunate that these early machines had small memories—comparable to today's portable computers— otherwise the production of Dumps would have deforested the North American continent.

ON TOWARDS INTROSPECTION

To further complicate matters, these early machines were relatively slow; so even modest computations could get dumped by hardware failure. Sound like fun? Machines were unreliable, slow, and only had small memories—all were characteristics shared by the programmers. However machines were expensive while programmers were cheap.

This cost factor guaranteed that the programmers would only approach the machine when they were quite sure that the program would work—otherwise they wouldn't. Combine this attitude with the pain of long delays for key-punches and access to the machine, and the idea of interactive computing becomes even less attractive. Furthermore, the kinds of problems that were considered fit for computers did not lend themselves to exploration and experimentation. The real problems were worked out with paper and pencil, and the computer only carried out calculations that implemented the solution.

Of course, most of these technological conditions are no longer true. Today's machines are compact, very rapid, and highly reliable, with large memories

CAN THIS MARRIAGE BE SAVED?

available at low cost. Unfortunately, programmers have not evolved at a comparable rate. They are neither compact, nor fast, nor reliable, nor has their memory capacity increased substantially. Their major change is an increased appetite for money.

The type of problems that we now expect to solve with computers has also evolved. No longer are we dealing with nice numerical problems; now we're using machines more as organizers of complexity. Operating systems keep programs out of each other's hair; word processors help create deathless prose. Data base systems keep track of everything from ducks and pigs, to airline reservations. Yet the tools

that we use to create these programs are slightly re-hashed versions of the old techniques: text editors act like card punches; operating systems have all the sympathy and understanding of our ancient

Machine Operator; and, bleaagh, we use the same old, tired, numerically-based languages. It is time that "common sense" says something about the way we interact with computers.

To begin, these new ideas say that computing should be **interactive**. For example, when we use a word processor to create prose, we don't write the material out by hand first, and then copy it into the system. We should think a lot about what to say and how to say it; we may even

make some notes. But when it comes to the actual writing, we sit down and compose interactively. We experiment with phrasing, with style, with formatting, and frequently with spelling. We enjoy the freedom to make mistakes and explore language. One effect of this is a more fluid —one might even say "drippy"—style of writing, called "ego-less writing". This does **not** mean that the writer doesn't care about the content or style; rather, it means

that the process of phrasing ideas is sufficiently painless that the author feels free to modify and experiment with the presentation.

In contrast, if the creation of a particular paragraph has taken a long time to create, its author will resist the suggestion of modification or—gasp!—deletion. Ego gets in the way—"how can I throw away all that effort!"

Of course, a good text editor is only a good tool, and mindless wordy waffles will flow from finger tips as well as from pen nibs. So we are not advocating that English Composition be replaced with Word Processing/4U, any more than we'd consider replacing Calculus with Computer Programming/2GO. The point is that a sharp tool in the hand of a skilled individual will give better results than a dull tool in the hand of a skilled individual, or a sharp tool in the hand of a dull individual. Gee, two platitudes in the same book!

PLATITWODES

And what does this have to do with computer languages? We would suggest that exploratory programming is the creative writing of computing. As such, it requires the same kinds of flexibility that writing in natural languages requires. It requires mind-training; it requires good,

ON TOWARDS INTROSPECTION

sharp tools; and it requires a language that will allow the writer to say what needs to be said, in the most expressive and natural way.

Elegance counts in both programming and writing, but there is one important distinction between the writer and the programmer: the programmer's work must not be fiction.

A program must meet some specifications before it is blessed. And therein lies the next common sense rule of modern computing. Any time a collection (covey? gaggle? swarm? sleaze? pride?—system is too fancy a term) of programs is being developed, we must expect change. We may have a faulty idea of what to program, or there might be bugs in the program, or we might just plain change our mind. All these conditions will involve changes in the programs; that process of change is called debugging. Debugging requires two things:

• That we are able to recognize that a bug exists and are able to isolate that insect.

• That we are able to modify the programs to exterminate the bug.

And how do we perform these wondrous things? We have seen hints about how to do the second task: run can take a list and execute the elements as Logo expressions. So, if we think about our Logo programs as lists, we can use Logo's list operation (first, bf, . . . list, etc.) to change programs, and then turn run loose on the new list.

The first problem—the bug diagnosis phase—is more difficult. That's not suprising since this skill separates good automotive or medical mechanics from the hackers and quackers in the non-computing fields. Where do **we** start? We need to

ask "where it hurts" and we need to take temperatures. These requests translate to questions like:

• What is the current value of :xxx?

• Who gave me this ghastly value?

• How did I get inside this Logo function?

Answers to these What-Who-How questions require that the Logo computation leave a trail of "bread crumbs" that shows the path that the Logomotive was following when it crashed. And how do we do that?

In this chapter we will develop a Logo calculator that is able to give a Logo physician information about what it thinks it is doing. Naturally, this calculator will be written in Logo. Once that is done, we will suggest how one could extend this system so that it would be able to look over its

```
to fl my [:key rc]
  cond [[any [(:key = 'l') (:key = 'L')] lt 45]
        [any [(:key = 'f') (:key = 'F')] fd 10]
        [ow throw "up
                  [string ['what does ' :key ' mean?']]]]]
  fl
end
```

own shoulder to detect bugs and correct errors. Physician, cure thyself.

One major part of such an endeavor is the ability to plant this programming tool in an environment that supports high quality interaction. We must be prepared to poke and prod at a program at any time; when we suspect a bug, we must be able to find it, isolate it, and mark it with a "B." One powerful advantage that Logo has in this quest is the ability to write these programming environments in Logo itself.

As a simple example, assume that our Logo didn't have the single-key f-l language, and that we wanted to define it. We can use the pre-defined function **rc** to read a character.

Recall that **throw** passes the value of its second argument out to the surrounding **catch** that matches the **throw**'s label. So, we might start our **fl** interpreter by typing:

catch "up [fl]

then **fl** would continue to interpret keystrokes until something other than **f** or **l** was typed. For example, we hit a **b**, we would see the string **'what does b mean?'**.

This simple single-key interpreter is a prototype for the top level of an interactive language system. From this two-note instrument we can build an orchestra by:

• Adding more recognizable operations. We could add more clauses to the **cond**, but we'll see better ways to do the same thing.

ON TOWARDS INTROSPECTION

• Adding useful error information.
Instead of just throw-ing "up an error
message, we could display a history of
how we got into that indelicate condition,
and ask the user's advice.

• Adding an editor.
We could integrate the program production
and testing under the umbrella of an editor
that could be used anywhere, anytime, on
anything. We'd define a Logo function, edit,
that could even operate on functions while
they executed.

• Adding interactive bug fixing.
When an error is discovered, we would
have access to the internal workings of the
computation. We could make changes in
that internal state and continue the
computation.

The list goes on and on. But before **we**
go on and on, we need some experience
with the insides of the devices that evaluate our Logo expressions. That's the task for
the remainder of this Chapter. We begin
with a couple of examples. The first is simple arithmetic; the second is simple list-
processing.

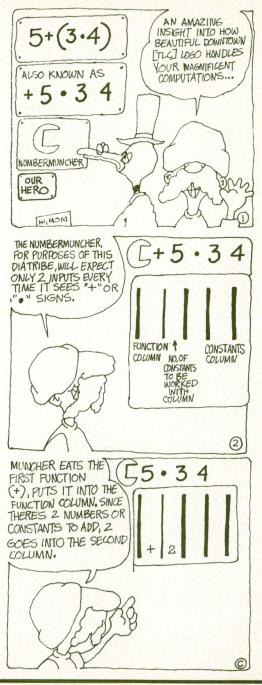

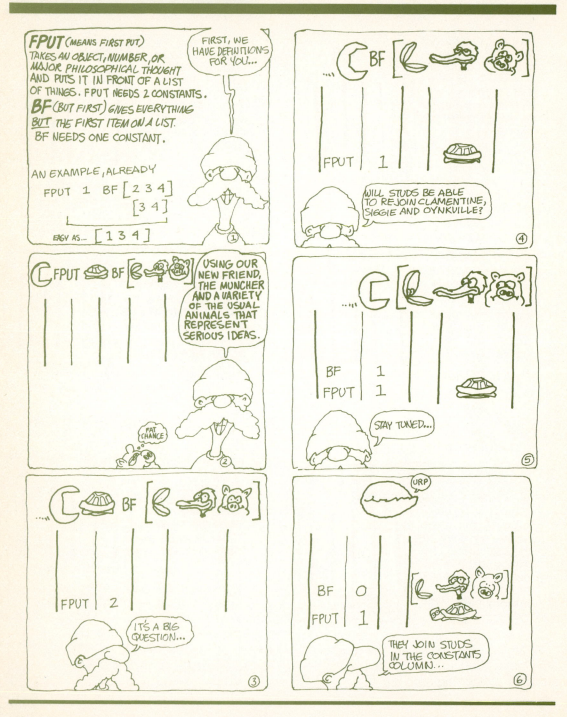

I. The input stream will be a list. For example: [+ **5** * **3 4**] seems a good start for the first of the previous examples.

II. The columns that contain the names, counts, and constants will again be lists. We will add elements by using fput; we will remove elements by using first and bf.

III. And we will represent the munching in a Logo program that manipulates these lists. This function, named munch, will expect four inputs: the input string to munch (:str), the column for functions (:fnc.col), the column for counts (:cnt.col), and the column for constants (:cnst.col).

```
to munch :str :fnc.col :cnt.col :cnst.col
   cond [[zero.first :cnt.col munch :str
                            bf :fnc.col
                            sub1.first bf :cnt.col
                            apply.fnc first :fnc.col
                                       :cnst.col]

         [empty :str      check.first :cnst.col]

         [is.const first :str    munch bf :str
                            :fnc.col
                            sub1.first :cnt.col
                            fput first :str
                                 :cnst.col]

         [is.fnc first :str    munch bf :str
                            fput fval first :str
                                 :fnc.col
                            fput arity first :str
                                 :cnt.col
                            :cnst.col]
end
```

So just as we can "play turtle" and "play junk mailer" we can also "play muncher". One question, of course, is: can we teach this to our friendly local Logo machine? Of course we can. To do so we need:

• Some way to express the pieces of the munchtoon to the machine: the input, and the columns for names and constants.

• A program to mimic the decisions that the munchketeer makes as it moves through the input.

We'll use lists to represent the pieces of the computation, and we'll use Logo to write the mimicking program.

where check.first is used to get the final answer out of the constants column when all the work is done. If there is no answer there, it simply returns the empty list, otherwise the answer is the first element in the constants column:

```
to check.first :l
  empty :l
    iftrue [:l]
    iffalse [first :l]
end
```

Even with the TLC-cond expression, the munch code looks like an e. e. cummings poem. But please try to spend some time relating the clauses in the conditional to actions in our munchtoon. You'll see that

munch uses several sub-functions to pick at the pieces. For example:

```
to is.const :x my [:tie type :x]
  any [(:tie = "fix) (:tie = "float)]
end
```

where :tie gets the type of :x. The recognizer is.const gives true only for an integer or a

floating point number (one with a decimal point in it somewhere), whereas a full-scale Logo muncher would also handle lists, words, and strings. This slight simplification will make it easier to see what's going on.

The implementation of is.fnc requires a bit of care because we also need to know how many arguments each function requires. Again, for the sake of this example muncher, we use a very simple scheme. We represent all the functions in a list called opr.list (operator list). Each element is itself a list; the first element is a name of a function and the second element is a number that tells how many arguments are needed. For example:

```
make "opr.list [[ + 2] [- 2] [* 2] [= 2] ]
```

A real system would have a large list of operators that it knew about, but this simple list will make the point.

Using :opr.list, we can write is.fnc as:

```
to is.fnc :obj
  (find :obj :opr.list) = "false
  iftrue [false]
  iffalse [true]
end
```

where find searches the opr.list for a function entry, and either returns the entry if there is one, or just false:

```
to find :n :list
  cond [[empty :list    false]
       [(first first :list) = :n    first :list]
       [ow    find :n bf :list]]
end
```

Thus, find "+ :opr.list gives [+ 2], while: find "honest.man :opr.list gives false.

When a function object is recognized, we need to select information about the function and the required number of arguments. We use fval and arity for these tasks, and they both use find:

```
to arity :x              to fval:x
  nth find :x :opr.list 2   find :x :opr.list
end                      end
```

Next, we have the functions that manipulate the constant counter, represented by the list :cnt.col. sub1.first subtracts one from the first element of the given list, and zero.first checks if the first element in the list is 0.

```
to sub1.first :l          to zero.first :l
  empty :l                  empty :l
  iftrue [ [] ]             iftrue [[]]
  iffalse [fput (first :l -1)  iffalse [(first :l) = 0]
            bf :l]          end
end
```

That takes care of all the business except apply.fnc. This function is used only when all the constants are ready and waiting for the top function on fnc.col. apply.fnc has the awesome responsibility of stripping off the right number of constants from the constants column, applying the first element of fnc.col to those constants, and then depositing the result as the new top element in the constants column.

```
to apply.fnc :fnc :cnst.col my :opr :num :bef.aft
  make "opr nth :fnc 1
  make "num nth :fnc 2
  make "bef.aft split :cnst.col :num
  fput do :opr first :bef.aft
      bf bef.aft
end
```

:fnc has two pieces of information bundled up in it. First, the name of the function, and second, the number of constants that it needs. Those two pieces get popped out into the my-variables named :opr and :num. Then we go to work on the list of constants that the muncher has made. We used split to rip off the first :num elements.

```
to split :l :n          to split1 :l :n :l1
  split1 :l :n []          :n = 0
end                       iftrue [(fput :l1 :l)]
                          iffalse [split1 bf :l
                                          :n - 1
                                          fput first :l :l1]
                        end
```

The result of split is a list whose first element is a list of the first :n elements of :l and the rest of the list contains the remaining elements of :l. split1 does all the work. Watch the way that split1 builds its answer. It uses a sneaky (but very useful) technique to build up a list in a new place as it gets torn down in another. For example:

```
split [1 2 3 4] 2   = >   split1 [1 2 3 4] 2 []
                    = >   split1 [2 3 4] 1 [1]
                    = >   split1 [3 4] 0 [2 1]
                    = >   [[2 1] 3 4]
```

Note that split reverses the order of the constants being taken off of cnst.col. But that is exactly what we want, since that puts them back in the order they originally occupied in the input stream :str.

And what does do do? It is the gateway into the subconscious of the muncher. The first argument to do is a primitive Logo function, and it is applied to do's second argument. For example:

```
do "+ [2 3]    is    5
```

Notice that do is related to our friend, run (do is, of course, run's papa). run expects a list representing a Logo expression, whereas do expects to see two arguments: (1) a word representing a function that we want to apply, and (2) a list representing the values that function will use. Thus:

```
do "+ [2 3]    equals    run [+ 2 3]
```

In our case, apply.fnc has the list of arguments and the name of the function, so do is more convenient than run.

Well, that's the magic number muncher in all its glorious Logo detail. So now we can munch things like:

```
munch [+ 3 * 4 5]  []   []   [] or
```

```
munch [fd 10 rt 90 fd + 4 5]  []   []   []
```

This simple collection of programs implements a prefix polish two-stack calculator. (Can **you** say "prefix polish two-stack calculator"). That's just a fancy name for a program that does arithmetic for expressions written with the function **pre**ceding the arguments—for example we'd write + *2 3* instead of *2 + 3*. This simple calculator is a start towards a program that will evaluate Logo expressions. Let's see how far we can go with it.

Well, we can't go very far with just constants; the next major breakthrough in cultural awareness allows names for constants just like a real Logo does. For example, if the value of :x is **5**, then the result of munch-ing on the list [+ 3 :x] should be **8**.

We'll add this naming operation in two steps—the old munch-a-bunch two-step. First, we'll add a separate table for variables, similar to opr.list for function names.

Next, we modify munch slightly to make naming a bit more dignified.

Below is the fast-food variety of a name-calling muncher. Rather than redo the

whole munch definition we simply describe the clause that we must add to the conditional.

```
[is.var first :str    munch bf :str
                         :fnc.col
                         sub1.first :cnt.col
                         fput lookup first :str
                              :cnst.col]
```

with:

```
to is.var :x          to lookup :x
  find :x :var.list      nth find :x :var.list 2
end                   end
```

where find was introduced for is.fnc's use. Notice also that if :x is not in :var.list, then find returns false, which is also returned as the value of is.var (as expected); however, if :x **is**

in :var.list, then find returns the entry containing it, which is also returned by is.var. But shouldn't the result of is.var be true or false?

When we discussed cond in Chapter 6, we said that the *actions* of a clause are executed if the *test* of the clause is not false. Usually our *test*s are either true or false, but they don't have to be. In TLC-Logo, anything other than false is as good as true. In fact, in our old-fashioned conditional expression, iftrue will work whenever the *test* evaluates to anything but false. Furthermore, examination of the code for cheap.cond in Chapter 6 will reveal an implementation of this true-is-not-false strategy. . . . but back to lookup, please.

There are much more efficient ways to perform storage and retrieval than lists and lookup, but efficiency is not at issue here. We're interested in exploring the ideas; remember, however, that real implementations of Logo and Lisp don't store tables of

names and values in this simple list fashion.

Ok, no more junk food computation. Let's do it right. The problem with the current scheme will become apparent when we add the ability to munch to-definitions. In that case we'll be changing the values of variables rather frequently and var.list will just get worn out. Instead, we will add another argument to the munch form-letter. This addition—called an environment, and named :env—will carry the tabular information that has been the responsibility of var.list. The changes to munch are minimal:

• Every call on munch has to include one more slot for :env, and

• lookup will use :env rather than :var.list.

```
to munch :str :fnc.col :cnt.col :cnst.col :env
  cond [[zero.first :cnst.col munch :str
                        bf :fnc.col
                        sub1.first bf :cnt.col
                        apply.fnc first :fnc.col
                            :cnst.col
                            :env
                        :env]

        [empty :str check.first :cnst.col]
        [is.const first :str munch bf :str
                            :fnc.col
                            sub1.first :cnt.col
                            fput first :str
                                :cnst.col
                            :env]

        [is.fnc first :str munch bf :str
                            fput fval first :str
                                :fnc.col
                            fput arity first :str
                                :cnt.col
                            :cnst.col
                            :env]

        [is.var first :str munch bf :str
                            :fnc.col
                            sub1.first :cnt.col
                            fput lookup first :str
                                :env
                            :cnst.col
                            :env]
end
```

with:
```
        to lookup :x :env
          first bf find :x :env
        end
```

We're getting so sophisticated—gloat, gloat—that we should be able to recognize more constants now, too:

```
to is.const :x my [:tie type :x]
  any [(:tie = "fix) (:tie = "float)
       (:tie = "list) (:tie = "string)]
end
```

With the new environmental monuments we can munch things like:

```
munch [fput :x :y]   []   []   []   [[:x 2] [:y [3]]]
```

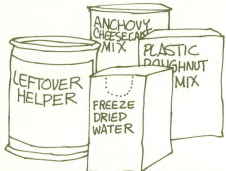

To be a serious muncher, however, we need still more. The major piece of code that's needed to make a full-strength Logo-like evaluator will handle user definitions. Before we dive in, let's think about what has to happen.

1. The system has to realize that a to-definition has been presented. We can see it coming a mile away: we'll run into the word **to** in the input. Once that's seen, we have to:

a. locate the name. That's easy.
b. locate the :-ed parameters
c. locate the body of the definition. That's easy; it's terminated with **end**.

The only part that's a problem is **b**. In normal Logo, we know when we run out of formal parameters because we see the

end of the line, but we don't have lines in our Logo dialect. So we'll assume that the parameters are already collected in a list, as in:

```
[to foo [:x :y :z] fput :x fput :y :z end foo 1 2 [3]]
```

With this slight modification we can handle definitions. That handling consists of stuffing them into **opr.list**. What we'll add to the table is: the name, the number of arguments, and the actual definition. Thus, **foo** would be stored as:

```
[foo 3 [:x :y :z] fput :x fput :y :z]
```

We use the name and the number just as we have all along; we use the rest of the information when we are ready to compute a value with the function. That brings us to the second problem:

2. To use a defined function, we must get the definition out of the **opr.list**, and perform the substitutions required by the JMC Model. We're lazy, though. Substituting all those values in all those slots in the form letter?—Man, that's tiring! So what we'll do instead is fake it. Instead of substituting, we'll build a new environment using the parameter names—:x, :y, and :z in the example—, and tie them up with the values

I'M NOT A REAL PARKING METER—*I'M* A PARAMETER!

we computed for them. And where, oh genius, are those values? They're on the top of the constants column! Armed with this new environment, we go off to hack and hew at the body of the definition. Thus, using the example:

munch [foo 1 2 [3]]   []   []   []   [] becomes:

munch [fput :x fput :y :z] [] [] [] [[:x 1] [:y 2] [:z [3]]],

and we already know how to do that.

Rather than repeat all of the muncher, we'll just highlight the pieces we'll add for handling to:

```
[is.to first :str
   munchto bf :str :fnc.col :cnt.col :cnst.col :env]
```

where:
```
         to is.to :x
            :x = "to
         end
```

and

```
to munchto :str :fnc.col :cnt.col :cnst.col :env my :def
   make "def to.end bf :str
   make "opr.list fput fput first :str
                        fput length nth :str 2
                           first :def
                     :opr.list
   munch bf :def :fnc.col :cnt.col :cnst.col :env
end
```

to.end is similar to split. It strips the definition out of the input by munching the stream up to the occurrence of end. to.end works like split except it splits up to end, rather than splitting up to a particular number; then it stuffs the appropriately decorated definition on opr.list. Then, with munchto gusto, munch snarfs the input that comes after the end.

SLURP

```
to to.end :l         to toend1 :l :l1
   toend1 :l []         (first :l) = "end
end                     iftrue [fput :l1 :l]
                        iffalse [toend1 bf :l
                                    lput first :l :l1]
                     end
```

Ha! to.end isn't **quite** like split. It has to make sure that the stuff it hacks off the front is kept in the right order, so it uses lput (last put) rather than fput.

Now here's the new model of apply.fnc:

```
to apply.fnc :fnc :cnst.col :env my :opr :num :bef.aft
   make "opr nth :fnc 1
   make "num nth :fnc 2
   make "bef.aft split :cnst.col :num
   is.prim :fnc
      iftrue [fput do :opr first :bef.aft
              bf :bef.aft]
      iffalse [fput munch body :fnc
                    []
                    []
                    []
                    mkenv dummies :fnc
                          first :bef.aft
                          :env
                bf :bef.aft]
end
```

Yeech! What's happened to our nice, simple apply.fnc? If :fnc is a primitive function—the kind we've come to know and love— then things act as before. The new stuff handles the user's definitions. Well, let's see what the situation is. mkenv takes three arguments: the first is the list of formal parameters; the second is the list of the constants, and the third is the old environment. With this information, mkenv makes a new name-value table.

```
to mkenv :names :vals :env
   empty :names
      iftrue [:env]
      iffalse [mkenv bf :names
                     bf :vals
                     fput list [first :names first :vals]
                          :env]
end
```

```
to is.prim :x        to dummies :x        to body :x
   empty bf bf:x         nth :x 3            bf bf bf :x
end                  end                  end
```

. . . and that's the new muncher.

One further ingredient in a healthy muncher is the ability to handle conditional expressions. For example:

```
member :stitch :time
   iftrue [save 9]
   iffalse [spend 200]
```

We know what such an expression means:

• Evaluate member :stitch :time

• If the value is false, evaluate spend 200 without evaluating save 9.

• If the value is not false, evaluate save 9 and ignore the iffalse clause.

• In either case, continue evaluating the input after iffalse.

• And just to make things difficult, either iftrue or iffalse may be missing.

ON TOWARDS INTROSPECTION

Now let's translate these informal directions into a bite for munch. Being optimistic, we'll do the iftrue case.

1. We'll evaluate member :stitch :time just like any other expression, and so the value will be found as the first element of :cnst.col when we see the iftrue.

2. We recognize the iftrue by running into it as the first element of :str.

3. At this point, we look at first :cnst.col. If it is true, we evaluate [save 9] and scrub the iffalse clause. If first :cnst.col is false, we ignore [save 9] by butfirst-ing down :str.

Here's the new cond-clause for munch:

```
[is.iftrue first :str    first :cnst.col
                  iftrue [munch.if.t bf :str
                                :fnc.col
                                :cnt.col
                                bf :cnst.col
                                :env]
                  iffalse [munch.if.not.t bf bf :str
                                      :fnc.col
                                      :cnt.col
                                      bf :cnst.col
                                      :env]]
```

So if an iftrue is seen, we check the value on the top of the constants column to see if the iftrue's list should be executed or skipped over.

There are two cases that munch.if.t can see at the front of :str immediately following an iftrue:

[*a*] iffalse [*b*] *c* . . . or [*a*] *c* . . .

In either case (assuming that first const.col was true) the list [*a*] is to be evaluated; but in the first case, iffalse [*b*] must be skipped over afterward.

```
to munch.if.t :str :fnc.col :cnt.col :cnst.col :env my :thos
   make "thos munch first :str
                    :fnc.col
                    :cnt.col
                    :cnst.col
                    :env

is.iffalse nth :str 2
   iftrue [munch bf bf bf :str
                 :fnc.col
                 sub1.first :cnt.col
                 fput :thos :cnst.col
                 :env]
   iffalse [munch bf :str
                  :fnc.col
                  sub1.first :cnt.col
                  fput :thos :cnst.col
                  :env]
end
```

where:
```
to is.iffalse :x          to is.true :x
   :x = "iffalse             :x = "iftrue
end                       end
```

First, look at the make in munch.if.t; that little beauty computes the [a]-expression, using the my-variable :thos to keep the result for a moment so we can catch our breath. bf bf bf—yeech, yeech, yeech what does that do? It lets us skip over the [a] iffalse [b] piece of the conditional. Gasp; then we hop on munch again after fiddling with :cnt.col. This little number is needed to let conditional expressions supply values to operators (remember **every** TLC-Logo expression has a value, even if it is nothing). For example:

fput (:x = 1 iftrue [2] iffalse [3]) [4] will give [2 4] if :x is 1 and will give [3 4] otherwise.

By now, our simple little calculator has grown and grown. And groan, it's hard to

see what's going on inside this muncher. So this might be a good time to take another look at the graphical munchtoon that graced our pages a while ago. Perhaps

we can get a better understanding of the added complexity by upgrading that graphical calculator. Let's do it.

Well, the same basic ideas will drive our new, improved, munch machine only now we will require a names-and-values column. Since to-definitions are just another form of names-and-values, we'll add them into the names-and-values column as well. These changes take care of the :env argument to munch.

Below is a carefully contrived example—three definitions, and a couple of expressions, are set up as input, and the munchers columns are empty:

```
[to gak [:x :n] + nth :x :n :n end
   ; notice we used the prefix form of +
 to foo [:x :y :z] fput :y bar :x :z end
 to bar [:y :u] lput :u [3] end
 foo "a gak [b 3] 2 6 rt :canal]
```

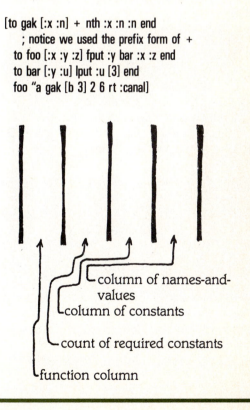

column of names-and-values
column of constants
count of required constants
function column

ON TOWARDS INTROSPECTION

In reality, the names-and-values column would not be empty now, but would contain representations of the primitive Logo functions. For example, fput would appear with (1) an indication that it requires two arguments, and (2) an incantation that will convince the demons of the netherworld to accept two offerings and return the fput of them. Thus, we'd see an entry like:

[fput   2   {pathway into the subconscious implementation of fput}]

The subsconcious of munch is a dreadful place, echoing with the shrill cries of the Scavenger, and where only Assembly Language is spoken. We'll not venture down **that** pathway!

Gasp, back to civilization at last; let's see what munch will do. First, in quick succession, we munch the definitions into the names-and-values column. We decorate

them appropriately so that we can quickly locate the number of required constants:

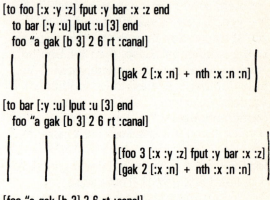

```
[to foo [:x :y :z] fput :y bar :x :z end
  to bar [:y :u] lput :u [3] end
  foo "a gak [b 3] 2 6 rt :canal]
```
| | | | [gak 2 [:x :n] + nth :x :n :n] |

```
[to bar [:y :u] lput :u [3] end
  foo "a gak [b 3] 2 6 rt :canal]
```
| | | | [foo 3 [:x :y :z] fput :y bar :x :z] |
| | | | [gak 2 [:x :n] + nth :x :n :n] |

```
[foo "a gak [b 3] 2 6 rt :canal]
```
			[bar 2 [:y :u] lput :u [3]]
			[foo 3 [:x :y :z] fput :y bar :x :z]
			[gak 2 [:x :n] + nth :x :n :n]

That little exercise installs the definitions. Now what? We see a name (foo). We recognize it as a function, and stuff it in the function column. We don't care now if it is a primitive or a to-definition; that trauma comes later. Thus:

```
["a gak [b 3] 2 6 rt :canal]
```
foo	3		[bar 2 ...]
			[foo 3 ...]
			[gak 2 ...]

Next, we digest the "a. Recognizing it as a constant, we stuff a in the constants column, as we drop the 3 to a 2 in the count column:

[gak [b 3] 2 6 rt :canal]

foo	2	a	[bar 2 ...]
			[foo 3 ...]
			[gak 2 ...]

Next comes another operation (gak) and it graces the function column, depositing its count on top of the count column:

[[b 3] 2 6 rt :canal]

gak	2	a	[bar 2 ...]
foo	2		[foo 3 ...]
			[gak 2 ...]

Does this madness never stop? The next object—the list [b 3]—is munched, giving:

[2 6 rt :canal]

gak	1	[b 3]	[bar 2 ...]
foo	2	a	[foo 3 ...]
			[gak 2 ...]

Swallowing our pride, we get another object—the 2:

[6 rt :canal]

gak	0	2	[bar 2 ...]
foo	2	[b 3]	[foo 3 ...]
		a	[gak 2 ...]

Finally, some variation! The count of the top function has gone to zero. This means that the top two elements in the constants column are ready as values for the top operator (gak). Now we discover that gak is a to-definition. Gak, indeed! What do we do?

We drop everything in the current munchful after extracting the needed inputs for gak, . . .

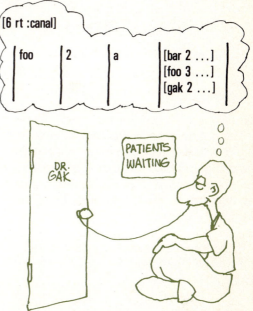

[6 rt :canal]

foo	2	a	[bar 2 ...]
			[foo 3 ...]
			[gak 2 ...]

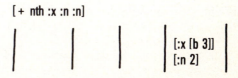

. . . but, we tie a string around our mental molar to let us know that the [6 rt :canal]-computation is patiently waiting. With that in mind, we begin to digest gak's definition:

[[:x :n] + nth :x :n :n]

Since gak needs two inputs, we decorate the top of a new name-value column with the names (:x and :n) and values ([b 3] and 2):

[+ nth :x :n :n]

			[:x [b 3]]
			[:n 2]

The first thing we see is +. Something's fishy.

The only names in the current table are :x and :n. Never fear, however; we tug on the string and discover that + is known at the previous level. It is a primitive requiring two inputs. We locate nth in the same fashion.

Being impatient to see the end of this story, we'll swallow the + and the nth at once:

[:x :n :n]

nth	2		[:x [b 3]]
+	2		[:n 2]

Now we see a variable (:x). We find its value ([b 3]) in the name-value slots and stuff it into the constants column:

[:n :n]

nth	1	[b 3]	[:x [b 3]]
+	2		[:n 2]

Grabbing another variable (:n), we find its value:

[:n]

nth	0	2	[:x [b 3]]
+	2	[b 3]	[:n 2]

Will wonders never cease? The count has gone to zero. Time to look at the function. It's a primitive, so we **do** it:

[:n]

+	1	3	[:x [b 3]]
			[:n 2]

We discover that nth [b 3] 2 is 3. Not astounding, but at least comforting. And we proceed to the next edible object. It's a :n that gives us a 2 as value:

[]

+	0	2	[:x [b 3]]
		3	[:n 2]

The count is now zero; we apply the primitive +. An incantation to the spirit world gives rise to 5, and **munch** takes the value and runs to:

[]

		5	[:x [b 3]]
			[:n 2]

Finally, a new situation: we have run out of food for thought. Now we untie the mental molar and follow the string back to the suspended meal. We take the value 5 back as the value of the computation, and decrease the count on the top of the count column:

[6 rt :canal]

| foo | 1 | 5 <br> a | [bar 2 ...]
 [foo 3 ...]
 [gak 2 ...] |

Well, we knew it couldn't last, so it's back to the ordinary world of eating constants and functions:

[rt :canal]

| foo | 0 | 6
 5 <br> a | [bar 2 ...]
 [foo 3 ...]
 [gak 2 ...] |

A familiar sight: the count is zero, so look at the definition. It's a non-primitive, so we drop the current task, associate the necessary values (a, 5, and 6) with the names (:x, :y, and :z), and leave cookie crumbs back to the interrupted feast:

[rt :canal]

| | | | [bar 2 ...]
 [foo 3 ...]
 [gak 2 ...] |

Notice that the columns have emptied out as a result of this sub-computation. munch won't notice until it returns; and then it won't care anyway. But now we have to take care of foo:

[fput :y bar :x :z]

| | | | [:x a]
 [:y 5]
 [:z 6] |

Since fput will be found in the previous state, we can now dispense with fput and :y in short order:

[bar :x :z]

| fput | 1 | 5 | [:x a]
 [:y 5]
 [:z 6] |

But here's a problem: the computational state ([:x a] [:y 5] [:z 6]) is dry—it has no bars. So we chase the cookie crumbs back to the interrupted computation and look there. Success! We note that bar needs two inputs, and keep on munching.

[:x :z]

| bar <br> fput | 2
 1 | 5 | [:x a]
 [:y 5]
 [:z 6] |

We find values for :x and :z and quickly arrive at:

[]

| bar <br> fput | 0
 1 | 6 <br> a
 5 | [:x a]
 [:y 5]
 [:z 6] |

The world gets complex now: bar has its inputs ready (a and 6), and we find bar's definition in the immediately preceding state. We're ready to go, so we set up a new environment associating :y with a and :u with 6, as we save yet another string to a suspended computation:

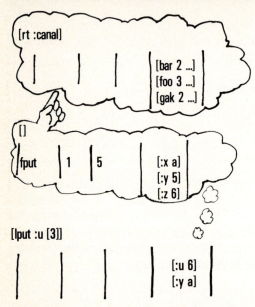

```
[rt :canal]
|     |     |     | [bar 2 ...]
                    [foo 3 ...]
                    [gak 2 ...]

[]
| fput | 1 | 5 | [:x a]
                 [:y 5]
                 [:z 6]
```

[lput :u [3]]

```
|     |     |     | [:u 6]
                    [:y a]
```

So, here we are finally. Ready to dissect the body of bar. The first thing we see

SAMURAI FERN BAR

before us is lput. It is not in this world, not in the prior world, but is finally discovered in the prehistoric world—it's a primitive.

[:u [3]]

```
| lput | 2 |     | [:u 6]
                   [:y a]
```

lput wants two arguments, and we can supply them without difficulty, and arrive at:

[]

```
| lput | 0 | [3] | [:u 6]
            6      [:y a]
```

lput is ready to go now. That gives us [3 6] as value to return to the patiently waiting computation:

[]

```
| fput | 0 | [3 6] | [:x a]
            5        [:y 5]
                     [:z 6]
```

Now we can fire off fput, giving [5 3 6]. Then it's off to the previously suspended computation, to grab the next object:

[rt :canal]

```
|     |     | [5 3 6] | [bar 2 ...]
                        [foo 3 ...]
                        [gak 2 ...]
```

and then gobble up rt:

[:canal]

```
| rt | 1 | [5 3 6] | [bar 2 ...]
                     [foo 3 ...]
                     [gak 2 ...]
```

Since this is supposed to be a realistic example, it has a bug. No, not the [5 3 6] on the top of the constants column; we don't care about that. The real problem is :canal; it has no value in **any** of the name-value tables. Of course, one of the things that greatly interests us is what to do about bugs. The remainder of this chapter builds to a discussion of the care, feeding, and extermination of bugs. But before we go into

the details of computational entomology, let's rummage through the rubble that has been accumulated during our excavation of munch.

The munch programs on the preceding pages of this chapter cover some of the most interesting and important ideas in computing. (You see, there's a **reason** it was so hard!) These programs describe how a computer works, using a notation that is far more understandable than the language of circuits and electronics.

And, if you think munch is complicated in TLC-Logo, just try writing it in machine language, or BASIC! These languages would insist that you use—ugh, bletch —numbers to represent programs. But Logo lets us use lists to represent programs and, by manipulating those lists, we can illustrate how the information is passed through the machine in a very high-level description. For example, we can see how substitution of the JMC-model is simulated by using the mkenv mechanism, without "hacking the bits."

The munch program, itself, is an example of a program called an interpreter, so-called because it interprets expressions, decoding them, and telling us what they mean. But one of the most fascinating features of the munchers is that the language the muncher munches (that is, TLC-Logo) is the same language that is used to write the muncher! Now that sounds like munch is an "echo-program"—like our Japanese mimic of Chapter 1—full of sound and fury, signifying nothing.

THIS PICTURE HAS NO MEANING

Yet, you **do** learn something by going through the evaluation of Logo expressions in munch; much knowledge about how Logo works has been gained. In fact, it is tempting to say that munch and Co. effectively **define** Logo. That is, we could say: "Well, Bozo, if you have a question about what Logo does with a particular expression, then just convert it into a list (even a Bozo can do that, we think to ourselves), and see what munch does with it." If Bozo is paying attention he'd respond: "Ok, fuzz face, the particular expression I'm interested in is munch [bf [a b]] [] [] [] []. And that says I should look at:

ON TOWARDS INTROSPECTION

```
munch [to munch [:str ...] end
       to sub1.first [ ...] end
```

(translations of all definitions used by munch)

```
       ...
       munch [bf [a b]] [] [] [] []
       []
       []
       []
       []
```

Does that bother you?"

If **we're** paying attention, our lightning response is: "Not a bit, because the **first** occurrence of the word munch is the the name

I STOPPED PAYING ATTENTION 5 CHAPTERS AGO.

of the function, while the munches in the function column are just elements in lists. As long as we precede the munch [bf [a b]] [ ] [] [] [] with the to-definitions that make up munch, then all's well."

This says that Logo list-representations of Logo programs can be manipulated by munch to simulate or mimic the behavior of a Logo machine, and thus munch can serve as a description of Logo. It gives us a recipe that describes how to implement munch. Careful analysis of munch will reveal that several assumptions are hidden within that

program. First, munch relies on the existence of primitives like fd, rt, and friends—not suprising, since we always have to assume that **something** exists before we can do anything. Next, munch assumes that someone has the ability to manufacture constants like 2, "J.Flanders, and [time [of day]]. Now, numbers are easy; we all know that computers like numbers. Right? Wrong. They like **their** numbers, but probably don't like ours. For example, most machines will choke on numbers like 123986126145379374 6212, saying that it is too large to store.

We know that one of the properties of numeric objects is that there is no largest such animal. If mere mortals can understand this, why can't mighty machines? The hardware difficulty arises because only a small fixed-size space has been set aside for each integer; if the number we want to represent is larger than that, we lose. The problem could be fixed in software, but typically isn't.

Similarly, many languages have restrictions on the number of letters in a symbol, again because only a fixed amount of space is allowed. Thus they'd allow "J.Flan and ignore the 'ders'. And lists? We can't have lists because lists don't have a fixed number of elements.

These three examples are symptoms of a more serious disease: Pre-objective Machinitis—making ideas fit the confines of machines. Fortunately, the affliction need not be terminal; its cure can be seen in an examination of fput. fput takes two existing objects:

. . . and creates a new object with the old parts as components:

Objects can come into being at arbitrary times, without explicit directions from the user. The effect is to give the user flexibility and give the implementor a headache. But that's as it should be; implementations happen occasionally, while applications are written frequently.

So down in the subsconscious of munch we find object management, primitive instructions, and tools for getting information into and out of the munch machine. Above this level we should find a smooth user interface, and a graceful notation in which we can express our ideas; . . . and

chickens have lips. Machines, languages, and implementors have all been too inflexible in the past. The acceptance of Logo and the appearance of high-performance personal machines are hopeful signs. We must dig deeper though, into the notational level, to see the long-term substance.

One key idea in the munchers is the appearance of lists that represent instructions. We have already seen some of the power of this technique in Chapter 6's discussion of run. Once we have program elements available as objects that we can manipulate, then we are on the way out of the implementation swamp. The idea that we could manipulate real programs of a real language using that language was novel in 1958 when Lisp transported the theoretical idea from mathematical logic to practical programming practice. Unfortunately, the power of the idea has still not been fully recognized in traditional programming circles.

Most languages have their roots firmly wedged in ancient implementation notions, that tend to be based on outdated notions of the cost of programmer time versus the cost of machine time. It has resulted in a cycle that is as hard to break as the dominance of the QWERTY keyboard. Q-W-E-R-T-Y are the first characters, left to right, in the second row of keys on a standard typewriter. The QWERTY keyboard was designed to minimize the jamming of keys on these original mechanical typewriters. The jamming problem has gone away, but the QWERTY keyboard remains. It continues to cramp fingers—just as traditional languages continue to cramp style—while superior designs go ignored. Never underestimate inertia.

Often, it is inertia rather than innovation that drives modern computing too. For example, we deal with lines and lines of characters to describe our computational ideas even though those ideas really involve relationships between objects. Why not express our programming ideas in terms of relations using graphical representations?

Or just look at the editors we use for writing programs. Many of them are "line editors", requiring each line of a program to have a "line number." These editors are a holdover from the days of punched cards and sequenced card decks. Others are "string editors." No line numbers are supplied to locate yourself in the program; rather, arcane search commands are given to position the editor at the desired text. These editors are a holdover from the early days of paper tape or, worse yet, a remnant of ancient Egypt's papyrus scroll technology.

Yet a program is neither a card deck nor a papyrus scroll. It represents a structure—the programmer's ideas expressed as interrelationships between programs and data objects. A pride—or even a sleaze—of programs involves an interrelated collection of functions; and each function has parts and subparts. A program-editor should supply commands so that the user may move through this structure, locate functions, or ask about relationships between components ("who calls this function", for example.) The key to such a system is the representation of programs as objects that the system can manipulate.

Just as programs-as-objects is a critical part of editing in an interactive environment, there is a comparable facility that is necessary for a high-quality model of debugging. And since we have implied that there is a very strong relationship between debugging and thinking, it is appropriate to examine interactive debugging and program modification.

So, let's go back to our last graphical example, and let's assume that we had mistyped the definition of bar as:

[to bar [:y :u] lptt :u [3] end]

Now we could have complained that lptt was undefined when the definition was entered into the table by bar, and stopped the process right then. Traditional languages do this kind of thing; in fact, most will require that all definitions be completed and checked before one even thinks about execution. But this kind of hand-holding error detection only works for the simplest kinds of mistakes. What could have been done, for example, if lptt **had** been defined, but we really wanted lput? Nothing short of mind-reading would have found **that** error!

So errors will happen, and programs will have to be modified. What, then, can be done when a change is needed? The traditional way out is very anti-social: throw away the computation, go get the editor, make the change, reload the program, and start the computation all over again. But why not just use common sense—a loaded

question if there ever was one! Tell the user the source of the difficulty, and let the user decide what to do. If, for example, a definition is missing, supply it and continue; if a function name is misspelled, correct it and continue. If the computation is in a muddle because of the error, perhaps we can reset some of the computation and continue. This forgiving attitude is particularly useful if the computation is long and involved (as is the case in many of the more modern applications.) Computation should be like life: only with the greatest reluctance should we consider throwing away everything and starting over. By George, another platitude!

But how do we bring rational behavior to computation? We have to get access to the "state of mind" of munch: what's it think the values of variables are; what was being computed when the roof fell in? To do this we must get the inner workings of munch available as outer workings. That way we can examine, and modify if necessary, all the environments and saved state that munch is munching on. After wading through munch, you should be able to find the areas that involve environments; the state information is harder to find (as usual, bureaucracies are good at hiding information).

We'll need to see one more generation of the munch family before we can think about writing that kind of code. But let's see what the code should do. It should tell the user the source of the difficulty. In the case of lptt, it encountered a function name that was not in the dictionary. It could tell the user what computation was being performed by supplying the values in :str, :fnc.col, and the other slots in munch.

What's not explicitly available yet is the history of the computation. In this case, lptt was called by bar, which was called by foo, which was called by gak. This history of who's doing what to whom, is called the control information. The control information is visible in the graphical representation, but where is it hiding in the Logo version of munch and friends? A thorough investigation will reveal that the control information is hidden in the very way munch calls munch. That is, the information that describes the control—or flow—of the computation is in munch's subconscious. Before munch can tell the user about the flow of control, we must make those subconscious computations available at the conscious level. We are not about to drop munch on the psychiatrist's couch, but we can analyze its behavior so that this control information becomes available as an explicit part of munch's vocabulary, just like :str, :fnc.col, and the other names we have come to know and love.

Behold:

```
to munch :str :fnc.col :cnt.col :cnst.col :env :dump
  cond [[(first :cnt.col) = 0
         do.fnc :str :fnc.col :cnt.col :cnst.col :env :dump]

        [empty :str   (empty :dump)
                      iftrue [check.first :cnst.col]
                      iffalse [munch str.part :dump
                               fnc.part :dump
                               sub1.first cnt.part :dump
                               fput first :cnst.col
                                    cnst.part :dump
                               env.part :dump
                               dump.part :dump] ]

        [is.fnc first :str   munch bf :str
                             fput fval first :str
                                  :fnc.col
                             fput arity first :str
                                  :cnt.col
                             :cnst.col
                             :env
                             :dump]

        [is.var first :str   munch bf :str
                             :fnc.col
                             sub1.first :cnt.col
                             fput lookup first :str
                                         :env
                                  :cnst.col
                             :env
                             :dump]

        [is.const first :str   . . . ]

        [is.to first :str   . . . ]

            . . . ]
end
```

where,

```
to do.fnc :str :fnc.col :cnt.col :cnst.col :env :dump &
                                 my :op :num :bef.aft
; the ampersand is the line-continuation character
   make "op nth first :fnc.col 1
   make "num nth first :fnc.col 2
   make "bef.aft split :cnst.col :num
   cond [[is.prim first :fnc.col munch :str
                                 bf :fnc.col
                                 sub1.first :cnt.col
                                 fput do :op first :bef.aft
                                         bf bef.aft
                                 :env
                                 :dump]
         [ow munch body first :fnc.col
                              []
                              []
                              []
                              mkenv dummies :op
                                    first :bef.aft
                                    :env
                              mkdump :str
                                     :fnc.col
                                     :cnt.col
                                     :cnst.col
                                     :env
                                     :dump]]
end
```

and

```
to mkdump :str :fnc.col :cnt.col :cnst.col :env :dump
   list [:str bf :fnc.col bf :cnt.col :cnst.col :env :dump]
end
```

This munch encodes the control part of the graphical "tooth-tying" ceremony in the new component called :dump. This elegant name, dump, has its origin in a theoretical machine developed in the early 1960's by an English computer scientist named Peter Landin. That machine was named the SECD machine.

S—is for the stack. It contains the partially completed values that we carry in :fnc.col, :cnst.col, and :cnt.col.
E—is for environment. It is our :env.
C—is for control. It is our :str; and
D—is for dump. It is our :dump.

Put it all together and it spells SECD.

The :dump component of this SECD muncher is what's of interest now; it contains all the information about what munch thinks it is doing. All that information is now available as Logo lists, and therefore we can write Logo functions to analyze it. That is, it can tell the user what it was trying to do when the error occurred; the sad story that "lptt, called by bar, called by foo, called by gak" is all accessible and available for modification. Given access to this kind of information, munch can start to get clever about itself.

As humans, we expect and experience a similar degree of flexibility and "error recovery". For example, let's assume we're in Northern California and want to drive from San Jose to Berkeley—we won't argue about which is the frying pan and which is the fire. If we were not sure of the area we'd check out a route and then proceed. If we came to a detour, we'd try to find an alternate route on the spot; we would not insist on returning home, replanning the trip, and starting out again. That kind of behavior would be too strange even for California. No, "on-the-fly" error detection

and correction come as standard equipment on humans. Yet traditional computing languages impose such conditions on their users when they require the total abandonment of a computation whenever any error is detected.

The transformations we are planning for munch move us in the direction of sympathetic systems. Such changes require that the computer be able to analyze its own behavior.

The ability of a muncher to analyze its own state should not be restricted to just error situations. It should be able to analyze its own behavior at any time we choose. Note the phrase "we choose". No diabolical free will is expected to spring up suddenly inside munch. We have to write the Logo programs that will extend munch to be aware of its internal state. But that requires that we can talk about the internal state. We don't mean that it is against the law to discuss that part of computation; we mean that if your language has no way to describe a

specific idea, then you are—in effect —prohibited from talking about it. This goes back to the notion of notation. We need to have ways of describing new ideas, giving them names, and then using these new names to build up more complex ideas. It is a powerful feature of natural language, and it is a powerful feature of the artificial language, TLC-Logo.

Enough motherhood and apple pie; how can we make use of the control information now available in the SECD muncher? Well, we can include the munch-raker in an interactive program loop (like the one on page 173), and supply the user with commands to halt the computation, to examine the values of variables, to look at the history of the computation, etc. It is then up to the user to determine what information to look for and how to change things on the basis of that information.

The next step, of course, is to analyze what it is that the programmer looks for in debugging; then we write a program that can perform some of these details itself. For example, there may be common typographical errors that could be corrected automatically, by a program that knew about the specific programming language and could look at the state of the computation. For example, the Lisp programming language uses parentheses to designate the scope of expressions. So instead of saying something Logo-like, such as:

```
fput wurst :x bf liver :y :z
```

whose structure cannot be understood unless we know how many inputs wurst and liver need, Lisp would require that we make the grouping specific. For example:

```
(fput (wurst :x) (liver :y :z))
```
and

```
(fput (wurst :x (liver :y) :z)
```
are two possibilities.

Since (and) are upper-case characters —often shift-8 and shift-9 on our friendly

QWERTY keyboard, a fast Lisper may miss the shift and get mumble9 instead of mumble); or for (gaff you get 8gaff. InterLisp, one of the major Lisp dialects has a program—DWIM (Do What I Mean)— that is quite good at discovering errors like these and correcting them. The correction is possible because Lisp programs are represented as lists and therefore can be modified with list operations. The detection is possible because the needed data on who's doing what to whom is also available to DWIM. Much more

THE WURST IS YET TO COME!

sophisticated error detection and correction is also possible in these DWIM-like systems.

So the idea of having control information available for the system to manipulate is useful in whizzy applications. Are there other places? Sure. The implementation of our friends, **catch** and **throw**, can profit from such control information. Instead of hand-coding these operations, they could be written in Logo itself if such control objects were available. (They're not usually, so they can't usually.)

Explicit control objects are much like the explanatory information that we stored in our deductive computer of Chapter 6. That information contained a history of the derivation of each result in the system. This discussion of debugging brings up another possibility—the debugging of deductions.

That is, real-world situations aren't "logical" with the same degree of certainty that these mathematical substitution-and-replacement systems expect.

In a logical systems, a deduction, once made, will remain a valid forever. But in a "real world" situation, truth—or rather, one's beliefs—may change. If a belief changes, we have to examine how that change might influence other beliefs. Some beliefs may have to be discarded because their only justification was that faulty belief. Other beliefs may survive because they're independent of the changed belief; still others may be retained, but now have different justifications. How do we begin to model this complexity in a computational system? How do we reason about change? How do we design a notation that makes it easy to reason about change? These kinds of problems must be solved before it is meaningful to talk about intelligence.

Our goals are much more modest: just notations that will let us talk about computational ideas in a civilized fashion. The examples we've discussed in the last three chapters illustrate the power of the TLC-Logo notation. In Chapter 5, we saw a notion of a deductive system that can manipulate facts and rules in data bases. Again in Chapter 6, we saw how to describe substitution and replacement systems. We've seen a computational system that will allow us to represent and manipulate these facts and rules —TLC-Logo's list-processing and lists. We saw a view of what it takes to build a computational system that is able to talk about its own behavior in this Chapter's **munch** family. These examples are a long way from the old "light-switch" model of computing, but so is modern computation.

ON TOWARDS INTROSPECTION

The blending of deductive systems, computational notions, and belief systems —deduction, computation, and truth—is at the heart of modern computation. And we got here from the child's play of Logo.

Summer Time

Well, it's summary time again. Objects, objects, objects, and more objects: that's the summary. They have been the sustaining force that has allowed us to move from the simple turtle movements of the fl-language to a discussion of the internals of artificial intelligence systems.

The level of abstraction that computational objects give us has been the key. We need not continually describe computing notions in terms of bits and bytes; given a notation like Logo we can keep building up layer upon layer of description. At the bottom it's all the same rubble of bits, but the complexity of the computation can be hidden by defining new names and by defining new objects in terms of existing names and objects.

The **to**-construct is Logo's way of hiding implementation details. Obviously, when we define a new Logo function, we can use that name to refer to all the computations entailed in the body. **to** also works wonders when we want to define new objects. We use lists as the primeval building blocks for new objects in TLC-Logo, but instead of referring to the object's components by **first**, **bf**, or **nth**, we can ask—nay, demand that we set up selector, constructor, and recognizer functions to manipulate the representation. This has immediate notational benefit. Functions that deal with squares, for example, can talk about **sq.color**, **sq.pos**, and **sq.hd** rather than **nth :x 3**, **nth :x 17**, **nth :x :time-of-day**.

This additional level of naming between usage and implementation also gives us the ability to change that implementation without having to rewrite fourteen yards of code; that is no small benefit!

Well, enough of a sermon. Unfortunately, the school of hard knocks is the only place that lessons in virtuous programming will get learned. At least we can say "we told you so!"

Well, its time to wrap up all this stuff. We've had enough fun with reality and the languages of today. Here we want to put the issue of computing languages in a broader context.

Chapter 8 talks about the future directions of computing—the theory, the languages, and the implementation. We break the chapter into three sections: **History**, **Mystery**, and **Ballast**.

History deals with the fundamental principles that underlie computation and how those ideas will drive the future notions. Is computation anything more than electrical engineering, applied mathematics, and physics? Of course, we answer that with a resounding **YES**!

Mystery gives indications of how computational principles combine with programming practice to influence language

design. Though Logo is a good starting point, it is far from ideal. What can we expect tomorrow? Though Logo is just now taking off, it is about fifteen years old. Can we do better now?

Ballast suggests how these ideas are influencing the design of computer architecture and hardware. After all, someone has to do **some** work. How do we build objects into hardware? How do we compute with them? What hardware considerations do object-based languages suggest in the future?

It is encouraging to see the elements of the trilogy beginning to be positioned this way so that theoretical ideas drive hardware implementations.

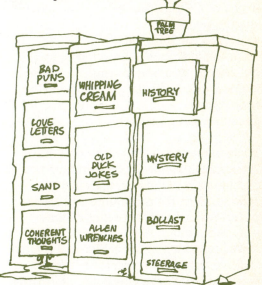

Then it's on to Section V. There —would you believe?—we get serious! Well, we warned you right up front that this is a serious book.

CHAPTER 8
HISTORY, MYSTERY, & BALLAST

This chapter moves from the general to the specific, so if you're interested in practicalities you might start from the end and work backward. One way or another you'll get to the next paragraph.

The axe we've been grinding all along concerns thinking—the care and feeding of the brain. Clearly, that is not a popular pastime. Even the most famous thinker couldn't afford a decent set of clothes.

We mentioned much earlier that mathematics was one of the more successful disciplines that have contributed to mental muscle tone through exercise and training. One particularly beautiful part of mathematics is mathematical logic—the formal study of the principles that underlie

scientific reasoning. This area has had, and will continue to have, a deep influence on

the principles and practice of computation. Given logic's importance in our story, we start with a historical tour of logical highlights.

History

Around the turn of the century several troublesome discoveries were made in mathematics.

A CENTURY AGO LATE LAST WEEK WHEN LOGIC WAS NOT SO OBLIQUE— WE JUST USED OUR HEAD BEFORE GOING TO BED, AND NOW I PUSH KEYS WITH MY BEAK!

A TERN FOR THE VERSE

Several of these difficulties had their origins in fundamental questions like "What is a proof?", What is truth?", and "What is a number?" You may recall that we raised a similar question in the Preface—"What is an object?" Compare our "It's a cloud in the blue sky of the mind" with the mathematician's "The number of things in a given set is the set of all sets that are similar to the given set." Sigh—driver, take us back to the clouds,

please. But the question is serious—for us, as well as for mathematics. We will come back to the issue of objects when we meet the Mystery section. In the remainder of this section we will explore the mathematical trail a bit further.

So we return to the thrilling days of yesteryear—back to the latter part of the nineteenth century— when mathematics was the queen of the sciences, and mathematical intuition was the king. Unfortunately for King Intuition, mathematical reasoning was about to dethrown him. The king, like the infamous emperor, was not properly dressed for the kinds of mathematical exercises that were becoming fashionable. For example, even one of the most tame and ancient areas of mathematical endeavor—geometry—had suddenly gotten quite nasty.

In the third century B.C., Euclid had developed a set of axioms that specified what we've come to know and love as plane geometry. These axioms described properties of points and lines that were positioned on a flat surface. Euclid's axiom

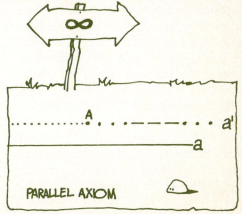

PARALLEL AXIOM

number XI—called the parallel axiom—implied that if *a* is a straight line and *A* is a point not on *a*, then there is at most one straight line *a′* that contains *A* and does not intersect *a*.

So, for example, the parallel axiom says that two parallel lines on a flat plane do not intersect. Seems intuitively obvious, doesn't it? So did other axioms like: "any two points (on the plane) determine a unique straight line." The axioms were supposed to reflect the truth of the universe—literally, capturing the notions of truth about real lines and real points; they were not just rules for some hypothetical game. But axiom systems, as such, **are** a game; they are used to replace fuzzy ideas, like "truth," with precise ideas, like "proof." One part of the precision is the establishment of a minimum number of axioms. If a fact can be proved from axioms, then don't include it as an axiom. Mathematicians believed that Axiom XI was provable from the other axioms, yet for centuries no one had been able to prove this, or refute it.

In true frying-pan/fire fashion, the troublesome axiom went away, to be replaced by the discovery that the parallel axiom need **not** be true! New definitions of the words "point" and "line" were discovered that made all of Euclid's other axioms true, but Axiom XI false! It may seem unfair to redefine "line" and "plane," however, but "You know what I meant!" is **not** a convincing argument. If words cannot be precisely defined, new interpretations are fair game (as any lawyer will gladly tell you, for a price.)

In fact, not just **one** alternate interpretation was found, but two "non-Eucildean" geometries were discovered. Even more surprising, perhaps, was the discovery that one interpretation was—in many ways—a better model of the real world than the plane vanilla choice. In that alternative view, a "plane" was the surface of a sphere (like the earth), a "point" was still a point—now on the surface of the globe. And a "line"? A "line" was the circle made by the intersection of the surface of the sphere and a plane passing through the center of the sphere. Such circles are called great circles, or geodesics. Behold:

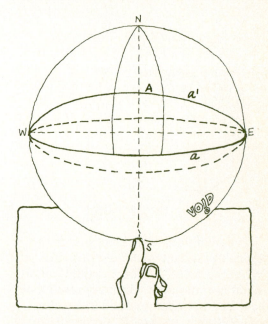

In this new interpretation, all Euclid's axioms were true, except for XI. Here, every line intersects any other line in exactly two points: one on each side of the sphere. Note too that this spherical interpretation is the kind of model on which air and sea navigation depends; airplanes and ships travel great circle routes to minimize distance. Locally, the "plane is flat"-interpretation is the one that fits everyday experience; globally, the "plane is a spherical surface"-interpretation is more adequate.

So here's the general situation: we attempt to use axioms to describe a "real" situation, so that we can manipulate the axioms using logic and deduction, rather than manipulate the real world using intuition and sweat. We hope to replace fuzzy ideas of reality and truth with formal,

game-like rules to manipulate axioms, and yet still discover all that we could know about the real world. The end result is supposed to be the same: we should not be able to prove results that are "false"; and we should be able to prove all "true" statements. In short, these axiom systems were supposed to exactly characterize reality. The discoveries of non-Euclidean

geometries showed that precise characterizations are quite difficult.

These geometric results, though surprising, were not catastrophic. The catastrophy occurred still later in the nineteeth century. In probing the extremes of mathematical thought, two fundamental ideas appear; the idea of a "set" as a collection of objects that possess some specific property; and the idea of the "infinite" as a quantity that outstrips our ability to measure.

For example, just as "point" and "line" are intuitive and obvious ideas, so too we feel comfortable with the idea of "same number of." This idea is as old as the barter system, predating even the integers and counting. We can compare two collections of objects simply by lining up the elements one-by-one and seeing if there are any left over in either set. If none are left over, then the sets are equal; otherwise the set with the extras is larger than the other set. Big deal, right? Well, try this: take the set of non-negative integers, $0, 1, 2, \ldots$, —call it I, and the set of even non-negative integers, $0, 2, 4, \ldots$ —call it E. We can match every element in I with its double in E, and thus there are the "same number of" elements in both sets. But common sense says that I has more elements. So just when you thought it was safe to go back in the math class, "same number of" strikes.

But perhaps comparison of sets like the integers is all we have to worry about. Are there sets that have "more" elements than the integers? Yup. In particular, let's see how many functions there are that take one integer input and produce an integer value; we've seen a lot of these functions just in Logo. Let's try to line them up and count 'em like we did with E and I. We'll write them as $f0(n)$, $f1(n)$, $f2(n)$, . . . ; and we'll write down a table of their values:

$f0(0)$	$f0(1)$	$f0(2)$ . . .
$f1(0)$	$f1(1)$	$f1(2)$ . . .
$f2(0)$	$f2(1)$	$f2(2)$ . . .
. . .	. . .	
$fi(0)$	$fi(1)$	. . . $fi(i)$ . . .
. . .	. . .	

Now consider the function defined as:

"given an integer, n, compute $fn(n)$ and add 1"

It's a function of a single argument, and so must be in the list of functions (if such a list exists). Let's assume that the index of the function is p; so fp is the function:

$$fp(n) = fn(n)+1$$

Look at: $\qquad fp(p) = fp(p)+1$

We've got a problem because that says the integer $fp(p)$ is equal to its successor. So something we assumed is fishy. In particular, the assumption that we could list all the functions is wrong. There **are** "more" such functions than there are integers! This combination of ingredients—the infinite and the intuitive—is an explosive mixture.

Unfortunately, it soon became clear there was no foolproof way of separating all the safe definitions from the explosive ones. It was known that you were on solid ground if you explicitly constructed such a set; that is, if you gave a recipe or computation that would eventually list every

single element of the set. But there were large pieces of mathematics that depended on "non-constructive" ideas, and mathematicians were not about ready to give all that up. Some of their prize possessions involved reasoning about infinite sets, and explicit constructions were not always possible. Some of their reasoning involved "non-constructive" proofs—proofs by contradiction, like we used in showing that we cannot "count" all the functions defined on the integers.

The general argument by contradiction uses the following pattern: "I want to prove that *blaah* is true of an object. Well, the object either has *blaah* or it doesn't. Assume it doesn't." They'd now go on to show that if the object was non-*blaah* a contradiction—like $0 = 1$—would result. Then they'd say: "Since non-*blaah* leads to a contradiction, it must be the case that the object has *blaah*." Pretty sneaky; they were allowed to prove that something existed without ever having to show one to us. Of course, we

use this kind of reasoning ourselves when we eliminate possibilities—it's either this or that; it's not this, so it must be that. Usually we can test our conclusions in the real world because we tend to be reasoning

about finite situations. And indeed, many cases of such reasoning in mathematics **are** just as safe; but too many "gotcha"s were being found.

Since these questions involved the very foundations of mathematics—what is a number, what is a proof, what is truth— the strength of the whole of mathematical reasoning was called into question. Clearly, some kinds of reasoning were valid, but how do we recognize the limits of specific reasoning techniques? The field couldn't continue using tools that would prove results that were wrong. So, just as axiom systems had been used in an attempt to clarify the meaning of point and line, such systems were again called upon, now to analyze notions like "set" and "proof." The intention was to give a complete set of axioms that would exclude the paradoxical results, while allowing us to prove all the wonderful, true results.

One particular characteristic of these axiom systems is that their description is finite. That is, they must be written down completely and therefore they must only use a finite number of letters and numbers. That doesn't mean that they only describe a finite number of objects, though. Think about a Logo program for drawing squares:

```
to square :n
  repeat 4 [fd :n rt 90]
end
```

There are about 40 symbols in that definition, yet it describes an infinite number of squares. As another example, the following

is true if the given integer, n, is even, and is false otherwise:

"Given an integer n, there is an integer, m, less than or equal to n such than m added to itself gives n."

We'll define "describable relations" to be those whose description is given in the

English alphabet, including punctuation symbols; furthermore we'll restrict the relations to those—like the even-test—that talk about properties of individual integers.

We can list the describable relations:

$d.1(n)$, $d.2(n)$, . . . where the occurrence of n names the integer variable that is referenced in the description. Now let's define a **new** description, similarly to the way we defined the new function fp on the previous page.

"Given any integer n, go get the n-th describable relation and compute its value for n. If that value is true, give false; if that value is false, give true."

This description seems to meet our requirements of finite description, and therefore is a describable relation. And so it has an index, say *p*. And what, pray tell, happens when we feed the integer *p* to the description $d_p(n)$? Ugh, bleagh, the value of $d_p(p)$ is the **opposite** of the value of $d_p(p)$; a most serious state of affairs.

Compare this situation with the previous example that counted the number of functions. There, we could show that the function must not be in the collection; it simply said that we could not list all the functions. Here we're not so fortunate, because we assumed that all the descriptions were constructed from a small, fixed, pot of symbols; and thus, we **can** list all the descriptions and the troublesome description **is** in the list. But it can't be. This little example is called Richard's paradox, and illustrates some of the pitfalls that we're up against when using words like "description."

one such system in Chapter 6, where we performed simplification and substitution in Logo expressions to illustrate the JMC model. Indeed, the kinds of rules that are generally acceptable are of this very constructive nature—the kinds of things that a mechanical device could perform. And what is a "mechanical device?" Sigh . . . so, as ground rules for axiom systems were laid down, rules for construction (or computation) had to be pinned down, too.

Where are we now? We started with the quest for Truth; we tried to reduce it to a question of proof; and finally ended up worrying about what we can compute. Thus, we now have a troublesome trio:

Truth
How do you know if something is true or false? This is not the "truth" of personal belief, but the notion of logical, mathematical truth.

The word "manipulate" is also up for grabs. We have to agree on what's an acceptable "move" in our game of mathematical symbol shuffling. We showed you

SYMBOL MINDEDNESS

Deduction

What can you prove? Can you develop a notation that can be used to represent fuzzy ideas in precise ways? What rules can you write down so that anyone who uses them with our notation will have some reason to believe that their proof will be accepted?

Computation

What is a mechanical process? Are there limits to what can be computed? If there are limits, can we tell what can be computed and what cannot?

It was hoped that there was a strong and healthy relationship between these three elements: questions about truth could be reduced to questions about deductions, and then computational systems could perform the deductions. Some parts of mathematics did yield to this attack, but initial optimism soon turned to disappointment. In the early 1930's, the mathematician Kurt Godel showed that any axiom system that was sufficient to describe the arithmetic of the integers would fail to completely capture the notion of truth. In particular, he showed that if we could write

down the axioms for integers—rules for +, rules for *, etc—in the language of our axiom system, then we could also write down statements that we would **know** to be true (because we knew what they **meant**), but those statements could not be proved in our system—unless our system could prove **everything**, like *0 = 1*, or *f(n) is not f(n)*. Such a system would be called inconsistent and, of course, would be totally useless since not everything is true.

Let's take a bit of time to analyze this last mouthful.

• First, what do rules for + and * look like? Well, here's a Logo-like rule for +:

```
to + :m :n
  :n = 0
  iftrue [:m]
  iffalse [add1 + :m sub1 :n]
end
```

so, assuming we have rules for = and rules for adding and subtracting 1, we have a rule for +.

• The next point is the difference between truth and provability. We can tell if a statement is true by understanding the **meaning** of the symbols. We know that the collection of symbols **3 + 2 = 5** is true, but a two year old child would not. How would you **prove** that **3 + 2 = 5**? You'd have to write down all the axioms and rules and show how to do the substitutions and replacements to end up with that string of symbols.

- Finally, what kind of statement would be obviously true, but not provable? That's the heart of Godel's trick. He created a statement that, if you knew how to interpret its symbols, meant that the statement itself was unprovable. Three questions:

1. Is that statement false? Well if it is, then it's provable, and the system is a loss because it would let us prove false things.

2. Is that statement true? Only if it's not provable! Because if we could prove it—that is, prove that it is unprovable— then the system is also a loser, because we'd again be able to prove false things. So the statement must be true but not provable.

3. Of course, the **big** question is: does such a statement exist?

Of course it does . . . we wouldn't have gone through all this for a joke. The germ of the idea is present in Richard's Paradox. Though Godel's construction is **not** paradoxical, it parallels the Richard argument using "proof", rather than "truth."

For example, in Richard's paradox we encountered the describable relation that is equivalent to:

- n does not satisfy the condition: $d.n(n)$

We'll mimic the notion of satisfaction—or truth—with provability, and formalize the describable relations with relations, A.i, in a Logo-like notation:

- Given n, it is not provable that: A.n :n

To parallel Richard, we'd have to show that this •-ed assertion was an element of the list A.i's. But the A's are assertions about numbers, and our •-ed buddy is an assertion about proofs. But assume for a minute that we **can** stick • in the list, as element **A.164**. What would A.164 164 mean? It would say that A164.164 is not provable. Exactly the assertion we're after.

So can we express • as an A? That exercise requires that we express the relationship "it is not provable that . . ." as an assertion about numbers. It turns out that we **can** represent such a relation, and in fact in a simplified piece of Logo restricted to the integers, recursion, and conditional expressions; but enhanced with notions from logic, like "for every integer", and "it is not the case. . ." This kind of a system will let us define Logo-like functions and then talk about their properties. We'll not give complete details for such an operation, but we'll present several of the major components.

We've done a lot of preparation for this construction already in Chapter 6, where we showed how to construct proofs of Logo assertions using the R- and S-rules. An expression was proved (or derived) by using commands, along with axioms and rules about conditional expressions. We kept a history of what rules were applied so we could see how a proof was derived; thus:

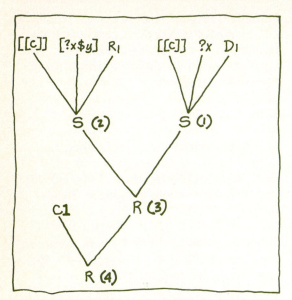

Now we want to turn things around and use that information to tell if an object is a proof. An object is a proof (of its last assertion) if it is an axiom, or it is the result of *R* or *S* and its parents are proved by the objects "above" them in the proof tree. In Chapter 6, we represented such proof objects as lists. Review that discussion, and then convince yourself that the following Logo function will give **true** if the list **:thm** represents a proof:

```
to is.proof :thm my [:tip the.last.formula :thm]
  cond [[is.axiom :tip true]
       [is.R.rule :tip all [:tip = replace main.parent :tip
                                            sub.parent :tip
                           is.proof main.parent :tip
                           is.proof sub.parent :tip]]
       ... ... ]
end
```

where **replace** performs the replacement, the = makes sure that the result matches **:tip**,

and the **all** makes sure that the historical chains are proofs—in fact, proofs of the components of the replacement.

Now, Godel's argument talked about properties of integers, and **is.proof** expects a list, representing a proof. We can certainly replace lists with numbers; we've been complaining that computer languages do this all the time. Our replacement operation—called a Godel numbering—has to be done carefully, however, so that we'll be able to detect what object is encoded in the number: is it a proof? is it an assertion like $f=g$? is it a symbol? a number? We'll call the Logo function that does the magic decoding **the.object.represented.by**. We can now define a Logo function to tell if one number is the Godel number of the proof of a specified Logo expression:

```
to proves :m :n my :proof.n :exp.m
  make "exp.m the.object.represented.by :m
  make "proof.n the.object.represented.by :n
  all [(the.last.formula :proof.n) = exp.m
       is.proof :proof.n]
end
```

This allows us to replace questions about proofs with questions about numbers.

The other thing we need this a way of talking about the substitution operation to make A.164 164. We've got that too, courtesy of Chapter 6's **subst** operation. If we were being quite precise, we'd have to demonstrate the Logo-like notation, and show that it was powerful enough to translate the necessary relations. However, this is not a book on logic.

HISTORY, MYSTERY, & BALLAST

For us, the real important consequence of these logical explorations was the much improved understanding of computation. Two models of computation are of particular interest: Turing machines, and the Lambda Calculus.

Turing machines: The Light Switch Model

The Turing Machine is named for the English mathematician, Alan Turing. In this scheme of computation we have an unending roll of paper divided into squares, called the tape. On each square we may write a *0* or a *1* and roll or unroll the paper one square at a time. A Turing Machine computes the value of a function by beginning with an initial collection of *0*'s and *1*'s and a

program that defines how to manipulate the tape. For example to define the function that adds *1*, we could could say that the representation of any number, *n*, is a sequence of *n 1*s on the roll, surrounded by *0*'s; to compute *n+1*, move past the last *1*, change the *0* found there to a *1*, move once more, write a *0* and stop. It can be shown that any possible computation (using a very general notion of computation) can be computed by such a machine. A Turing Machine is a mathematician's delight, and a programmer's nightmare.

Lambda Calculus: The Functional Model

This model of computing evolves from the notion of a mathematical function. For example, recall the dreary example from high-school algebra:

*f(x,y) = 2 * x * (3 * x * y + 4)*

Your seventh-grade math teacher, Gak, (recall him from chapter 2) would insist that you calculate the value of *f(5,6)*. To this day, few really know the reason. Nevertheless:

f(5,6) is the same as *2*5*(3*5*6 + 4)*, which is the same as *10*(3*5*6 + 4)*, or *2*5(15*6 + 4)*, either of which reduces to *940*.

This kind of system should look familiar: it's a variation on the JMC-theme, where we perform substitutions, and then we do simplifications. In Logo's JMC model, the order in which we carried out the operations would make a difference: fd 10 rt 90 is not the same as rt 90 fd 10. However, in functional mathematics the order of simplifications does not matter.

In its pure mathematical form, axioms for the JMC model can be given. The system that results is called the Lambda Calculus, and was developed by Alonzo Church in the late 1930's. Instead of the tape-moving instructions of the Turing Machine, Church's instructions formalize the substitution and simplification rules that we used in the JMC model. It can be shown that anything that can be computed using Turing's model, can also be computed using Church's Lambda Calculus.

The objects that these theories dealt with were numbers and functions that computed numeric values from numeric inputs. Mathematically speaking, this made perfect sense, since it is easy to show that all computation can be reduced to manipulations of *0* and *1*—the old light switch bug-

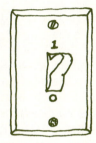

a-boo again. John McCarthy made the important innovation for modern computation: that instead of computing with numbers, we could compute with objects. McCarthy's formalism—called Lisp—used tree structures as building blocks for complex objects. At the ends of a tree's branches we could deposit symbolic objects. Symbols, called "literal atoms" in Lisp and "words" in Logo, allowed us to talk about individuals, while the tree structure let us demonstrate relationships between the individuals. Thus:

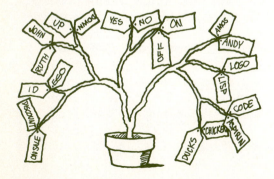

We will come back to Lisp in the Mystery and Ballast sections. The importance here is to note that Lisp is a mathematical system of the same power as that of Church's and Turing's work. Mathematically speaking, there is no difference between the systems; it can be shown that whatever can be computed in one formalism can also be computed in the other. The important distinction between the systems is expressibility, not computability. What's hard to formulate in Turing's formalism is easy in Church's arithmetic. What is hard in Church's arithmetic is easy in McCarthy's Lisp.

In terms of effective communication, the difference is enormous. Modern computation needs languages that have even more expressive convenience built into them than Lisp. In fact, the artificial intelligence community now uses Lisp as a "machine language" in which to implement higher-level tools that let them say more with less notation. However, it is important that the language development be driven by concern for mathematical elegance.

Now where is the elegance in dealing with deductions? The point of the deductive system was to reduce the search for truth to a formal manipulation of symbols. Given a rule and some objects that satisfy the requirements of that rule, we may apply the rule. Furthermore the test for satisfaction is also mechanical—it's a question of whether two patterns of symbols match. But creativity and elegance are required in the judgement of which of the possible rules to apply at what time. Like the monkey at the typewriter, a machine or an

URBAN GORILLA

uninspired person may "hit the keys" long enough to derive an interesting result; however, it takes insight to apply those rules in an intelligent fashion to drive the process—computation or deduction—to a speedy, elegant conclusion.

In everyday terms, it's the difference between:
• finding a path through a maze, and
• checking that a proposed solution really is a path through the maze.

The first alternative requires creativity; the second only requires persistence. A similar condition has been present in computing languages. Traditional languages —including Logo and Lisp—are of the "checking" variety. That is, the programmer has been responsible for the creation of the path; the machine has only been required to follow it. A more enlightened approach would require more of the machine. Why not supply a description of a problem, and let the machine decide to solve it—that is, get through the maze?

Since mind-reading is not allowed, we have to supply problem-solving rules, and we have to supply bookkeeping techniques for controlling the application of these rules. We saw some of this activity in Chapter 5; here we want to emphasize that model: a collection of logical "axioms" and a collection of "rules of thumb" for applying those rules. The realization that we can view computation as the application of logical rules, with a sideorder of insight, has been a long time coming. Most programming languages—including Logo— muddle the two ideas. This brings us to a third model of computing.

In the same stew that contained Turing machines and the lambda calculus, simmered a third ingredient called the predicate logic. In this scheme of things, one represented facts as statements like:

Owns(Melvin, Chopper)   or   *Duck(Pauline)*

These statements represent assertions that may (or may not) hold between objects. Thus they are either true or false.

We will have further assertions that relate classes of objects. Thus if we want to state that every duck has feathers, we might write:

Feathers(?x) if Duck(?x)

This collection of explicit facts and implicit relationships makes up our world. We manipulate the objects in this world by making deductions. The spirit of these deductions is similar to that of Chapter 5, only here we emphasize the mathematical aspect of that discussion. In particular, we can specify formal axioms—like those of plane geometry—that will describe the objects and their relationships. This specification can then be manipulated to deduce new facts about the objects, much in the same way that one does computation in other formalisms. This leads to computing languages called logic-programming languages. We go more deeply into these languages in the Mystery and Ballast sections.

Of course, proofs and computations are purely formal, meaningless manipulations, as mathematicians have known for a long time. The value of this work is its relationship to truth. The study of the relationships between these topics—truth, deduction, and computation—is fascinating and rewarding. What can you know? What can you prove? And what can you compute? What are the interrelationships, and the limitations? These are all questions of modern computer science, and yet, are all rooted in the centuries-old quest of the mathematical and philosphical mind:

"A mathematician never defines magnitudes in themselves, as a philosopher would be tempted to do; he defines their equality, their sum and their product, and these definitions determine, or rather constitute, all the mathematical properties of magnitudes. In a yet more abstract and formal manner he lays down symbols and at the same time prescribes the rules according to which they must be combined; these rules suffice to characterize these symbols and give them a mathematical value. Briefly, he creates mathematical entities by means of arbitrary conventions, in the same way that the several chessmen are defined by the conventions which govern their moves an relations between them."

L. Courturat, De l'infini mathematique, Paris, 1896

So, almost one-hundred years ago we have a description of how to deal with objects (through descriptions of their properties), and of how to compute with them (using formal deductive rules). The fundamental notions of mathematics and logic come back through computation.

And where do we begin? How can we generate interest in a field as profound as modern mathematics? We begin with Logo Not Logo as a programming language, but Logo as a hatrack—a place to hang and hide ideas about computation, deduction, and truth . . . from turtles, ducks, and chairs to Truth, Deduction, and Computation.

Mystery

At the more "practical" level, we examine some of the features we've encountered while phrasing problems in the language of Logo. The point of a language —either "natural" or "artificial"—is to express thoughts and ideas. Some languages make it easy to express simple thoughts, while falling short when complex or abstract ideas are required. The key ingredient of any language is the range of its expressive power. If the listener's language is baby-talk and you're trying to describe a payroll problem, then you're in trouble. One major problem with personal computers is their dependence on baby-talk. If these machines are **really** going to be of use to the general populace, then the quality of their language must improve —and of course it wouldn't hurt to see the humans take a course or two in self-expression.

In Chapter 7, we examined the historical forces that gave us programming languages designed for the convenience of the machine or convenience of the language implementor. However, it is now time to grow up; we must have languages that allow us to express our ideas in a convenient and comfortable way. It is more than a practical issue of programming. The quality of one's language directly affects the kinds of thoughts one can express. Unfortunately, the usual computing languages are not thought-provoking. This is not to say that these languages have not been useful. Successes in engineering and business say otherwise. The point is that most aspects of the quality of life have little to do with either of these endeavors. Personal machines had better be able to deal with more than engineers and bankers.

Both the success and the failure of modern computing stems from the same source: the tyranny of numbers. When you want to do arithmetic, of course numbers can't be beat. But they're a lousy way to represent non-numeric information, as our little tour of Godel numbering illustrates. Yet traditional programming languages inflict Godel numbering on us everyday, when we're forced to reduce all problems to numbers and relationships between numbers. We code the problem; we compute a number; and then we re-interpret that number as an answer to our problem.

In the past, if your problem wouldn't fit the tools of mathematical analysis, it was too bad for you. It wasn't until the late 1950s with the Symbolic Expressions of Lisp that a mathematical tool—a language—let us compute on real machines using notions that had not been reduced to numbers. Computation with objects had arrived. This improvement in the expressibility game was the use of Symbolic Expressions rather than numbers. These symbolic expressions gave a voice to notions that involved relationships between objects—relationships that could change even as the computation proceeded. There were programming languages before Lisp that had this freedom to compute directly with such relations—the IPL family is the most notably. The elegance that Lisp brought to the situation, was notational—the language and expressibility issue again. The IPL's were machines for non-numerical languages; Lisp was their Fortran.

The Symbolic Expressions that Lisp introduced have a dual role: they are a programming tool of substantial power, and they are the basis for a mathematics of computation. As a tool, they are a close cousin of Logo's lists. As a tool kit, Lisp gave the object builder a large supply of a few kinds of parts from which objects of all shapes and sizes could be constructed. This is in contrast to "general purpose" languages that give a fixed collection of many different kinds of parts. Lisp can generate objects dynamically; Brand X requires that the size of the stockpile be declared before computation begins. Lisp supplies vectors or strings, for example; Brand X gives strings of length 4, or strings of length 22, or vectors of 5 integers.

Lisp's collection of parts, plus the ability to name new functions (the to operation in Logo), gave the Lisp programmer a substantial advantage when building complex programs. The early 1960s saw a large number of elegant results in AI, due in large part to the power of Lisp as an executable notation for thoughts.

We chose these last words carefully: Lisp was executable. After all, this wasn't philosophy, it was computer science. Since Lisp was a notation for thought, it was more than just a programming language. This dual perspective on programming languages has been carried over from Lisp to Logo.

A key ingredient in the advance of knowledge and understanding has been our ability to create notations in which we can express our problems. Given those

DEAR [ABBEY]

notations, we can manipulate expressions on paper, rather than have to juggle the ideas in our heads. We can use the notation for abbreviation, as well as a starting point for reasoning, generalization, and abstraction.

We see this ability to manipulate representations of problems as a key ingredient that is missing from most programming languages. In traditional languages, programs are "cast in concrete"; they cannot be read, let alone be reasoned about. Since they cannot be combined in meaningful ways to discover solutions to other problems, there is no elegance, no poetry, just an executable mess! Some very "clean" parts of languages like APL, Lisp, and Prolog, do have this purity that lends itself to mathematical elegance. Hopefully, this trend will continue.

So the future of languages is elegance, simplicity, and expressibility, with the expectation that the machines will be powerful enough to compute answers from our scribblings. But that is as it should be. One step toward this goal is the development of notations that describe only the logical relationships between objects, leaving open the issue of how to fulfill them. Such a notation is said to be descriptive rather than prescriptive. Most languages—including Lisp and Logo—are prescriptive, that is, they insist on telling (or prescribing) how, and in what order, computations are to occur. That's really quite fascist. Just as in dealing with people, the less detailed the direction, the better they like it; and the better we like it, too.

Perhaps the best-known systems that contain a descriptive flavor are the "spreadsheet" programs. We can define relationships between columns of data, and the machine must maintain those relationships as we vary the information in the columns. This notion is related to the idea of constraint-based programming. That is, the descriptive part of such a program limits (constrains) the kind of solution that the machine may pursue. For example:

*Fahrenheit temperature = 32 + 9/5 * (Celsius temperature)*

expresses a relationship between two quantities. Given a Celsius reading, the equation can be used to find the corresponding Fahrenheit reading and, given a Fahrenheit reading, we can find the corresponding Celsius reading. One cannot be changed without changing the other; that says there is a constraint between the two temperatures.

Now what happens if we want to write a program to compute values with this formula? We have to write **two** definitions:

```
to fahren :c          to centi :f
  32 + 9/5 * :c         5*(:f - 32)/9
end                   end
```

And the elegance is gone. We no longer have the nice mathematical equation that could be reasoned with and combined with other equations. We have two tacky little computational rules to contend with instead. The idea of constraint-based programming is to express or describe ideas using notations like equations, and let the system generate the necessary parts for a solution that will satisfy the constraints.

For example, consider:

fact (0) = 1

fact (x+1) = (x+1) * fact (x)

This pair of equations can be used as a definition of the factorial function. We could use our substitution and simplification rules to compute *fact(6)*. We can also translate the pair into logical assertions:

F(0, 1)

F(x+1, y) if F(x, u) and * (x+1, u, y)

where *and* and *if* are logical operators, and where *F(a, b)* says *fact(a) = b*, and **(a,b,c)* represents *a*b = c*. We can look at *F(a,b)* as a constraint between *a* and *b*. For example, we can compute *fact(6)* by *F(6,x)* and expect the result *x = 720*. Equally well, we can ask *F(y,6)* and should expect any reputable system to respond, *y = 3*. Finally we can ask *F(1,2)* and expect *false* as a response.

Systems based on this kind of expression and manipulation of logical relationships are called logic programming languages. The notion is that once a problem is specified logically—through axioms and deduction rules— it can then, in theory, be executed by a computer. We can augment the formal description with "helpful hints", called heuristics or control information, to influence the search for the solution. In this way, the programming task splits into two clear components: a logical, descriptive,

piece; and a prescriptive, control piece. As the control segment is varied, the elegance, or efficiency, but not the correctness, of the solution is affected.

And to come full circle, these kinds of systems first showed up in different dress in the artificial intelligence circles of the

late 1960s. About the time that Logo was splitting off from Lisp on one side, Carl Hewitt at the Massachusetts Institute of Technology was developing a descriptive programming formalism called Planner. Planner grew from the same kind of concern for notation that gave rise to Lisp. It too, spawned a programming language. This language, called micro-Planner, implemented several of the fundamental notions of descriptive programming. One major contribution, named pattern-directed invocation (PDI), gave the micro-Planner programmer the ability to specify conditions under which Planner programs would be invoked (or called). Thus, instead of calling a specified function, the micro-Planner "machine" was simply directed to "solve this problem". It would match the form of the problem against the possible programs whose patterns matched the current situation. Out of that nest of possibilities, the machine would pick a candidate and try to satisfy the parts. The system was able to try a different attack if a candidate failed.

Meanwhile across the Atlantic, at Edinburgh University, Robert Kowalski was proposing to separate the logic and contol components of programs by using a subset of Predicate Logic (called Horn clauses) as a programming language. The facts and rules that we used in Chapter 5 were in fact Horn clauses, as are the clauses used above to describe *F(a,b)*.

One can develop a data base of facts and rules (thought of as programs), and then ask questions of this data base, requiring the system to execute programs. As in Planner, the choice of methods or rules to apply is made in the system by pattern-matching. The programmer need not worry about **how** a computation is accomplished; she merely specifies **what** relationships must hold. This approach to Logic Programming is embodied in the language Prolog (**Pro**gramming in **Log**ic), which was first implemented in 1972 at the University of Marseilles by Colmerauer and Roussel. It is the major language used by the Japanese in the Fifth Generation Computer Project.

What is particularly important in both Planner and Prolog is that PDI separates the descriptive—the logical data base of possible methods—from the prescriptive—the specific approach that should be used for the current problem. Thus, more problem solving methods can be added to the system without having to recode humongous piles of programs. In this way, problem-solving routines become separate self-contained entities that communicate with each other. This allows the programmer to limit the amount that has to be said about the interactions between programs.

Another way of limiting the amount we have to say about objects is to say "I want widgets like those frobs, except that they have to be green and weigh less than four pounds." That is, we re-use the known information and only vary a small amount. We do exactly this kind of thing in TLC-Logo when we hatch a new turtle. The new one inherits all the characteristics of its parent, but then is free to change most of its turtle properties. This idea of viewing objects (like Studs, Tillie, Frieda) as instances of a class (the class of turtles) is a powerful programming tool. The simplest form of this idea is called a class hierarchy, meaning that classes are related to each other in a strict way. Thus:

This hierarchy goes from primeval ooze, to parallelograms, to rectangles, squares; each class of object in this hierarchy is a variant of the class above it.

To create a new instance of a class is to "hatch" a new object with predefined values. By virtue of the position of the class in the hierarchy, elements of a particular class will either respond to messages themselves, or boost the message up the hierarchy to someone who can handle the inquiry. Programming in this style becomes an issue of setting up appropriate classes, and defining the messages that these new classes can understand.

This is similar to the way we define a new kind of object by defining the constructors and manipulators for the new object. However, the inheritance mechanism of class hierarchies is distinct from this. It is similar in power to Logo's ability to define new words using to; only in class-construction we are defining object characteristics, rather than defining actions. The major modern advocate of such class-oriented, inheritance-based programming (my, that sounds impressive) is Smalltalk. The Smalltalk series of languages have evolved from the early Logo experience with languages for children, into a rather formidable creation called Smalltalk-80.

So systems are becoming more and more complex, but the complexity is becoming more controlled. It is controlled by being more descriptive in defining the objects and in defining the functions that are used on and by the objects. The critical problem, then, in these new systems is not computation, but communication. The systems act like complex societies of interacting entities, hopefully cooperating to achieve a common goal. Well, we know how common that is with humans. What's going to happen when we have 54,983 little entities, each sending messages around the country-side, when each entity is a separate computer with its own idea of reality? Clearly, something is going to go wrong. And how, pray tell, will anyone know if the basketful of little entities has gone into a paranoidal sulk?

We've got some work to do. The first order of future business is to develop a reasonable language for describing these interactions. Now language doesn't just mean a new programming language; it means a notation that will let us discuss, reason about, and manipulate representations of these societies. And it means investigating the logics of such societies. For example, the typical logic operates under some pretty unlikely assumptions. In particular, logic assumes that the world is consistent and that facts remain true; most logics have a hard time dealing with the notions of time

and change. Now, if you believe that none of these restrictions and assumptions in traditional logic have any importance to computing, we've got a really good deal on a bridge for you.

Ballast

We've finally worked our way down to machines. Now, machines to us don't mean the whirring and clicking of tiny transistors. Our machines build new objects and examine existing objects. Our machines have primitive operations like fput, first, type, and fd, rather than add and subtract. In the past, this kind of machine didn't exist in hardware, but had to be simulated in software. That situation has been changing lately, but for our discussion of object machine architecture, it doesn't matter whether the ideas are in software or hardware.

These object-oriented languages all have one common characteristic: they make a valiant attempt to make life easy for the user, while driving implementors or machine designers up the wall. Someone has to do the work that the traditional language required of that user. A particular concern is the creation of objects; once an object exists, the kinds of things a user can do to it is reasonably controlled. Since objects are the numbers of object-oriented programming, we can expect to use lots of them; however, each object takes up space. For example, a garden-variety TLC turtle takes about 20 bytes (and if you don't know what a byte is, it doesn't matter except to note that a small TLC-Logo has about 30,000 of them to eat). Each element

in a list takes 4 bytes; each word takes 8 bytes, plus a byte for each character in the word. The important point here is that object-based machines tend to require very large memories—the bigger, the better. But memory size is only part of the problem; the major concern is memory organization. How does an object memory keep track of all the different kinds of objects? How does it make a new object? What happens when it runs out of objects?

Traditional machines have been built with quite different design rules in mind. Traditional problems, and traditional languages have required lots of fast arithmetic and lots of fast code in general. The reasoning here is historical, as we mentioned in Chapter 7. You only showed up at the machine to compute an answer to a problem that had already been solved. For example "What's the square root of *123.567*?". In contrast, object-machines have grown out of the problem-solving quest. A more likely question here is "Gee, how can I find a good algorithm for computing square roots?". The issue is debugging and exploration.

Machines and languages that are designed for exploration and debugging will emphasize modification—modification of programs, and modification of data. Externally, these requirements translate into interactive programming environments; these are important, but peripheral, hardware and software considerations. Of more fundamental concern is the management of objects—their birth, growth, and death. Clearly, objects come from somewhere; primitive objects are assumed given:

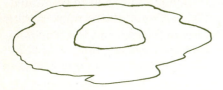

Non-primitive objects are made up of references to other objects. Thus:

These fuzzy pictures are translated into concrete terms by representing objects as storage in a machine, and references as pointers to blocks of storage. Thus:

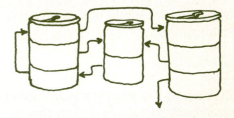

Storage space that is not in use is kept in a "free space" area. Any computation that needs a new object simply asks for enough space to put it in. That space magically appears for the user as it disappears from the free area. That is, space cannot be created or destroyed; however, it can get lost. During a computation, we may discard objects and wander off, leaving the object behind. Unlike Little Bo Peep's sheep, discarded objects don't come wandering after; instead, object-based systems contain components called "garbage collectors" whose purpose is to collect stray objects and deposit them in the free area so their space can be recycled. The garbage collection process can become quite involved, since one computation's garbage is another's pride-and-joy. Before any object is collected, the collector must verify that no one has any claim on it. This is a non-trivial problem in systems like Logo and Lisp.

In the past, garbage collectors and object management systems have been built in software. Recently, however, several of these operations have been implemented in hardware, giving improved performance as well as reducing the burden on the system's designer. Further hardware for object-based systems can be expected. In particular, one bottleneck is the insistence on executing one instruction after another.

A traditional machine would execute something like:

$(2+4)-(4*5)$

by computing $2+4$, then computing $4*5$ and then performing the subtraction. Now if we had two machines, one could compute $2+4$, while the other was computing $4*5$. They could meet later and one of them compute the difference. Of course, all computation is not this easy; we can't always compute pieces in parallel because the order of the computing may matter (f I versus I f), and there is the further problem of coordination betweeen the computations; but the idea has great merit.

The potential for parallelism is further advanced as we move toward more descriptive languages. Recall the distinction we made between descriptive and prescriptive languages—a prescriptive language contains explicit directions for computing a quantity; a descriptive language will specify a relationship that must be satisfied, and leave open the issue of how to satisfy it. The fewer directions we give the machine, the more freedom the computer has for fulfilling the computation. In particular, languages based on deductive principles, like logic or purified Prolog, Logo or Lisp, can exploit their lack of control to let the machine make control decisions.

Of course, there is no free lunch. As more and more pieces are are performed in parallel, the problem of communication becomes more severe. How do pieces communicate their results to other computations? What happens when one of the pieces encounters an error situation? And we're back to the issue of notation. For we have two choices: (1) to "hack it"—that is, to make it work at the hardware or software level, or (2) to "solve it"—that is, to develop a mathematics of communication between computational objects. Future computation should refuse either choice to the detriment of the other. That's what makes computation exciting—a blend of theory and practice in mental exploration.

OBJECTION SUSTAINED

This Section Almost Intentionally Left Blank

A great deal of the current discussion about computing—the languages, the future, and the educational applications—has a highly personal, almost religious, flavor.

One group expects high technology to be the savior of modern society. Another says that it's just snake oil. Another group says computers should be used interactively to develop programs. Another says that all careful thinking should be done away from the machines and all parts of the program be specified before addressing the machine.

Of course, the truth lies somewhere in the midst of this mess. To begin, we have to recognize computing as a field with substance and the potential for mind training. We must get over the notion that computing is just programming, or just hardware, or just video games. The point of this book is to start you thinking and exploring computational ideas that are more indicative of the substance behind the superficial fast talk and hyperbole. QWERTY languages, and other assorted historical artifacts **can** be filed in their appropriate bit bucket; but time is running out.

An 1898 poem called "The Calf Path" conjures up an image of a city whose major artery—long, twisting, and tortured—remains unchanged and held in great reverence by its travelers, though its course resulted from the random wanderings of a calf many centuries before. One verse sums up the situation:

For men are prone to go it blind
Along the calf paths of the mind
And work away from sun to sun
To do what other men have done.

Unfortunately, computer-related endeavors already have an overabundance of QWERTY "cow paths." We see the pasture pastries in this country's schools, industries and, most unfortunately, in personal computing. Personal computing —free from externally imposed and institutionalized dogma—should reflect the most innovative and exploratory kinds of thinking. Yet "New Wave" computing involves the transportation of ancient operating systems to personal computers, or the arrival of the latest programming language copyrighted—in true "Catch-22" fashion—by the Department of Defense. How to reverse this trend? We see hopeful signs in Logo's acceptance; we see hopeful signs in the concerns for quality education. Whether those signs will bear fruit, remains to be seen. It **is** clear, however, that the rest of the world will not wait for us to make up our minds.

The Fifth Generation Project announced the Japanese intention to use Artificial Intelligence as their stepping stone to an information-based society. By 1990 they intend to have advanced AI machines available. These machines are to influence every segment of their culture: industry, art and science, education, and daily life. The project involves the integration of several decades of hardware, software, theory, and AI research, into a knowledge-based computing engine that will be available to the Japanese populace—consumer-oriented AI. The United States has a substantial lead in the AI field, yet the major sponsor and beneficiary of this work is the U.S. military, not the consumer.

AI is a coming reality, like it or not. And questions of its application and control cannot be answered by a society that is ignorant of the principles that implement it. Superficial "computer literacy" courses will not suffice; neither will movies like "The Artificial Pig that Ate Cleveland." Rather, the educational system needs to capture the knowledge as well as the excitement that modern computation represents. Yet we must do that without down-grading mind training into technological training. It would be a dreadful error to simply teach the "new technology." Technology is only a tool; one teaches ideas—ways of thinking—and technology can be used to enhance (or stifle) creative thought.

An underlying theme of Pirsig's "Zen and the Art of Motorcycle Maintenance" is the interplay between creativity, technology, and humanism. Many people already feel resentment and suspicion towards computation in general, and AI in particular. The vision of unforgiving, omnipotent devices represent a threat to those who feel disenfranchised by modern society. These are real concerns of real people. Distrust of technology stems in part from ignorance of the devices, and in part from the all too often blatant misuse of that technology by its keepers.

Many non-computer professionals are put off by the numeric dogma surrounding computation: how can psychologists, for example, relate their perception of the mind to a device that does nothing but dull arithmetic? In the Preface, we noted that our quest for "paying attention" is well-known to the acting profession. In Chapter 8, we showed that—contrary to a popular misconception—computational ideas did not begin in the "silicon valley" in the latter part of the twentieth century. We also pointed out that computers don't really do arithmetic; they simply change state. And only by historical accident were these changes interpreted as arithmetic operations. We can equally well interpret these states and changes as patterns and pattern manipulations. In Chapters 5, 6, and 7, we saw how to analyze a large part of intelligent behavior as pattern-directed activity. Thus the ideas we're after are every bit the intellectual legacy of the philosophers and the psychologists, the artists and the actors. Unfortunately, this broader view of computation is not well-known and so the myth, the numeric cow path of the mind, remains.

Of course, these views of computation will threaten some beliefs in the same way that Galileo's and Darwin's visions did. It is always a challenge to the optimism of the human spirit when future progress requires letting go of past beliefs. Several facets of society are required to "let go". The professional computerist must realize that the personal machine can be made accessible to large numbers of people. The ordinary citizen must be willing to trade the fear of "The Giant Electronic Brain" for the acceptance that machines can do several things previously reserved for human intelligence. This horse trade can be made palatable—indeed, rewarding—if the person can gain an understanding of how machines are able to exhibit this "intelligent" behavior. Trading fear for understanding is always a win in the long run. This kind of trade is a major component in our view of computation-based education: to make such complex systems understandable, and use the resultant fascination to motivate deeper study of the substantive parts of the topic, leading to the fundamental theoretical issues.

Neither hardware nor software are the critical issues in understanding computation; both are transient technology. The theoretical principles will persist across technological change. It is this kind of thinking that we are trying to motivate with this book. But ours is a dynamic and visual generation; printed matter—even decorated with ducks—is static. How best to channel this restless energy? One need only step inside a video arcade to see what can be done with young minds, personal computation, and graphics. What's happened to imagination between the arcade and the classroom?

Given that computers **can** attract inquisitive minds, the issue then becomes what to teach. One shouldn't teach programming, any more than one teaches shoveling as part of a civil engineering program. But programming, itself, **is** valuable because it helps develop self-confidence, helps crystallize ideas, and generally prepare the individual for further exploration of ideas. Languages like Logo are a good way to seduce people into thinking about some deep ideas. Unfortunately,

though, the potential for the misuse of Logo is great. Many see Logo as "Basic with graphics", as yet another programming language, and therefore as representing evolution rather than revolution. The potential exists for a disaster similar to that experienced by classical mathematics in the hands of the New Math experiment. There too, the goal was to improve education by popularizing deep subjects; there too, the material was frequently presented by people who were unable to convey the scope and grandeur of the ideas. However, in contrast to the New Math, Logo has a strong seductive, experiential component based on computation, rather than the more formal, less intuitive basis in set theory.

And what are the ideas of computation? Some of the ideas are found in the notions of the munchers and the evaluation of expressions; and they are found in the deductive reasoning that supports the JMC models. These two ideas—functional languages and axiom systems—are part of the mathematics of computation. They can stand on their own merits, or can be used to motivate more traditional pieces of mathematics, like high school algebra or plane geometry.

If the notions of functional languages and axiomatic logic are so powerful, easily presented, and potentially so practical, why don't we teach such topics in our schools? Besides the issue of making the information available, there is a deeper problem: the society is schizophrenic. The educational system can't decide whether it should train minds, or train hands (become a "market-driven" corporation). Industry can't decide if it wants educational systems driven by "technological imperatives" (that means "trade schools") or by search for knowledge. Finally, society in general wonders if education really matters, or is immediate gratification more important? The answers in this country aren't encouraging, and the current mixture of technology, education, and politics is a sure recipe for disaster.

Quality education cannot be spread about like warm peanut butter, regardless of the whizzy technology that is used to apply it. It requires a personal commitment on the part of the participants—a notion of quality, if you wish. And it is this notion that we must cultivate. That spirit of quality, of mind, of individual responsibility, is well represented in the Japanese culture. As Pirsig wrote in "Zen and the Art of Motorcycle Maintenance", "assembly of Japanese bicycle require [sic] great peace of mind". The Japanese concern for "mind" is no post-war phenomenon: Zen, Kabuki, Haiku, even their preparation of food, all reflect an exquisite concern for contemplative excellence. Slick technological packaging is no substitute for mind-training and quality. Without that "peace of mind", educational reform will not work.

And how do you get knowledgeable people to bring the principles behind modern computation into mainstream education? How do you build programs that can put some fundamental substance behind the technological form. Many teachers get burned out dealing with the "Calf Path" mentality that asks "is it rele-

vant?" which translates to: "Is it an employable skill?" Students, administration, and industry all contribute to bring this pressure to bear; if the courses aren't "relevant", the students don't enroll; if the students don't enroll, the courses are cancelled, and the teacher is then forced back to "calf path" courses.

And "calf path" leads to "half path" as we see many students leave the universities without completing a graduate degree. They are followed by their professors, who are seduced by higher pay and fewer headaches. And as those who know go, we'll see much more "high tech" education that consists of superficial programming and literacy courses. Those who move into the computer field on the basis of such courses are potential victims, as surely as the Detroit auto-workers were. Whether they are enticed by educational institutions who dread falling enrollment or industries in search of inexpensive labor, they are still potential victims.

The underlying theme throughout this discussion is "thinking". That is the business of education. "High tech education" is not hardware or software, but mind training; that is accomplished by stressing fundamental principles. It is the discovery and understanding of these fundamental principles that will determine a country's excellence at basic research. To achieve these goals one needs a rare combination of innovation, mind-training, and self-discipline. These issues have been the reason for the book. The mind and the computer are both valuable resources, and the misuse of either is troublesome to us.

SPARE PARTS

Dirty Laundry

A thumb-nail description of what's wrong with vanilla Logo.

The turtle is a special case: This violates the notion of first-class data. A cardinal rule of modern language design must be that any type of object must be available in a general setting.

Lists are the only structuring object: They are universal, but not always best. Vectors and strings should also be supplied—again as first-class objects.

A weak notion of function: Most Logos are based on the notion of procedure, wherein computation is driven by a side-effect. Functions and relations are better. Again first-class, please.

Dynamic scoping: Given Logo's ability to define new control constructs, name clashes are unavoidable in dynamic scoping.

A Prescriptive language: Something must be done to encourage "descriptive programming"—emphasizing the "what" rather than the "how."

Class System: Following the lead of Smalltalk, a general class system is desirable, whereby we can describe the intended behavoir of objects without getting mired down in the implementation.

Less emphasis on sequential ideas The ideas of communication between cooperating entities is a powerful human notion. Message passing is start; multi-processing notations must be designed.

If Logo is to replace BASIC in the Fifth Generation, these issues must be addressed.

Eye Catchers

Allen, J., **Anatomy of Lisp**. McGraw-Hill, New York, 1978.

Abelson, H., and DiSessa, A. **Turtle Geometry**. MIT Press, 1982.

Abelson, H., and Sussman, G., **Structure and Interpretation of Computer Programs**. MIT Press & McGraw-Hill, New York, 1984.

Bell, E., **Men Of Mathematics**. Simon Schuster, New York, 1937.

Bronowski, J., **Ascent of Man**. Little, Brown & Co., Mass, 1973.

Goldberg, A., and Robson, D., **Smalltalk-80**. Addison-Wesley, Mass, 1983.

Georgescu-Roegen, N., **The Entropy Law and the Economic Process**. Harvard University Press, Mass, 1971.

Henderson, P., **Functional Programming**. Prentice-Hall, New York, 1980.

Hofstadter, D., **Godel, Escher, Bach: An Eternal Golden Braid**. Basic Books, New York, 1979.

Kowalski, R., **Logic for Problem Solving**. North Holland, New York, 1979.

McCarthy, J., **LISP—Notes on Its Past and Future**. Proceedings of the 1980 Lisp Conference, The Lisp Company, 1980.

Moore, S., **The Stanislavski Method**, The Viking Press, New York, 1960.

Papert, S., **Mindstorms: Children, Computers, and Powerful Ideas**. Basic Books, 1980.

Pirsig, R., **Zen and The Art of Motorcycle Maintenance**. Bantam Books, New York, 1974.

Simon, H., **Is Thinking Uniquely Human**. University of Chicago Magazine, Fall 1981.

Paint by Numbers

In several places throughout the book we make reference to colors, shapes, and other values, by using names like :blue, :arrow, or :up. Below we relate some of those names to numerical quantities. The definitions of colors and shapes will be dependent on the machine you are running your TLC-LOGO on. See your user manual for details. You may install names in your Logo by using the make operation; for example:

```
make "down 1
```

Penstates
```
up 0
down 1
```

Visibility States
```
hide 0
show 1
```

SPARE PARTS

Hairy Words

Logo Primitives

Book Functions